Wireshark® Workbook 1
Practice, Challenges, and Solutions

Laura Chappell
Founder, Chappell University™
Creator of the WCNA Certification Program
(formerly referred to as the Wireshark Certified Network Analyst program)

Edited by James Aragon

*Always ensure you have proper authorization
before you listen to or capture network traffic.*

Protocol Analysis Institute, Inc.
59 Damonte Ranch Parkway, #B340
Reno, NV 89521 USA

Chappell University
info@chappellU.com
www.chappellU.com

Copyright Notice

Dedication

This book is dedicated to Lindsey Faye Poulsen.

We miss your humor, bright smile, and clever insights...
every minute of every day.

Laura

About the Author

Laura Chappell has been a protocol analyst for almost 30 years – yes, she has gray hair! Back in the 1990s, Laura became a networking evangelist and member of the IEEE while working at Novell.

Laura is the CEO and Founder of Protocol Analysis Institute, Inc., and Chappell University.

Laura began using Wireshark as her sole network analysis tool when it was in its infancy (under the Ethereal name). Laura teaches courses online and onsite and continues to research and write about troubleshooting, optimization, and security techniques for both terrestrial and interplanetary network systems.

Laura's customers include many of the Fortune 100, as well as local, national, and international law enforcement agencies. Visit chappell-university.com for more information on Laura Chappell's projects, join her newsletter and read her blog (*In Laura's Lab*).

Laura's courses are available online at *chappell.talentlms.com*.

Ms. Chappell can be reached at laura@chappellu.com.

In 2006, with the encouragement of Gerald Combs (creator of Wireshark), Laura founded *Wireshark University* to evangelize network analysis skills and promote a baseline of knowledge with the *Wireshark Certified Network Analyst (WCNA)* program. [1]

Laura Chappell remains an adamant supporter of the network analysis developer and user community and the open source Wireshark project.

Is This Book Available as a Training Course?

Yes. You can take this *Wireshark Workbook* as a pre-recorded course online through Laura Chappell's **Wireshark Training All Access Pass** training portal (*chappell.talentlms.com*).

Wireshark Versions Used in These Labs

This *Wireshark Workbook* was written using several Wireshark 3 versions. If you are still stuck in the world of Wireshark 1.x, it's time to update your version. Wireshark versions 2 and 3 offer numerous advantages over the earlier versions, such as a native installation for Macintosh users, USBpcap support, Intelligent Scrollbar, much better graphs, a Related Packets Indicator, Npcap support, Cisco Remote Capture, and more.

---

[1] In 2019, Riverbed (the "sponsor" of the Wireshark project) prompted the Wireshark Foundation to take over the "Wireshark University" name in their quest to "monetize Wireshark assets." The certification program is simply referred to as the "WCNA Certification program" because of trademark issues enforced by Riverbed's attorneys. Don't ask her what she thinks of Riverbed, their former employees who pushed to "sell off" the "Wireshark University" name for money, or her thoughts on the secretive workings of the "Wireshark Foundation."

How to Use This Wireshark Workbook 1

This *Wireshark Workbook* contains 16 sets of lab questions with fully-documented solutions to each question. It is designed to test your knowledge of Wireshark and TCP/IP analysis by focusing on your ability to locate answers to network traffic questions.

If you've participated in Laura Chappell's wildly successful Packet Challenge during *SharkFest*, the Wireshark user and developer conferences, then you know what you're in for! The difference, however, is that now you'll be able to see the step-by-step processes used to get the answer to those challenging questions.

Step 1: Lab Preparation

Start with the **Lab Preparation** section on page 1. That will walk you through creating your *Wireshark Workbook 1* profile that is referred to throughout the book.

Step 2: Book Supplements

Next, visit the book supplements page at *https://www.chappell-university.com/books* to download the trace files and blank Answer Sheet document used with this book.[2]

Step 3: Warm-up Lab

Finally, complete **Lab 1: Wireshark Warm-Up** to get an idea of the type of questions asked and the detail level of the solutions provided.

From that point on, feel free to skip around to different labs as you wish.

Suggested Prerequisite Knowledge to Run these Labs

Before you delve into this *Wireshark Workbook* (or network analysis in general), you should have a solid understanding of basic network concepts and TCP/IP fundamentals. For example, you should know the purpose of a switch, a router, and a firewall. You should be familiar with the concepts of Ethernet networking, basic wireless networking, and be comfortable with IP network addressing, as well.

This *Wireshark Workbook* assumes that you may not know how to use some of Wireshark's features. This is why the workbook will walk you step-by-step through the processes used to get the answers – and, in many cases, show more than one method to get the answers.

---

[2] Consider capturing your traffic when you download the book trace files! You will see where we actually keep our book supplements and have a nice file transfer trace for later analysis.

[This page intentionally left blank.]

Table of Contents

Lab Preparation

Hello fellow Wireshark and packet analyst enthusiasts!

If you've ever joined me at *SharkFest*, the Wireshark user and developer conference, you've likely seen and hopefully participated in my Packet Challenge. I began the packet challenge many, many years ago as a contest at the conference. The shark fin awards would be presented on the last day of the conference to the contestants who were the closest to 100% correct on their answer sheets.

This book is based on my Packet Challenges, but I've included lots of detail on how I got the answers. There are often many ways to get the answers, so you might find alternatives – as long as we get the same answer, that's ok!

Step 1: Download the Lab trace files and Answer Sheets *from* www.chappell-university.com/books

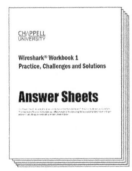

The *Answer Sheets* document does not contain the answers. The *Answer Sheets* document offers an organized, efficient method for answering the lab questions rather than writing in a book or just jotting your answers on a blank sheet of paper.

Download the *Answer Sheets* document and the set of *Wireshark Workbook 1* trace files from *www.chappell-university.com/books*.

*I recommend that you write your answer **and** make a note of how you got that answer. Did you add a specific column? Did you use a certain display filter? Did you look at one of the statistics windows? When you look at the answers, you will see how I got the answer and you can compare your method to mine. Quite often there is more than one way to get an answer.*

Step 2: Create your **Wireshark Workbook 001** *profile*

In Wireshark, profiles enable you to customize Wireshark columns, dissector preference settings, display filter buttons, and more.

Right-click on the *Profile* column on the Status Bar and select *New*.

Name your new profile *Wireshark Workbook 001* and click *OK*.

That's it! Now you have created a new profile that can be used as you work through the labs in this book.

Step 3: Check out the online **Wireshark Workbook 1** *course*

If you are already a **Wireshark Training All Access Pass** member, you can take the **Wireshark Workbook 1** course set to watch how the labs are solved. You can skip around to different lab solutions as desired.

Visit *chappell-university.com* for more information on online and onsite training courses.

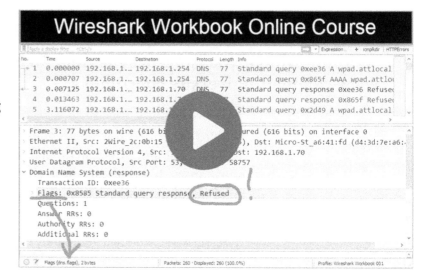

Ok! Once you have the trace files, *Answer Sheet*, and your *Wireshark Workbook 001* profile, you are ready to go! Fire up Wireshark and let's get started!

Lab 1: Wireshark Warm-Up

Objective: Get Comfortable with the Lab Process.

Completion of this lab requires many of the skills you will use throughout this lab book. If you are a bit shaky on any answer, take time when reviewing the answers on page 9 to ensure you have mastered the necessary skill(s).

`Trace File: wwb001-http.pcapng`

Skills Covered in this Lab

In this lab, you will have a chance to work with many key functions in Wireshark. The answers to this lab demonstrate how to use functions, including, but not limited to:

- Perform address detection
- Measure DNS response time
- Add and sort columns to detect the highest/lowest field values
- Determine the trace file capture location
- Analyze conversation statistics
- Apply display filters on request and response packet values
- Detect HTTP host names
- Filter on TCP flags with && (and) and == (eq)
- Use automatic display filter packet counts
- Compare TCP flag summaries in display filter results
- Detect HTTP request URI values with display filters
- Apply display filters to detect HTTP error responses
- Use the packet relationship indicator
- Evaluate port usage statistics in TCP conversations
- Identify TCP handshake option definitions
- Determine highest and lowest HTTP response times
- Change TCP preference settings
- Reassemble HTTP objects

- Identify TCP and UDP stream numbers and counts using display filtering
- Determine throughput
- Identify the capture application
- Analyze spurious retransmissions
- Use the right-click conversation filtering method
- Analyze the TCP Calculated Window Size value
- Display filter based on subnet/CIDR (Classless Interdomain Routing) values
- Identify the TCP conversation Initial Round-trip Time (iRTT) value
- Detect IP fragmentation
- Measure peak bandwidth utilization

Lab 1 - Q1. What is the IP address of the DNS/HTTP client in this trace file?

_____

Lab 1 - Q2. What is the IP address of the DNS server?

_____

Lab 1 - Q3. What DNS response time is seen in this trace file?

_____

Lab 1 - Q4. Do you think this trace was taken closer to the HTTP client or closer to the HTTP servers?

_____

Lab 1 - Q5. What are the IP addresses of the HTTP servers to which the client successfully connected?

_____

Lab 1 - Q6. What are the HTTP host names of the target HTTP servers?

_____

Lab 1 - Q7. How many TCP SYN packets did the client send to the HTTP servers?

_____

Lab 1 - Q8. What Uniform Resource Identifier (URI) does the client request first in this trace file?

_____

Lab 1 - Q9. What HTTP error response(s) are seen in this trace file?

_____

Lab 1 - Q10. **What requested web object could not be found on the HTTP server?**

_____

Lab 1 - Q11. **What TCP port numbers did the client open to communicate with the HTTP server?**

_____

Lab 1 - Q12. **What TCP options are supported by the client?**

_____

Lab 1 - Q13. **What TCP options are supported by the HTTP servers?**

_____

Lab 1 - Q14. **What is the slowest HTTP response time seen in this trace file?**

_____

Lab 1 - Q15. **What is the fastest HTTP response time seen in this trace file?**

_____

Lab 1 - Q16. **What words are seen in the _featureb.jpg_ image?**

_____

Lab 1 - Q17. **What is the average bits-per-second throughput rate in this trace file?**

_____

Lab 1 - Q18. **What application was used to capture this trace file?**

_____

Lab 1 - Q19.   What is the largest Calculated Window Size advertised by the client?

_____

Lab 1 - Q20.   What is the fastest initial round-trip time seen in this trace file?

_____

Lab 1 - Q21.   How many UDP streams are in this trace file?

_____

Lab 1 - Q22.   How many TCP streams are in this trace file?

_____

Lab 1 - Q23.   What is the purpose of TCP stream 7?

_____

Lab 1 - Q24.   How many packets allow IP fragmentation in the IP header?

_____

Lab 1 - Q25.   How many times does the packets-per-second rate reach over 125 in this trace file?

_____

[This page intentionally left blank.]

Lab 1 Solutions

Trace File: wwb001-http.pcapng

Lab 1 - A1.   **The IP address of the DNS/HTTP client is 192.168.1.72.**

Frame 1 is a DNS request sent from 192.168.1.72. Frame 3 is a TCP SYN packet sent from 192.168.1.72 to an HTTP server at port 80. That is the IP address of the DNS/HTTP client in this trace file.

You could also look for GET requests to see the IP address of the HTTP client in this trace file.

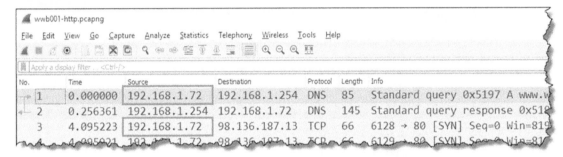

Lab 1 - A2.   **The IP address of the DNS server is 192.168.1.254.**

Frame 1 is a DNS packet addressed to 192.168.1.254. If the DNS traffic did not occur right at the top of the trace file, you could apply a display filter for dns to find the IP address of the DNS server.

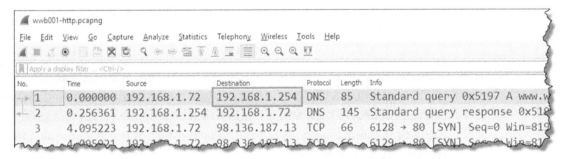

Lab 1 - A3.   The DNS response time seen in this trace file is 0.256361[3] seconds.

You can look at the *Time* column for this value since the DNS request and response packets are the first two packets of the trace file. The *Time* column indicates the DNS response arrived 0.256361 seconds (just over 256 ms) after the DNS request.

Alternately, you can expand the DNS section of the DNS response packet and look for the *[Time:]* value. This is Wireshark's measurement from the related DNS request to this DNS response in the trace file.

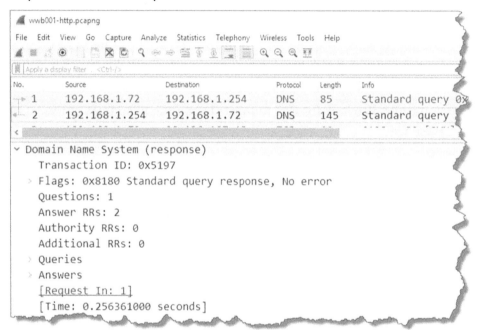

 If you need to analyze a lot of DNS response times in a trace file, consider right-clicking on this Time *field in any DNS response packet and selecting* Apply as Column. *Once the field is added as a column in the Packet List pane, you can click twice on the column heading to sort DNS response times from high to low.*

Wireshark can measure the response times for several applications including DNS, HTTP, and SMB/SMB2. The response time measurement is based on when the related request is seen and is contained in *.time* fields. For example, the *dns.time* value of 0.256361 seconds is a measurement from the DNS request in frame 1 to the DNS response in frame 2.

---

[3]   Throughout this book, we will only focus on time values to the millisecond-level, removing any trailing zeroes.

Where you capture the traffic does matter.

These response time values will be more accurate if you capture close to the client or even on the client system. If you capture closer to the server, your time does not include the time required to get the request to that point in the network or the time required to return the response to the client from that point in the network.

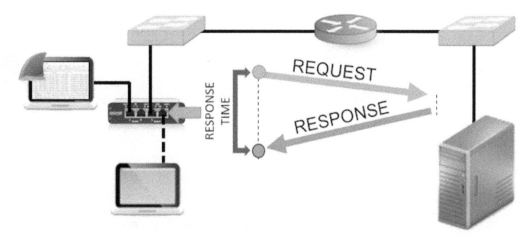

 In the image above, I have placed a TAP[4] (Test Access Point) between the client and the upstream switch.

Although you might be tempted to use port spanning on switches, please consider placing a TAP on your network instead.

Too often I see Wireshark's Expert indicate "ACKed segment that wasn't captured" on trace files captured using a port spanning process. This means that the trace file contains an ACK that doesn't have a corresponding data packet. This is what you see when a switch drops data packets during the span process.

When I see these indications, I throw away that trace file. I cannot perform analysis on a "partial picture" of the communications. It can be very misleading and waste a LOT of time.

TAPs are well worth the investment – get them in place before you need them!

---

[4]   The tap in this image is a Portable Gigabit Copper TAP from Profitap (*www.profitap.com*). Visit Profitap's website to check out some great white papers and case studies from many of my friends in the network analysis industry.

Lab 1 - A4. **This trace file was taken close to (if not directly on) the client, 192.168.1.72.**

We can use the TCP handshake to determine where the capture was taken. In the image below, notice that frames 3, 5, and 6 depict the TCP handshake between 192.168.1.72 and 98.136.187.13 using ports 6128 and 80.

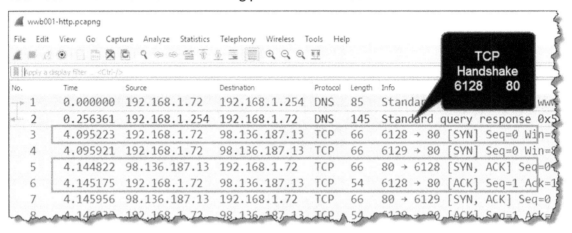

Frame #	Time Value	Packet Type	Traffic Direction	Delta
Frame 3	4.095223	SYN	Client to Server	N/A
Frame 5	4.144822	SYN/ACK	Server to Client	0.049599
Frame 6	4.145175	ACK	Client to Server	0.000353

When the delta time is remarkably smaller between the SYN/ACK and ACK (2nd and 3rd packets of the TCP handshake), the capture was likely performed close to the system that sent the SYN packet.

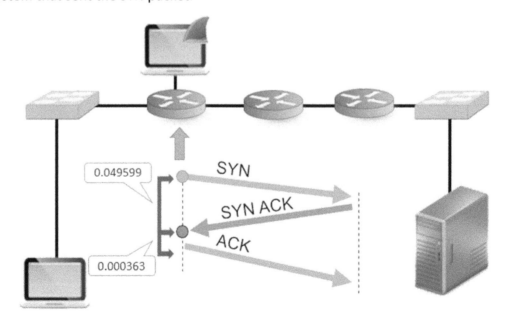

Lab 1 - A5.   The IP addresses of the HTTP servers to which the client successfully connected are 98.136.187.13 and 98.139.206.151.

There are many ways to obtain this information. You can select *Statistics | Conversations* and look under the *TCP* tab. For clarity, sort the *Address B* column and you can clearly see the two HTTP servers listed with port 80.

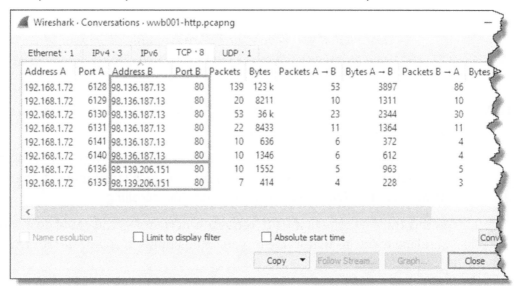

Alternately, you can apply a display filter for `http.response` to view all HTTP responses and focus on the *Source* field, as shown below.

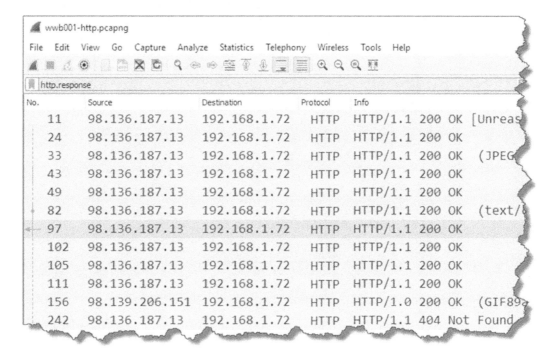

In the previous image, the TCP setting Allow subdissector to reassemble TCP streams *is off. If the setting is enabled, you will see the same number of packets, but the HTTP response code will be associated with the last packet of the object download, rather than the first packet of the object download.*

As of Wireshark v3, we have a No Reassembly *profile automatically installed. If you keep your TCP reassembly on in your other profiles, you can quickly switch to the* No Reassembly *profile when desired.*

Lab 1 - A6. **The HTTP host names of the target HTTP servers are *www.wiresharktraining.com* and *visit.webhosting.yahoo.com*.**

HTTP requests contain a *Host* field (`http.host`). Although you could scroll through the packets to look for this field separately in each HTTP request, there is almost always a better way to locate something than scrolling.

In this trace file, the first HTTP request is in frame 9. You could do a small bit of scrolling to locate that frame or you could apply a display filter for `http.request`.

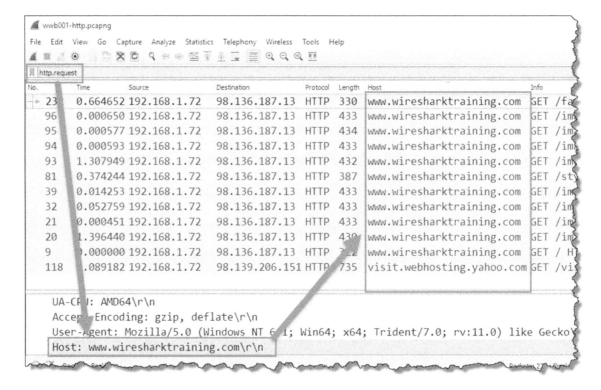

Just 12 packets match this filter. Each of these packets has an `http.host` field in the HTTP section of the Packet Details pane.

Expand the HTTP section in the Packet Details pane, right-click on the *Host* field and select *Apply as Column*. Now you can clearly see the *Host* field values contained in the trace file. In the previous image, we've sorted on the HTTP *Host* column to make it easier to identify the various host names.

```
> Frame 9: 322 bytes on wire (2576 bits), 322 bytes captured (2576 bits)
> Ethernet II, Src: HewlettP_a7:bf:a3 (d4:85:64:a7:bf:a3), Dst: PaceAmer_1
> Internet Protocol Version 4, Src: 192.168.1.72, Dst: 98.136.187.13
> Transmission Control Protocol, Src Port: 6128, Dst Port: 80, Seq: 1, Ac
∨ Hypertext Transfer Protocol
  > GET / HTTP/1.1\r\n
    Accept: text/html, application/xhtml+xml, */*\r\n
    Accept-Language: en-US\r\n
    User-Agent: Mozilla/5.0 (Windows NT 6.1; WOW64; Trident/7.0; rv:11.0)
    Accept-Encoding: gzip, deflate\r\n
    Host: www.wiresharktraining.com\r\n
    DNT: 1\r\n
    Connection: Keep-Alive\r\n
○ ⚡ | HTTP Host (http.host), 33 bytes                          Packets: 273 · Displa
```

The only time I scroll through a trace file is when I want to understand how a protocol or application works.

In that case, I examine each packet of the process looking for the startup routine, request format, response format, timing, packet sizes, packet counts, closing process, etc.

As you go through this workbook, you will see that I make a TON of display filters to find items of interest. When I am learning a protocol or application, I create filters and buttons for anything I would like to locate quickly later.

*When troubleshooting that application or protocol, I know what I am looking for – whether it is an error response, timing issue, unexpected packet counts, or another anomaly. You need to know how things **should** work before trying to find the cause of problems.*

Lab 1 - A7. **The client sent eight TCP SYN packets to the HTTP servers.**

Note that we are not counting SYN/ACK packets, just SYN packets. So, let's consider creating a filter for what we really want to see; packets that only have the SYN bit set and not the ACK bit.

```
tcp.flags.syn==1 && tcp.flags.ack==0
```

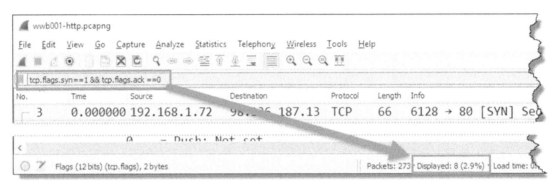

You may have found the answer another way.

In classes, one or more of my students often suggests that we create and apply a filter based on the Flags summary line (`tcp.flags==0x002`), as shown below.

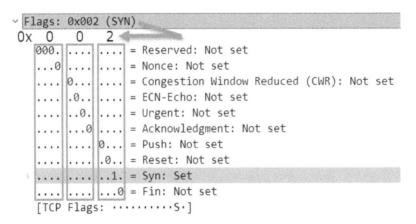

Using `tcp.flags==0x002`, you would still see 8 packets in this case, but the filter has a flaw. This *Flags* summary line includes the *Reserved, Nonce, Congestion Window Reduced (CWR),* and *ECN-Echo bits*, as well as the TCP *Urgent, Acknowledgment, Push, Reset*, and *Fin* bits. Your `tcp.flags==0x002` filter will not match TCP SYN packets where any bits in the *Flags* field are different from how they are set in this packet.

You could build a display filter based on the TCP Flags line below the FIN flag. Simply right-click on this TCP Flags summary line and select *Apply as Filter*. Wow! What an ugly filter! This filter is literally looking for UTF-8 middle dots in all positions except for an "S" in the next to last position.

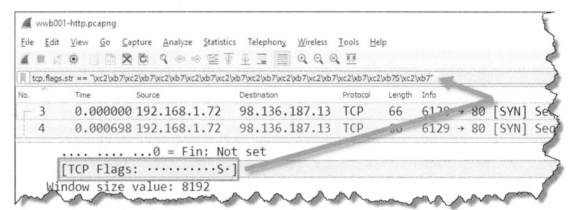

In Wireshark, there are often many ways to find specific packets. Sometimes, however, using summary lines from the Packet Details window will not yield the desired results.

Lab 1 - A8. **The first Uniform Resource Identifier (URI) requested by the client is "/" (the default page).**

You could simply look at the Packet List pane and find this answer quickly by looking at the *Info* column of frame 9.

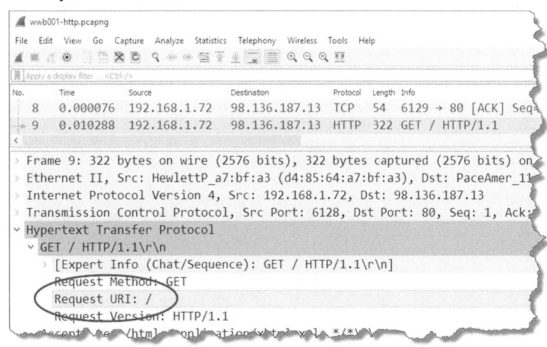

Alternately, you could use a `http.request.uri` display filter to view only packets that contain this field, as shown below.

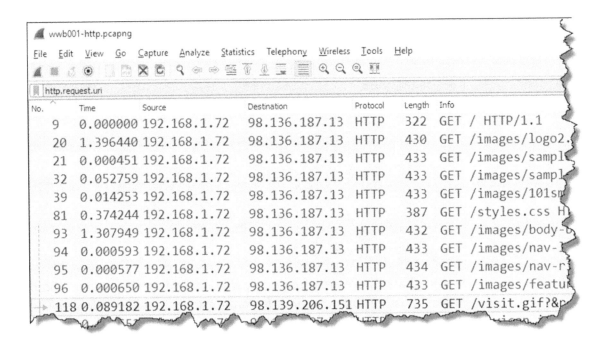

Another option would be to add the `http.request.uri` field as a column in the Packet List pane, as shown below. Note that you will need to expand the request section of the HTTP packet to see the *Request URI* field.

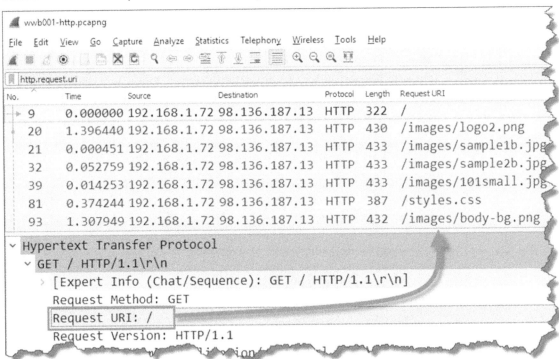

You can probably already tell that adding columns to the Packet List pane is a powerful feature. If you don't have the screen space to handle all the columns you want to add, right-click on a column and deselect it to hide it temporarily. This powerful feature justifies the need for more than one monitor on your desk! You will be a much more efficient analyst if you have more space available to add columns and keep statistics windows open as needed.

Lab 1 - A9.   There is a single 404 Not Found HTTP error response in frame 242.

This is where a display filter will quickly help you locate application error responses. You need to know two things:

1. What is the response code field name?
2. What response codes constitute errors?

In HTTP, any response code greater than 399 indicates an error.

>   4xx   Client Errors
>   5xx   Server Errors

In the image below, we applied a display filter for `http.response.code > 399`. There's the 404 response in frame 242.

Lab 1 - A10. **The web object that could not be found on the HTTP server is *favicon.ico*.**

Now we want to find the URI value that triggered the 404 response in frame 242.

Wireshark detects related packets and denotes that information within the Packet Details pane and to the left of the frame number value in the *No.* column of the Packet List pane, as shown below.

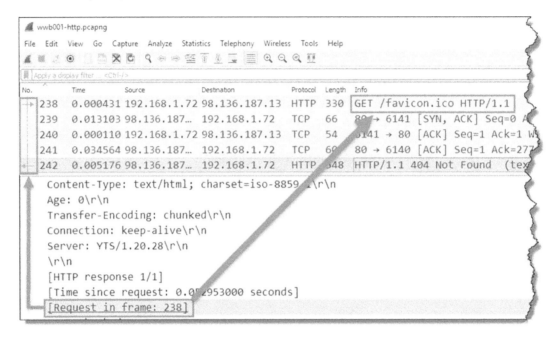

Lab 1 - A11. **The HTTP client opened TCP port numbers 6128, 6129, 6130, 6131, 6135, 6136, 6140, and 6141 to connect to the HTTP servers.**

This information is readily available in the *Statistics | Conversations | TCP* view, as shown in the following image.

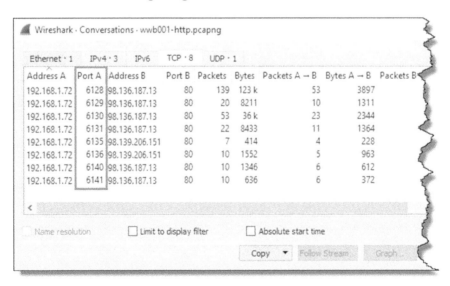

Lab 1 - A12. **The client supports a Maximum Segment Size (MSS) of 1460 bytes, Window Scaling with a multiplier of 4, and Selective acknowledgment (SACK).**

This information is contained in the client's SYN packets. You don't need to look inside those SYN packets in the Packet Details pane, however. Just look at the *Info* column of the Packet List pane. The *Info* column contains all the TCP options information, so you can quickly determine the capabilities of both sides of a TCP connection.

In the image below, we applied the display filter `tcp.flags.syn==1 && tcp.flags.ack==0` to view just the SYN packets in the trace file. (Note that we removed some columns from view to fit the desired information in the image.[5])

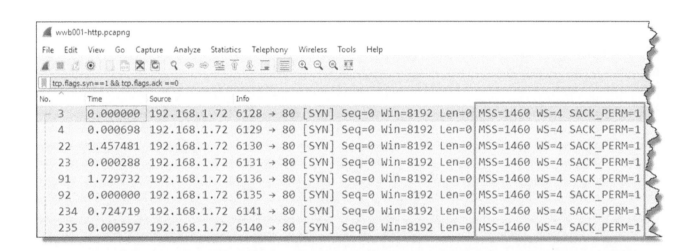

 As much as I love to delve into packets and spend time looking at their contents, time is usually of the essence. It's important to find the issues as fast as possible so we can "point the finger" to the problem area on the network.

The Info *column offers so much information about the TCP handshake packets that I rarely need to look into the SYN, SYN/ACK, or ACK packets.*

---

[5] You should have at least two monitors on which to analyze traffic. As you add more and more columns to your profile, you will find that one monitor slows you down tremendously!

Lab 1 - A13.   The TCP options supported by the HTTP servers are:

- 98.136.187.13: Maximum Segment Size (MSS) of 1460 bytes, Window Scaling with a multiplier of 256, and Selective Acknowledgment (SACK)

- 98.139.206.151: Maximum Segment Size (MSS) of 1460 bytes, Window Scaling with a multiplier of 128, and Selective Acknowledgment (SACK)

To obtain this information quickly, we can look at the second packet of the TCP handshake, the SYN/ACK packet. In the image below, we applied the display filter `tcp.flags.syn==1 && tcp.flags.ack==1` to view the server capabilities.

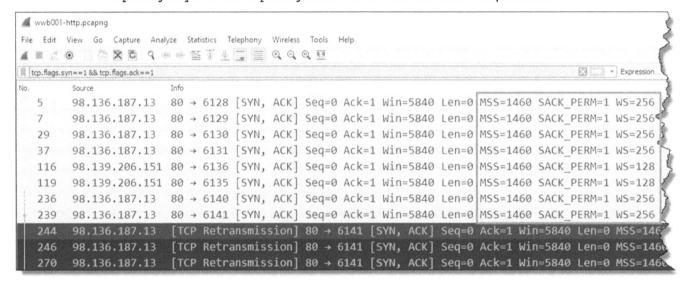

 We will go over this later in this workbook, but now is a good time to mention that a server will not advertise certain options in its SYN/ACK packet if the client didn't mention those options in the SYN packet.

For example, if the client had not advertised that it supported SACK (SACK_PERM=1), the server would not have included that in it's SYN/ACK.

This is true for options such as SACK, Window Scaling, and TCP Timestamps. It is not true for the Maximum Segment Size (MSS) option. Each side of the TCP connection states its MSS value independently.

This means that if you want to know if a connection will support SACK, Window Scaling, and TCP Timestamps, you can just look at the SYN/ACK packet.

Lab 1 - A14. **The slowest HTTP response time seen in this trace file is 0.109500 seconds (frame 156).**

In order to measure the HTTP response time properly, we must disable the TCP preference setting *Allow subdissector to reassemble TCP streams*. Why? Well, with this setting enabled, Wireshark measures response time from the HTTP request to the **end** of the object download.

We want to measure the time from the HTTP request to the HTTP response (with the numerical code, such as *200 OK*). With this preference setting disabled, Wireshark does just that.

Right-click on any TCP header in the Packet Details pane and select *Protocol Preferences.* If the TCP reassembly preference is enabled, just click on it to disable it.

Any time you are looking for the largest or smallest number in a field (such as the *Time since request* field), consider adding that field as a column in the Packet List pane and then sorting the column.

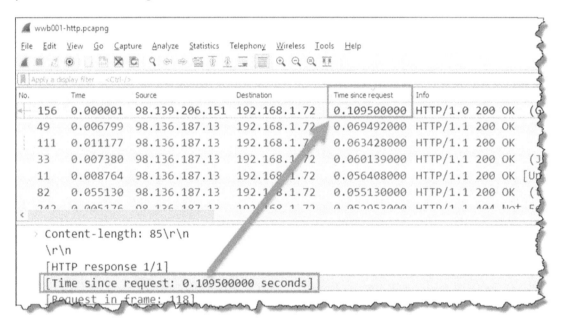

  Although it might be tough to see it, there is a small sort order indicator at the top of the columns.

In the image above, you might be able to see the small down arrow above the Time since request *column heading.*

As you get older, these little itty bitty indications get tougher and tougher to see... sigh.

Lab 1 - A15.   The fastest HTTP response time seen in this trace file is 0.047247 seconds.

Again, we sorted the `http.time` field (*Time since request*). This time, however, we added a filter to view only packets that contain the HTTP *Time since request* field. This filter only displays HTTP responses that have a corresponding HTTP request in the trace file.

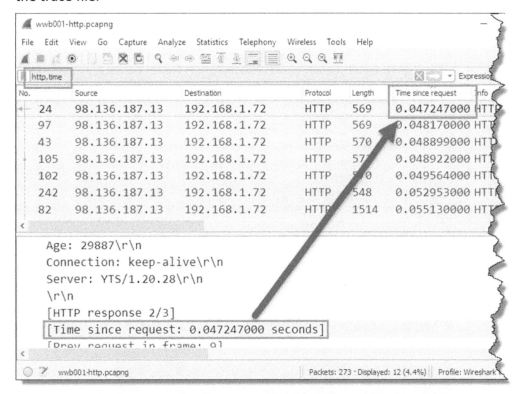

Lab 1 - A16.   The words "Get Deep" are seen in the *featureb.jpg* image.

In this case, we need to perform two key steps. First, we need to enable the TCP reassembly preference so we can reassemble the *featureb.jpg* file. Next, we need to export the reassembled image (also called an HTTP "object") and look for the words.

Right-click on any TCP header in the Packet Details pane and enable *Allow subdissector to reassemble TCP streams*.

When should you enable or disable this TCP preference setting? Essentially, I keep this setting disabled by default so the `http.time` value is the time from the request to the response, rather than the time from the request to the completion of the object download. I only enable it when I need to reassemble objects (as in this case) or work with TLS/SSL analysis.

Now you can select *File | Export Objects | HTTP.* In the image below, we see the desired file near the bottom of the object list. Select the file, click *Save*, and select a directory for the file.

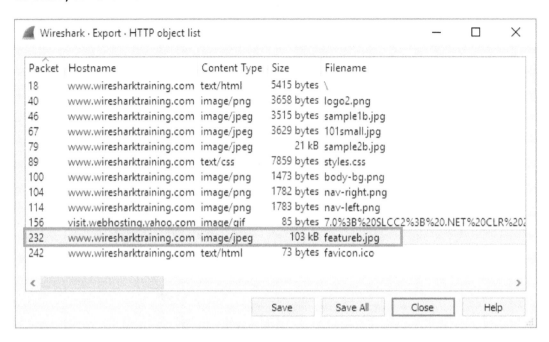

When you open the exported file, you will see the words "Get Deep" in the image.

 Remember to turn Allow subdissector to reassemble TCP streams *off after finishing this reassembly.*

Lab 1 - A17.   The average bits-per-second rate in this trace file is 37k.

Select *Statistics | Capture File Properties* to view statistics and comments related to this trace file.

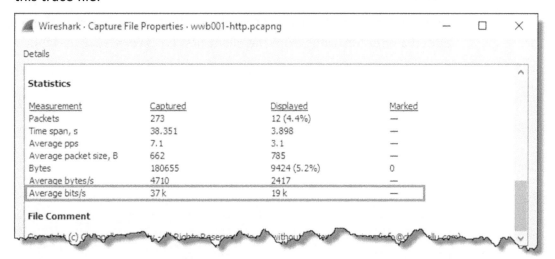

Alternately, click the *Capture File Properties* button on the Status Bar to open this window.

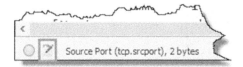

Lab 1 - A18.   Dumpcap v1.10.5 was used to capture this trace file.

This information is also in the *Capture File Properties* window.

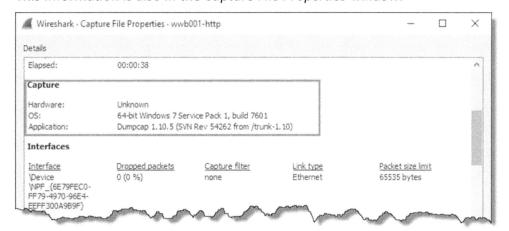

Lab 1 - A19. **The largest Calculated Window Size advertised by the client is 65,700 bytes.**

Earlier we learned that the client and HTTP servers in this trace file support Window Scaling.

Now, to determine the largest Calculated Window Scaling size of the client, we added a filter for traffic from the client first (`ip.src==192.0.0.0/8`).

Next, we added the *Calculated window size* field as a column and sorted the column.

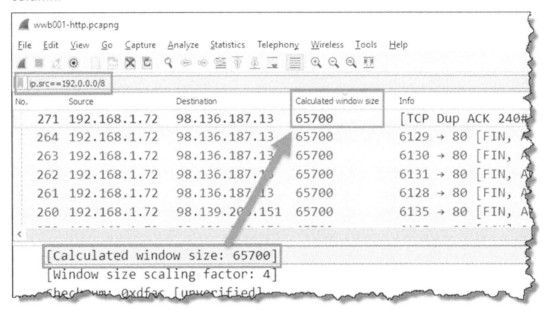

The `ip.src==192.0.0.0/8` *filter is a pretty lazy filter.*

If this trace file had other hosts with IP addresses starting with 192, this wouldn't have worked. We would have had to be more explicit in the IP address of the source to look only at traffic from our client of interest.

Lab 1 - A20.   The fastest initial round-trip time seen in this trace file is 0.048901 seconds.

Wireshark automatically calculates the Initial Round-trip Time (iRTT) for each TCP connection based on the time from the first to the third packet in the TCP handshake. This information is placed in all packets of a TCP conversation (except the SYN packet) under the *[SEQ/ACK analysis]* section, as shown below.

To find the fastest initial round-trip time, expand the *[SEQ/ACK analysis]* section of any TCP packet (except a SYN packet). Right-click on the *iRTT* field and select *Apply as Column.*

Now sort this column from low to high. Since many packets do not have this value in them (SYN packets and DNS packets), you will have some blank lines at the top of your sort list. Apply a filter for `tcp.analysis.initial_rtt` to only view packets that have this value.

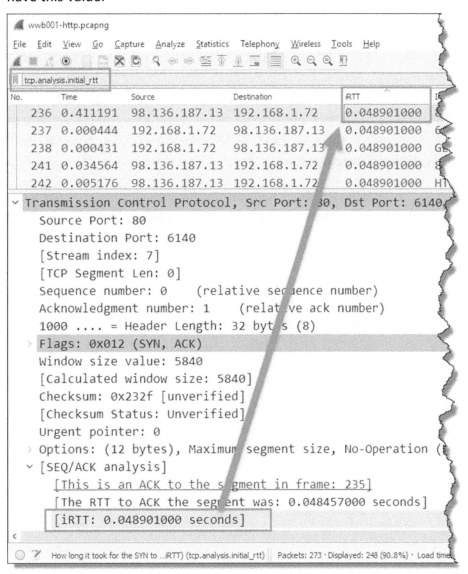

The connection that has the fastest iRTT is between 98.136.187.13 and 192.168.1.72 on ports 80 and 6140.

Lab 1 - A21. **There is one UDP stream in this trace file.**

You can use the *Statistics | Conversations* window to identify the number of UDP and TCP streams in a trace file.

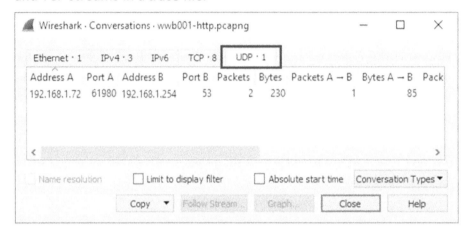

If you look inside TCP and UDP headers, you will see that every TCP and UDP conversation in the trace file is given a number by Wireshark (starting with 0). This is called the stream index number.

 When Wireshark adds information and interpreted fields that are not actually inside a packet, it places square brackets around the field in the Packet Details pane. The stream index numbers are provided by Wireshark – they do not exist in TCP or UDP headers.

In the following image, we right-clicked on the UDP *Stream index* field in the UDP header and selected *Apply as Column*.

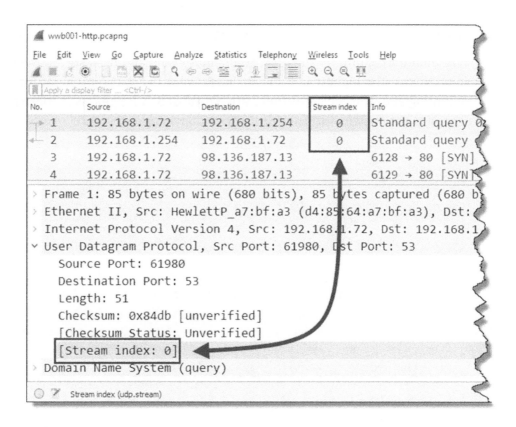

UDP stream index numbers and TCP stream index numbers are not related.

You can use these stream index numbers to filter on a conversation. For example, to apply a display filter for this conversation, the syntax would be udp.stream==0.

The stream indexing ability of Wireshark truly sped up the processing time for TCP and UDP conversation processing.

As you move ahead in this workbook, you will see how often I add a column for stream information.

Although you can get a conversation count by looking at the Statistics | Conversations window, you can also add the Stream index *column and sort from high to low to get the count.*

Lab 1 - A22.   **There are eight TCP streams in this trace file.**

We added a column for the *TCP Stream index* field and then sorted the column from high to low. The highest TCP stream index value is 7, but remember that we start counting at 0. This indicates there are a total of 8 TCP streams in this trace file. You can also get this answer using *Statistics | Conversations | TCP*.

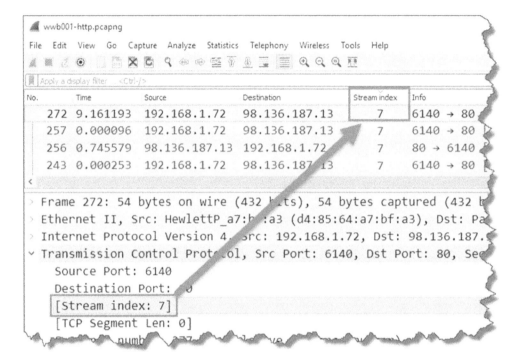

Lab 1 - A23.   **The purpose of TCP stream 7 is for the client to obtain the *favicon.ico* file from an HTTP server. This request is unsuccessful, however.**

We used the display filter `tcp.stream==7` to look at this one TCP conversation. Since we'd sorted differently when answering the last question, we had to click the *No.* column heading to re-sort in the original order.

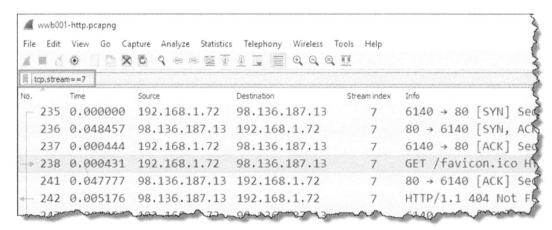

Lab 1 - A24.   One packet allows IP fragmentation in the IP header in this trace file.

In this case, we are looking in the IP header at the *Don't fragment* field. When this field is set to 0, IP fragmentation is allowed. When this field is set to 1, IP fragmentation is not allowed.

You can select any packet in the trace file, right-click on the *Don't fragment* field and choose *Prepare a filter*. If you selected a packet that does not allow fragmentation, simply edit the filter before you apply it.

You should be filtering on `ip.flags.df==0`.

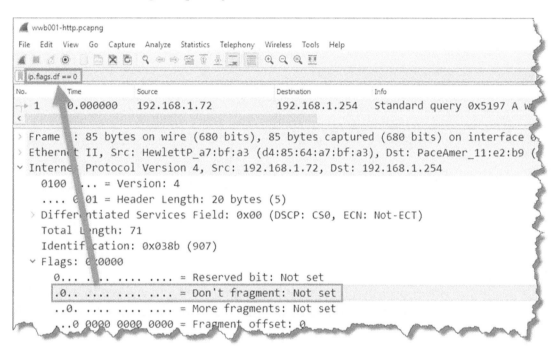

  If you want to know if there are IP fragments in a trace file, consider the following filter:

`ip.flags.mf==1 || ip.frag_offset > 0`

The first part, `ip.flags.mf==1`*, indicates that more fragments are to come in the fragment set. This will not catch the last fragment of a set, however.*

The second part, `ip.frag_offset > 0`*, means the fragment offset is greater than 0 – in other words, this is not the starting fragment. This will not catch the first fragment of a set, but it will catch the second through last fragment of the set.*

Lab 1 - A25. **The packets-per-second rate reaches over 125 in this trace file just once.**

Wireshark's IO Graph is the perfect tool to answer this question.

Select *Statistics | IO Graph*. By default, Wireshark provides the packets-per-second rate of all the traffic in the trace file and the TCP error count. In the next image shown, we can clearly see that the packets-per-second rate jumps above 125 just once in the trace file.

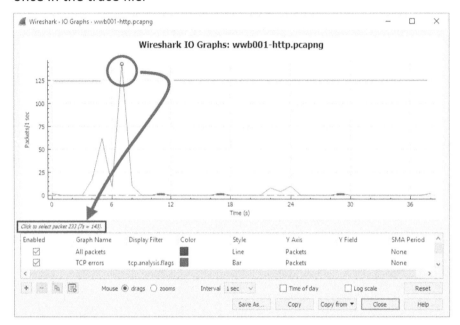

Hover over that high point in the graph and you will see that Wireshark indicates that the packets-per-second rate hit 143 at 7 seconds into the trace file.

Lab 2: Proxy Problem

Objective: Examine issues that relate to a web proxy connection problem.

Trace File: wwb001-pacing.pcapng

Skills Covered in this Lab

In this lab, you will have a chance to work with many key functions in Wireshark. The answers to this lab demonstrate how to use functions, including, but not limited to:

- Filter on SYN packets only
- Perform Maximum Segment Size (MSS) analysis
- Analyze TCP connection capabilities
- Detect HTTP *User-Agent* field values
- Detect HTTP request URI values
- Use the *Do not call subdissectors for error requests* TCP preference setting
- Analyze HTTP response time
- Detect HTTP server information
- Analyze HTTP response codes
- Create display filter buttons to detect HTTP errors
- Follow a TCP stream to identify an application
- Determine which host terminated a connection
- Use the Time Reference feature to measure delta times

Lab 2 - Q1. What is the IP address of the client?

_____

Lab 2 - Q2. What is the IP address of the server to which the client connects?

_____

Lab 2 - Q3. Analyze the TCP handshake process and explain the capabilities of the TCP peers and the features that will be available.

_____

_____

_____

Lab 2 - Q4. What browser is the client using to connect to the proxy server?

_____

Lab 2 - Q5. What file is the client requesting?

_____

Lab 2 - Q6. What type of file is a *.pac* file?

_____

Lab 2 - Q7. How many times did the client request the same *.pac* file?

_____

Lab 2 - Q8. What is the HTTP response time?

_____

Lab 2 - Q9.   **What version of web server software is running on the server?**

_____

Lab 2 - Q10.   **Why didn't the client load the *.pac* file?**

_____

Lab 2 - Q11.   **What software is used to block unsafe sites?**

_____

Lab 2 - Q12.   **Which side of the TCP conversation initiated termination of the connection?**

_____

Lab 2 - Q13.   **How long was this connection active before the client received an error response?**

_____

[This page intentionally left blank.]

Lab 2 Solutions

Trace File: wwb001-pacing.pcapng

Lab 2 - A1. **The IP address of the client is 192.168.9.49.**

Since the client is the one sending the SYN packets, we can see this information in the first packet of the trace file. If we did want to filter on SYN packets, the filter could be `tcp.flags.syn==1 && tcp.flags.ack==0` based on individual flag bits. Of course `tcp.flags==0x002` is also possible, but this filter is based on the TCP *Flags* summary line which includes other fields such as *Nonce* and *ECN-Echo*. For example, if the SYN and ECN-Echo bits are set, the TCP Flags summary value would be 0x042 and our filter would not display the packet.

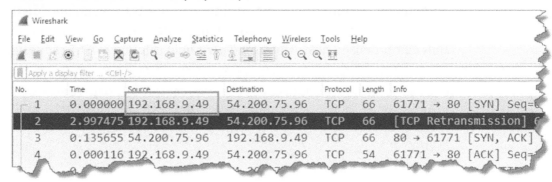

Lab 2 - A2. **The IP address of the server to which the client connects is 54.200.75.96.**

We don't really need to build a filter for this information because it is in the first packet of the trace file, as well.

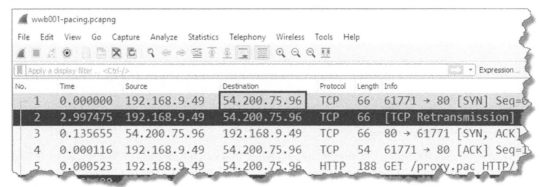

Lab 2 - A3. **Each side of the TCP conversation supports Window Scaling and Selective Acknowledgment (SACK). Each side advertises a different Maximum Segment Size (MSS), as noted below.**

In frame 1, 192.168.9.49 indicates its MSS is 1460 bytes. This means the server, 54.200.75.96, can send *up to* 1460 bytes of data after a TCP header[6] to this client.

```
1      0.000000 192.168.9.49   54.200.75.96   TCP   66
          61771 → 80 [SYN] Seq=0 Win=8192 Len=0 MSS=1460 WS=4 SACK_PERM=1
```

In frame 3, 54.200.75.96 indicates its MSS is 1200 bytes[7]. This means the client, 192.168.9.49, can send *up to* 1200 bytes of data after a TCP header to this server.

```
3      0.135655 54.200.75.96   192.168.9.49   TCP   66
          80 → 61771 [SYN, ACK] Seq=0 Ack=1 Win=5840 Len=0 MSS=1200 SACK_PERM=1 WS=128
```

Lab 2 - A4. **The client is using Internet Explorer v11 to connect to the proxy server.**

This *User-Agent* field is an interesting place to look in the case of network forensics. Sometimes, compromised hosts will send requests using unique identifiers in the *User-Agent* field. This can help you identify the malicious application running on that compromised host. The *User-Agent* field is found in GET requests.

```
> Frame 5: 188 bytes on wire (1504 bits), 188 bytes captured (1504 bits) on
> Ethernet II, Src: IntelCor_06:e2:8f (4c:80:93:06:e2:8f), Dst: MojoNetw_9d
> Internet Protocol Version 4, Src: 192.168.9.49, Dst: 54.200.75.96
> Transmission Control Protocol, Src Port: 61771, Dst Port: 80, Seq: 1, Ack:
∨ Hypertext Transfer Protocol
   > GET /proxy.pac HTTP/1.1\r\n
     Accept: */*\r\n
     User-Agent: Mozilla/5.0 (compatible; IE 11.0; Win64; Trident/7.0)\r\n
     Host: interproxy.ours.net\r\n
     \r\n
     [Full request URI: http://interproxy.ours.net/proxy.pac]
     [HTTP request 1/4]
     [Next request in frame: 6]
```

---

[6] The MSS value is the maximum amount of data bytes that can follow the TCP header. If the IP and TCP header are a minimum length of 20 bytes each, there is room for 1460 bytes of data. If, however, the IP and/or TCP headers have any options, the TCP data segment will be reduced by the number of bytes taken up by these options.

[7] See the previous footnote regarding the MSS size.

Lab 2 - A5.   **The client is requesting the *proxy.pac* file.**

This is evident in the Packet List pane *Info* column of frame 5.

If you were working with a trace file that had lots of traffic in front of the client's HTTP request, you could apply an `http.request.uri` filter to the trace file. Only packets that contain this field (HTTP request packets) would be displayed.

If you had lots of other hosts sending HTTP requests in the trace file, you could incorporate address information in your filter. For example, you could use `ip.src==192.168.9.49 && http.request.uri`.

```
> Ethernet II, Src: IntelCor_06:e2:8f (4c:80:93:06:e2:8f), Dst: Mojo
> Internet Protocol Version 4, Src: 192.168.9.49 (192.168.9.49), Dst
> Transmission Control Protocol, Src Port: 61771, Dst Port: 80, Seq:
v Hypertext Transfer Protocol
  v GET /proxy.pac HTTP/1.1\r\n
    v [Expert Info (Chat/Sequence): GET /proxy.pac HTTP/1.1\r\n]
        [GET /proxy.pac HTTP/1.1\r\n]
        [Severity level: Chat]
        [Group: Sequence]
    Request Method: GET
    Request URI: /proxy.pac
    Request Version: HTTP/1.1
```

Lab 2 - A6.   **A .pac file is a proxy auto-configuration file.**

This file contains the javascript function for a URL and host. An example of *.pac* file content is shown below.

```
function FindProxyForURL(url, host)
{
return "PROXY proxy.example.com:8080; DIRECT";
}
```

You can perform an Internet search for ".pac file extension" to find this information. One site that has great information regarding file types and file extensions is *fileinfo.com*.

Lab 2 - A7. **The client requested the same *.pac* file four times (frames 5, 6, 7, and 8).**

This information is visible right at the start of the trace file.

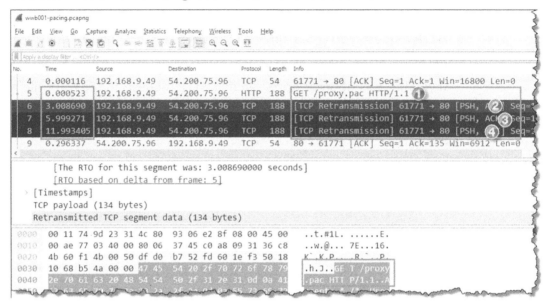

Wireshark automatically marks frames 6, 7, and 8 as TCP retransmission packets. The fact that these packets have the same sequence number as frame 5 and the same amount of data in the frames makes these retransmissions.

Note the time between the packets is almost exactly double for each retransmission. This is the nature of TCP's retransmission timer. It doubles the amount of time between successive retransmissions.

We should use a filter, however, to ensure we don't miss any of these *.pac* file requests later in the trace file. The filter `frame contains ==".pac"` will display the original request and three retransmitted requests.

If you filter for `http.request.uri=="/proxy.pac"` or even `http.request.uri contains ".pac"`, you may only detect one packet.

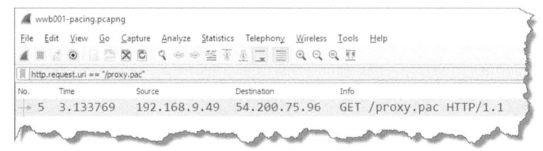

There are four packets requesting the *proxy.pac* file. Whether you see one or all four instances of the *proxy.pac* request depends on your Wireshark TCP preference settings.

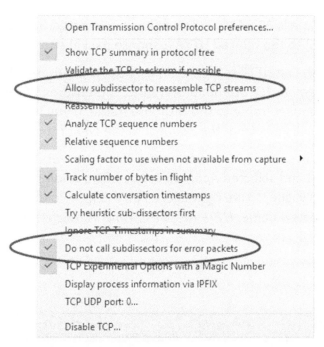

Turn off the TCP reassembly setting and disable *Do not call subdissectors for error packets* to see all four packets using a `http.request.uri=="/proxy.pac"` filter. If the HTTP dissector is not applied on these Retransmissions, you do not have an `http.request.uri` field on frames 6, 7, and 8.

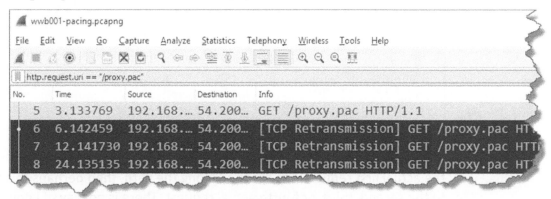

Now we see all requests. Before changing the TCP preference setting, three of the requests did not match the filter because the HTTP dissector was not being applied to the TCP retransmissions ("error" packets). The table below shows how the TCP preference settings affect the results of your filter.

Retransmitted GET Requests	TCP Reassembly ON	TCP Reassembly OFF
Do Not Call after Error ON	1 visible	1 visible
Do Not Call after Error OFF	1 visible	**4 visible**

Lab 2 - A8. **The HTTP response time is 22.647407. This value is calculated from the original GET request (frame 5) to the related HTTP response packet (frame 10).**

Any time you are analyzing HTTP response times, be sure to disable the *Allow subdissector to reassemble TCP stream* preference. This ensures Wireshark measures from the request frame to the response frame. If you have this setting enabled, Wireshark measures from the Request to the *end* of the object download.

In the image that follows, we right-clicked on the *Time since request* field in the HTTP response packet and selected *Apply as Column*. The column title, *Time since request*, was a bit too vague, so we right-clicked on the new column header and edited the name. The new name, *HTTP Response Time*, is much more descriptive.

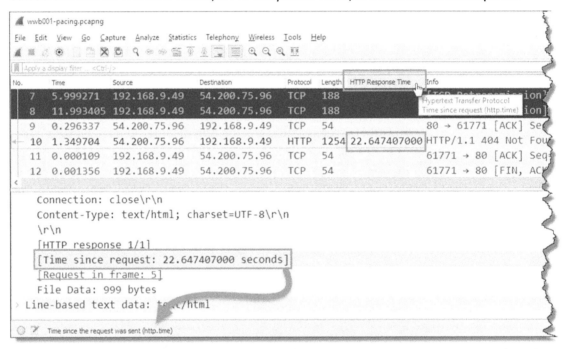

Wireshark measured the response time based on the first request in the trace file. If the actual first request was dropped along the path, then perhaps this response is to the second, third, or fourth actual request. There is no way of knowing if the original request arrived at the server. This is as much as we can tell from the packet-level view.

Lab 2 - A9.   Apache 2.2.3 (Red Hat) is the web server software running on the server.

```
∨ Hypertext Transfer Protocol
  ∨ HTTP/1.1 404 Not Found\r\n
    ∨ [Expert Info (Chat/Sequence): HTTP/1.1 404 Not Found\r\n]
        [HTTP/1.1 404 Not Found\r\n]
        [Severity level: Chat]
        [Group: Sequence]
      Request Version: HTTP/1.1
      Status Code: 404
      [Status Code Description: Not Found]
      Response Phrase: Not Found
    Date: Tue, 17 May 2016 22:05:01 GMT\r\n
    Server: Apache/2.2.3 (Red Hat)\r\n
```

There are numerous interesting fields that are returned with HTTP responses. These fields include the date information, server information and oftentimes, X- records (optional records that provide additional information about the server, user-agent, or connection).

The following are some sample filters to look for specific web server response attributes:

Filter	Purpose
`http.server contains "Apache"`	Find Apache web servers. "Apache" is case sensitive.
`http.server matches "Apache"`	Find Apache web servers using regular expressions. "Apache" is case insensitive.[8]
`http contains "X-"`	Find any custom options in web server responses.
`http.content_length > 500000`	Find server responses offering content that is greater than 500,000 bytes in length. (Try this on *wwb001-movietime.pcapng*.)

---

[8]   Prior to Wireshark v3, you needed to add "(?i)" in your regular expression to force case insensitivity (for example, `http.server matches "(?i)Apache"`). If you want to remove case insensitivity, add "(-?i)" at the front of your regular expression.

Lab 2 - A10. **The client did not load the *.pac* file because there is no such file at that location, and the server indicated that by sending a *404 Not Found* response.**

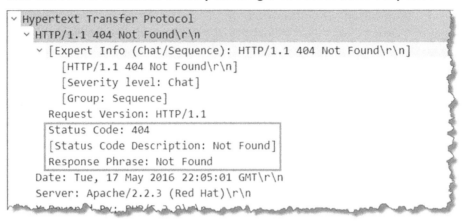

In this short trace file, it is pretty easy to spot the HTTP error response. If you are working on a larger trace file, you don't want to scroll to find any error responses. Instead, consider making a display filter button for `http.response.code > 399`.

To build this button, follow these steps:

1. Type the display filter into the *Display Filter* toolbar.
2. Click the + button on the right of the *Display Filter* toolbar.
3. Type the desired button label ("*HTTPErrors*" in our example).
4. Click *OK*.

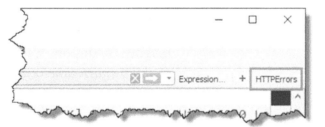

Display filter buttons appear to the right of the Display Filter input field.

Lab 2 - A11. Norton ConnectSafe is used to block unsafe sites.

This is a pretty short trace file containing only 25 packets and a single TCP conversation. This information must be in there somewhere.

Rather than scroll through the trace file and try to look for this information within each individual packet, right-click on any packet in the Packet List pane and select *Follow | TCP Stream*.

Wireshark's *Follow Stream* feature removes the network headers from view and shows you the application-layer commands and responses. This is a fast way to see the commands and responses used by applications.

Following streams is a great feature to use when you have unusual traffic on which Wireshark cannot apply a dissector. If an application uses a non-standard port number, Wireshark may not be able to identify the application and, therefore, would not apply a dissector to the traffic. For example, if a compromised host uses non-standard port numbers to communicate to a Command and Control (C2) server, following the stream might give you a hint as to what is being said between the hosts.

Notice the display filter that is applied when you follow a stream. The display filter is based on the stream index value.

Lab 2 - A12. **The client initiated termination of the TCP connection.**

In frame 12, the client sends a FIN/ACK packet to the server. The FIN indicates the Finish bit is set in the TCP header. This is an indication that the client is finished sending data to the server. Almost immediately, the client sends a RST/ACK, as well. The RST indicates the Reset bit is set in the TCP header. This bit is used to explicitly terminate a TCP connection.

Although the FIN bit is used to gracefully close the connection, it appears this client decided not to leave the connection in a half-open state by generating a RST. Until the server receives the RST, it can continue to send data to the client.

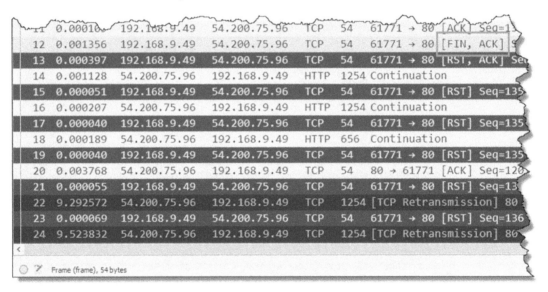

 Notice the stripes in the previous image.

Typically, stripes "do not look good" on a network. In Wireshark, they are often a sign of a problem. In this case, we have a client that has sent a TCP Reset to the server, but the server continues to send data to the client. The client is trying to terminate the connection, but it appears the server still has data coming to the client.

The location where you capture traffic can change the view of a process such as this. If capturing close to the server, you will see those data packets go out before the FIN and Resets arrive.

Lab 2 - A13.   **This connection is active 22.647930 seconds before the client received an error response.**

If we consider "active" to mean that the TCP handshake is completed, we would measure the time from the third packet of the TCP handshake to the *404* response packet for the answer.

To measure the time from the third packet of the TCP handshake to the *404* response packet, we will set a time reference by right-clicking on frame 4 and selecting *Set/Unset Time Reference*[9].

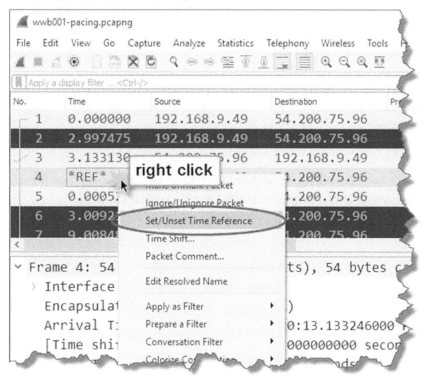

Time References are only temporary. If you close this trace file and open it again, the Time Reference will be gone. You can also right-click on frame 4 and toggle this setting off.

After setting the Time Reference, we can jump to the HTTP response packet using the hyperlink inside the HTTP GET request. Frame 10 contains the 404 response.

---

[9]   This is a good time to start looking at the keyboard shortcuts for Wireshark. You can find specific keyboard shortcuts by finding the operation in the menus. To obtain a complete list of keyboard shortcuts, view *Help | About Wireshark | Keyboard Shortcuts*.

The *Time since reference or first frame* field in the *Frame* section of the *404* response indicates that this packet arrived 22.647930 seconds after frame 4.

```
˅ Frame 10: 1254 bytes on wire (10032 bits), 1254 bytes captured (100
  › Interface id: 0 (unknown)
    Encapsulation type: Ethernet (1)
    Arrival Time: Jul 31, 2017 15:20:35.781176000 Pacific Daylight
    [Time shift for this packet: 0.000000000 seconds]
    Epoch Time: 1501539635.781176000 seconds
    [Time delta from previous captured frame: 1.349704000 seconds]
    [Time delta from previous displayed frame: 1.349704000 seconds]
    [Time since reference or first frame: 22.647930000 seconds]
    Frame Number: 10
    Frame Length: 1254 bytes (10032 bits)
    Capture Length: 1254 bytes (10032 bits)
```

 You can set multiple time reference packets in a trace file. Rather than right-click to remove each time reference separately, you can select Edit | Unset All Time References.

Lab 3: HTTP vs. HTTPS

Objective: Analyze and compare HTTP and HTTPS communications and errors using inclusion and field existence filters.

Trace File: wwb001-httpvshttps.pcapng

Skills Covered in this Lab

In this lab, you will have a chance to work with many key functions in Wireshark. The answers to this lab demonstrate how to use functions, including, but not limited to:

- Use an inclusion filter
- Use the *Conversations* window to analyze application use
- Apply "field existence" filters
- Compare related packet filters (`http.response_in` and `http.request_in`)
- Obtain packet counts based on port number filters
- Use Wireshark's autocomplete feature to filter on the TLS/SSL handshake
- Graph and compare port usage in a trace file
- Graph and compare protocol errors in a trace file
- Filter on HTTP errors
- Determine which TCP conversation contains the highest number of Expert Information warnings
- Determine why the window size scaling factor is shown as *-1* (unknown) by Wireshark

Lab 3 - Q1. What is the IP address of the client that is using HTTP and HTTPS?

_____

Lab 3 - Q2. What is the IP address of the HTTP server?

_____

Lab 3 - Q3. How many packets are to or from TCP port 80?

_____

Lab 3 - Q4. How many packets are to or from TCP port 443?

_____

Lab 3 - Q5. How many TLS/SSL handshake packets are in this trace file?

_____

Lab 3 - Q6. Build an IO Graph depicting the bits-per-second rate of HTTP traffic vs. the bits-per-second rate of HTTPS traffic. Based on your graph, did HTTP or HTTPS traffic have a higher bits-per-second rate in the trace file?

_____

Lab 3 - Q7. Again – build an IO Graph denoting TCP retransmissions seen in the HTTP traffic vs. TCP retransmissions seen in the HTTPS traffic. Did HTTP or HTTPS traffic experience the highest peak in the rate of retransmissions?

_____

Lab 3 - Q8. What HTTP error responses exist, if any?

_____

Lab 3 - Q9.   **Which TCP stream index number experienced the highest number of Duplicate ACKs?**

_____

Lab 3 - Q10.   **Why is the window size scaling factor shown as _-1 (unknown)_ in all the TCP header sections of this trace file?**

_____

[This page intentionally left blank.]

Lab 3 Solutions

Trace File: wwb001-httpvshttps.pcapng

Lab 3 - A1.   **The IP address of the client that is using HTTP and HTTPS is 192.168.1.70.**

There are several ways to obtain this information. In the example below, we applied a filter for `tcp.dstport in {80 443}`. The membership operator (`in`) looks for specified values within a field.[10] In this case, we are looking for the number 80 or 443 within the `tcp.dstport` field.

Once we applied this filter, we sorted on the *Source* field, looked at the first entry, and then jumped to the end of the trace and noticed the same value in the *Source* field. There is only one HTTP/HTTPS client in this trace file, 192.168.1.70.

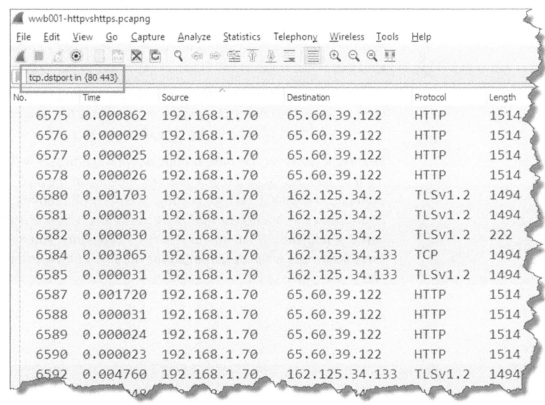

---

[10]   To look for a range of values, use "`..`" between the values. For example, to look for traffic from ports 650 and 780 through 810, use `tcp.srcport in {650 780..810}`.

You can also use the *Statistics | Conversations | TCP* window to obtain this information. In the image shown below, we see the only Address A value sending to ports 80 and 443 is 192.168.1.70.

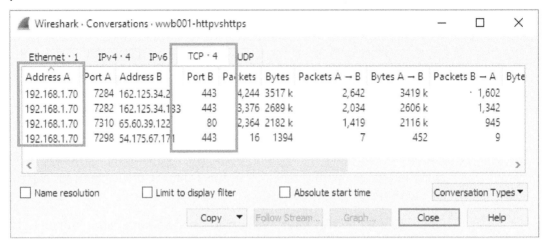

Address A	Port A	Address B	Port B	Packets	Bytes	Packets A → B	Bytes A → B	Packets B → A	Byte
192.168.1.70	7284	162.125.34.2	443	4,244	3517 k	2,642	3419 k	· 1,602	
192.168.1.70	7282	162.125.34.133	443	3,376	2689 k	2,034	2606 k	1,342	
192.168.1.70	7310	65.60.39.122	80	2,364	2182 k	1,419	2116 k	945	
192.168.1.70	7298	54.175.67.171	443	16	1394	7	452	9	

Another interesting statistics window is the Statistics | Endpoints *window.*

Statistics | Endpoints lists individual addresses seen in the trace file. If you want to know how many IPv4 hosts are in a trace file, you can open Statistics | Endpoints and look at the IPv4 or IPv6 tabs.

Be careful, however, because broadcasts and multicasts will show up in the IPv4 address list and multicasts will show up in the IPv6 list. For example, in wwb001-skyhigh.pcapng, Statistics | Endpoints *lists a total of 38 endpoints. There are six IPv4 multicast addresses, one IPv4 broadcast address, and one 0.0.0.0 address listed as endpoints. You must subtract these addresses when determining the number of IPv4 hosts in the trace file.*

Lab 3 - A2.   The IP address of the HTTP server is 65.60.39.122.

If you looked at the TCP conversations to obtain the answer to Lab 3 – A1, you would quickly see the HTTP (port 80) server is 65.60.39.122, as shown below.

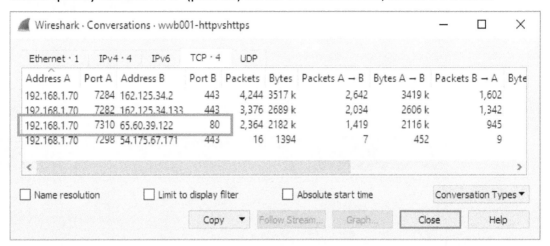

Alternately, you can create a filter for HTTP responses (which would only come from HTTP servers). For example, the filter `http.response` only displays a single packet from the HTTP server, offering a quick way to identify that server. This type of a filter (one without any parameters) is called a "field existence" filter.

Here's another interesting trick for HTTP display filtering. The display filter `http` displays only HTTP request and response packets in the trace file. You will not see the TCP handshake packets, TCP ACK/RST/FIN packets, or any of the data packets (if the TCP preference *Allow subdissector to reassemble streams* is on).

 There is another interesting trick with HTTP filters and related packets – the `http.response_in` *and* `http.request_in` *display filters. Normally, Wireshark does not have the ability to filter on one packet based on some characteristic of another packet. In the case of HTTP communications, however, Wireshark tracks the request-response nature of the communications and links requests to responses. When an HTTP request has a response in the trace file, Wireshark adds an* http.response_in *field to that request packet and provides the packet number of the related response. Applying a filter for* `http.response_in` *displays only HTTP requests that have responses in the trace file. Likewise, Wireshark adds an* http.request_in *field in response packets that have a related request in the trace file. Applying a filter for* http.response_in || http.request_in *will display only HTTP requests that have related responses and responses that have related requests in the trace file.*

An http.request && !http.response_in *display filter will show all the requests that do not have a response in the trace file.*

Lab 3 - A3. **There are 2,364 packets to or from TCP port 80 in this trace file.**

Apply a simple `tcp.port==80` display filter to view the count of displayed packets on the Status Bar.

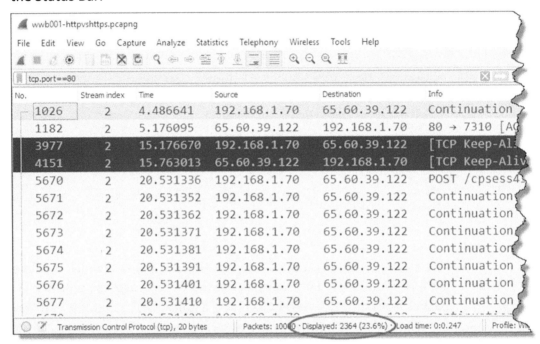

What if you wanted to focus on conversations that did not include TCP port 80 traffic?

There is a right and a wrong way to exclude traffic to and from a port.

The correct way is to simply put an ! *in front of the filter used above to create* !tcp.port==80.

The incorrect way (which people often try) is to use != *in the exclusion filter. For example,* tcp.port != 80 *will not remove any port 80 traffic from view.*

Why doesn't that filter syntax work? Because it is interpreted as tcp.srcport != 80 || tcp.dstport != 80. *In every packet, one of the port fields will not contain 80, so all packets will be shown. Nothing is excluded from view.*

Don't use != *with combo fields. A combo field is a Wireshark-generated field that expands to multiple real fields. For example,* tcp.port *means "*tcp.srcport *or* tcp.dstport.*" Other combo fields include* udp.port *and* ip.addr.

Lab 3 - A4.   There are 7,636 packets to or from TCP port 443 in this trace file.

Apply a simple `tcp.port==443` display filter to view the count of displayed packets on the Status Bar.

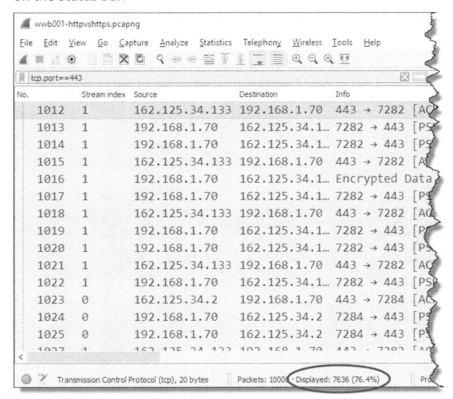

Lab 3 - A5.   There are no TLS/SSL handshake packets in this trace file.

If you just scroll through the trace file to find these packets, you'll waste a lot of time. Try the display filter auto-complete feature to find a suitable filter.

Wireshark v1 and v2 do not understand `tls` as a display filter.

If you are using Wireshark v1 or v2, type `ssl.` into the display filter area. Once you type the dot, Wireshark displays all the display filters that begin with `ssl`.

You will see `ssl.handshake` on the list of available display filters.

Once you apply the `ssl.handshake` display filter to the trace file indicates that there are no SSL handshake packets in the trace file.

Wireshark v3 and later support `tls` display filters. If you are using Wireshark v3, type `tls.` into the display filter area. Once you type the dot, Wireshark displays all the display filters that begin with `tls`.

You will see `tls.handshake` on the list of available display filters.

Once you apply the `tls.handshake` display filter to the trace file indicates that there are no TLS handshake packets in the trace file.

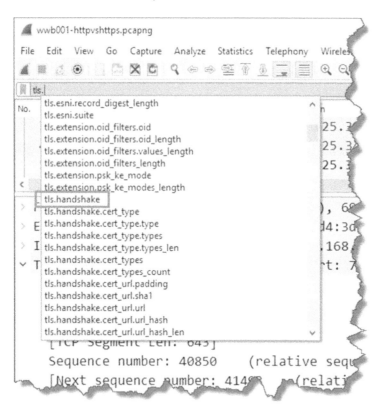

 When Wireshark v3 released, the NEWS.txt file indicated that "The SSL dissector has been renamed to TLS. As with BOOTP, the old "ssl." display filter fields are supported but may be removed in a future release."*

Do you read the NEWS.txt file when you update Wireshark? You should. There are sections listing bug fixes, new and updated features, removed features and support, new file format decoding support, new protocol support, new and updated capture file support, new and updated capture interfaces support, major API changes, and more.

The New and Updated Features section is one you should look at closely. For example, in Wireshark v3, the NEWS.txt file provided the information about this new display filter syntax.

Lab 3 - A6.   **An IO Graph depicting the bits-per-second rate of HTTP traffic vs. the bits-per-second rate of HTTPS traffic indicates that the HTTP traffic has a higher bits-per-second rate in the trace file.**

To build this graph, select *Statistics | IO Graph* and add two new graph lines.

Graph Name	Display Filter[11]	Color	Style	Y Axis
HTTP	tcp.port==80	Brown	Line	Bits
HTTPS	tcp.port==443	Green	Line	Bits

Based on the IO graph, we note that the HTTP traffic hit the highest bits-per-second rate in this trace file.

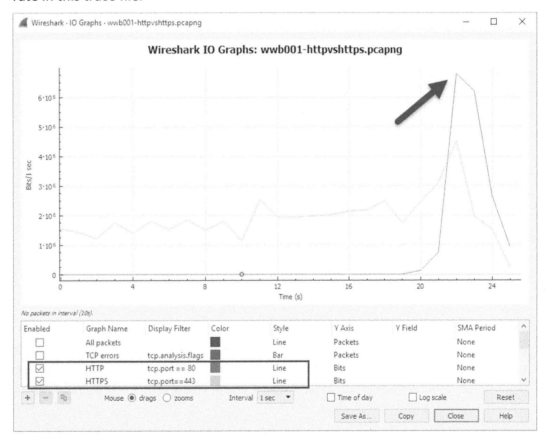

---

[11]   When filtering on applications that use TCP, remember to filter based on the port numbers rather than the protocol names. When you filter on the port numbers, you view the TCP overhead packets as well as request, response, and data packets. When you filter on the application names, you do not see the TCP overhead packets.

Lab 3 - A7. **An IO Graph denoting TCP retransmissions seen in the HTTP traffic vs. TCP retransmissions seen in the HTTPS traffic indicates that there is a higher rate of TCP retransmissions in the HTTP traffic (at the 24-second mark).**

To build this graph, select *Statistics | IO Graph* and edit your HTTP and HTTPS graph lines to use the following display filters.

Graph Name	Display Filter
HTTP	`tcp.port==80 && tcp.analysis.retransmission`
HTTPS	`tcp.port==443 && tcp.analysis.retransmission`

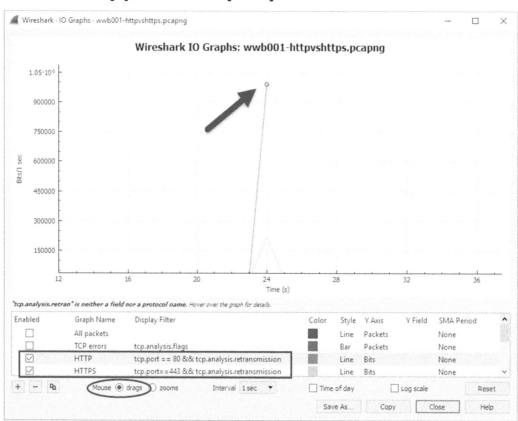

 Note the Mouse settings options at the bottom of the IO Graph. When set to "zooms," click and drag over an area to zoom into that area. Use "drags" to move the graph around. Click Reset to return to the original view.

Lab 3 - A8. **There is one HTTP error response in the trace file – *413 Request Entity Too Large*.**

We are interested in HTTP response codes that are greater than 399.

HTTP Response Code Sets

1xx   Information
2xx   Success
3xx   Redirection
4xx   Client Error
5xx   Server Error

The display filter `http.response.code > 399` will display all client and server errors.

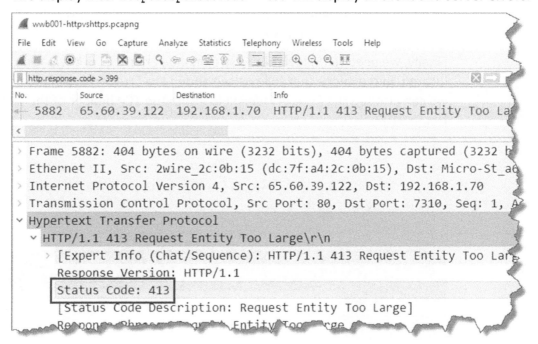

 If you were only interested in HTTP server errors, your filter could be `http.response.code > 499`*.*

If you only wanted to see HTTP client errors, your filter could be `http.response.code > 399 && http.response.code < 500`*.*

Lab 3 - A9. **TCP stream index number 2 experienced the highest number of Duplicate ACKs.**

To obtain this answer, we will (1) apply a display filter for
tcp.analysis.duplicate_ack and then (2) open the *Statistics | Conversations*
window. We next select the *TCP* tab and (3) check *Limit to display filter* in the
Conversations window.

Now we are only seeing packets that are TCP Duplicate ACKs in the *Conversations*
window.

We can sort the *Packets* column to identify the conversation that contains the
highest number of Duplicate ACKs.

To identify the stream index number of this conversation, (4) right-click on the top
conversation row and select *Find | A ⟷ B*.

Finally, we need to (5) look at the stream index number of the packet we just
located. In the image that follows, we added the *Stream index* field as a column, but
we can also see the *Stream index* field inside the TCP header of the highlighted
frame 9109.

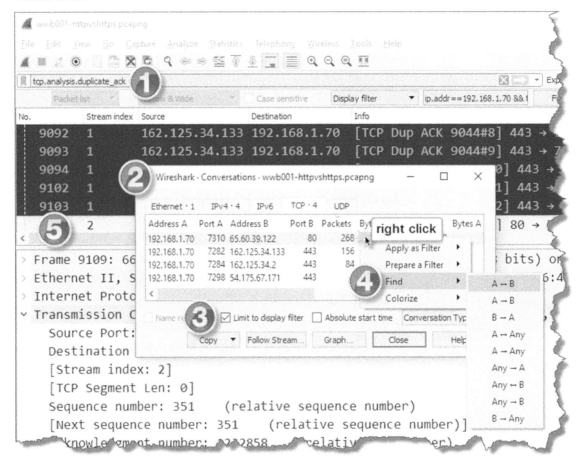

Lab 3 - A10. **The window size scaling factor (multiplier) is shown as *-1 (unknown)* in all the TCP header sections of this trace file because we did not capture the TCP SYN and SYN/ACK packets that are used to determine the window size scaling factor.**

In each TCP header of this trace file, you will see the "*[Window size scaling factor: -1 (unknown)]*" field.

The square brackets indicate this field contains an interpretation by Wireshark. Unfortunately, since we did not capture the SYN or SYN/ACK packets of these connections, we cannot know what window size scaling factors were advertised by the client and servers.

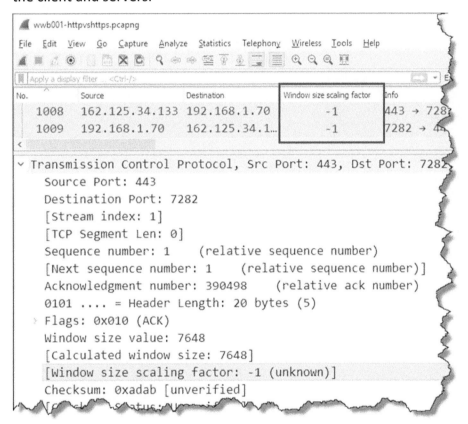

[This page intentionally left blank.]

Lab 4: TCP SYN Analysis

Objective: Filter on and analyze TCP SYN and SYN/ACK packets to determine the capabilities of TCP peers and their connections.

Trace File: wwb001-syns.pcapng

Skills Covered in this Lab

In this lab, you will have a chance to work with many key functions in Wireshark. The answers to this lab demonstrate how to use functions, including, but not limited to:

- Display TCP SYN packets only
- Analyze traffic coloring rules
- Analyze frame metadata
- Filter traffic based on the TCP Window Scaling option
- Filter traffic based on the TCP Selective Acknowledgment (SACK) option
- Filter traffic based on the TCP Timestamps option
- Filter traffic based on the TCP Maximum Segment Size value
- Limit conversation statistics to filters
- Analyze TCP SYN or SYN/ACK packets that are missing the MSS option
- Filter on TCP flags and network protocol
- Analyze true TCP sequence numbers
- Filter on data existence in frames
- Detect TCP Fast Open frames
- Determine the largest Window Scaling Shift Count
- Obtain the Initial Round-Trip Time (iRTT) between peers
- Determine whether TCP connections were terminated with FIN or RST

Lab 4 - Q1. Build and apply a filter to view only packets that have the TCP SYN bit set on. What is the syntax for this filter?

_____

Lab 4 - Q2. How many packets matched your TCP SYN filter?

_____

Lab 4 - Q3. Why are some of these packets colorized with Wireshark's Bad TCP coloring rule?

_____

Lab 4 - Q4. Why are some SYN packets colored green and others gray (using Wireshark's default coloring rules)?

_____

Lab 4 - Q5. How many TCP conversations support Window Scaling?

_____

Lab 4 - Q6. How many TCP conversations support Selective Acknowledgment (SACK)?

_____

Lab 4 - Q7. How many TCP conversations support TCP Timestamps?

_____

Lab 4 - Q8. How many SYN or SYN/ACK packets do _not_ contain a Maximum Segment Size (MSS) value?

_____

Lab 4 - Q9. What is the purpose of the MSS value in the TCP handshake?

_____

Lab 4 - Q10.   How will communication between TCP peers be affected if either peer does not advertise an MSS value during the handshake?

_____

Lab 4 - Q11.   How many SYN packets were sent over IPv6?

_____

Lab 4 - Q12.   Which SYN packet has the highest _true_ TCP sequence number?

_____

Lab 4 - Q13.   How many SYN or SYN/ACK packets contain data?

_____

Lab 4 - Q14.   What is the largest Window Scaling Shift Count?

_____

Lab 4 - Q15.   What is the largest Initial Round-trip Time (iRTT) seen between TCP peers?

_____

Lab 4 - Q16.   Were most TCP connections terminated using FIN or RST?

_____

[This page intentionally left blank.]

Lab 4 Solutions

Trace File: wwb001-syns.pcapng

Lab 4 - A1. **To view only packets that have the TCP SYN bit set on, the display filter is** `tcp.flags.syn==1`.

Don't be tempted to use the TCP *Flags* summary line, *Flags: 0x002 (SYN)*, as that filter includes all the flags bits and packets will match the filter only if they have that exact combination of bits set.

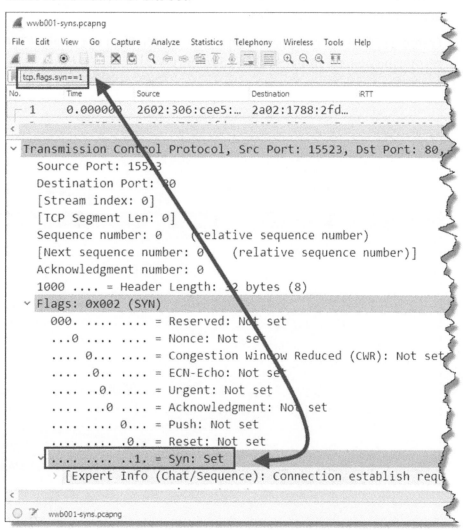

Lab 4 - A2. **Eighteen packets matched the TCP** `tcp.flags.syn==1` **filter.**

It is typical to see an even number of packets with the SYN bit set. We see two packets with the SYN bit set in every complete handshake in the trace file, the SYN packet and the SYN/ACK packet. If we are missing part of a TCP handshake or a retransmission of the first two handshake packets occurred, we may see an odd number of packets matching this filter.

Lab 4 - A3. **Packet 4 and Packet 216 are colorized with Wireshark's Bad TCP coloring rule because they are TCP retransmissions.**

In the image below, we associated the TCP retransmissions with the original packets. The frame 4 SYN/ACK is a retransmission of frame 3. We can see the match of the port numbers easily. Both the original TCP SYN/ACK and the retransmission are from port 80 to port 15523.

Frame 216 SYN is a retransmission of frame 215. Both the original TCP SYN and the retransmission are from port 15626 to port 443.

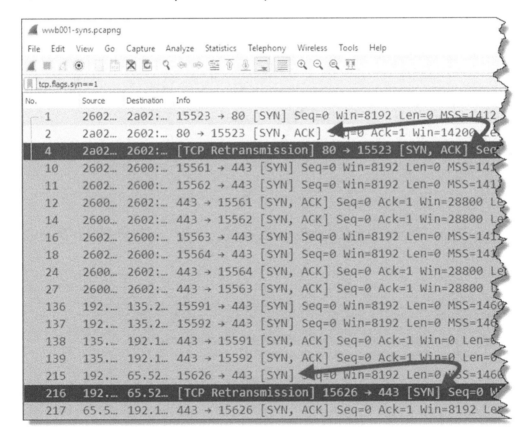

Select *View | Coloring Rules* to add, modify, delete, and deactivate coloring rules.

Lab 4 - A4. **The SYN packets colorized in green match the HTTP coloring rule string while the SYN packets colorized in gray match the TCP SYN/FIN coloring rule string.**

The *Frame* section (at the top of the Packet Details pane) contains metadata about each packet. This information is gathered from the trace file header, the packet header, or added by Wireshark during packet processing.

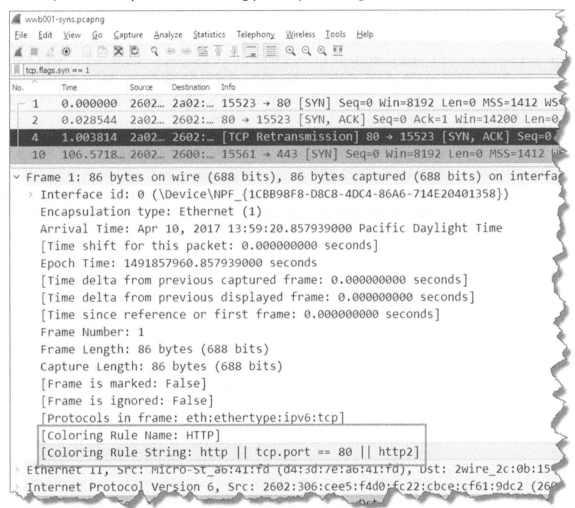

Let's take a closer look at the different lines in the *Frame* section of frame 1 and identify how each item is obtained. Keep in mind that all information in square brackets is a Wireshark interpretation. All other information comes from the trace file header, packet header, or the packet itself.

.pcapng *(the "ng" stands for Next Generation) is a more robust trace file format than the traditional* .pcap *format and is the default for Wireshark captures. We will focus on* .pcapng *captured trace file formats in this section. The* .pcapng *format specification is held at the GitHub repository (*https://github.com/pcapng/pcapng*).*

- **Frame 1: 86 bytes on wire (688 bits), 86 bytes captured (688 bits) on interface 0**
Wireshark often creates summary lines with basic information. In many cases, you can look at the summary line to obtain all the information you need about the collapsed section that is summarized.

- **Interface id: 0 (\Device\NPF_{1CBB98F8-D8C8-4DC4-86A6-714E20401358})**
This information is situated in the *Interface Description Block (IDB)* container of the trace file. This is the container for information describing an interface on which packet data is captured. Since Wireshark (and other capture tools) can capture on more than one interface at a time, this block differentiates the interfaces used to capture separate packets.

- **Encapsulation type: Ethernet (1)**
This information is also inside the IDB container in the *LinkType* field. This field contains a value that identifies the link layer type for the interface that captured this packet. The possible Encapsulation type values (Standardized Link-Layer Type codes) are available in the *tcpdump.org* link-layer header types registry at *http://www.tcpdump.org/linktypes.html.*

- **Arrival Time: Apr 10, 2017 13:59:20.857939000 Pacific Daylight Time**
Inside the trace file we also have an *Enhanced Packet Block (EPB)* container. This is where the timestamp information is stored during the capture-to-file process. The timestamp is a 64-bit unsigned integer that represents the number of units of time (seconds and microseconds) that have elapsed since 1970-01-01 00:00:00 UTC. When you send a trace file across time zones, the arrival time will be based on the capture file UTC value (the local offset to UTC, such as +1 in Berlin) and the local time zone setting. The image on the previous page depicts the time in Pacific Daylight Time because that is the time zone setting on the computer used to write this book. If the computer's time zone setting is changed to Venezuelan Standard Time, this field will display *"Arrival Time: Apr 10, 2017 16:59:20.857939000 Venezuela Standard Time."*

If you spend time analyzing trace files sent to you from other time zones, take a moment and test how the arrival time information changes as you alter the time zone setting on your computer. For example, if you on the East Coast of the United States, your computer is likely set to use the EST time zone. If you open one of my trace files for this book, you must change your computer's time zone setting to Pacific Standard Time to see the same arrival time that I saw while writing this book.

- **[Time shift for this packet: 0.000000000 seconds]**
  Here we see square brackets. This means that this field is a Wireshark interpretation. Time shifting is a feature that is used to change the timestamp of a packet or entire trace file. Although rarely used, if time shifting had been set on this packet, we would know it.

- **Epoch Time: 1491857960.857939000 seconds**
  This field is the time from 00:00:00 1/1/1970 UTC.

- **[Time delta from previous captured frame: 0.000000000 seconds]**
  Another Wireshark interpretation, this is the time delta from the previous captured frame to this frame. Frames are timestamped upon full receipt, so this is the delta time from the end of the previous frame to the end of the current frame.

- **[Time delta from previous displayed frame: 0.000000000 seconds]**
  You probably get this time area now. Wireshark has calculated and is displaying the time from the end of the receipt of the previous displayed frame to the end of the current frame.

 This is a great time field when you are looking for large gaps of time in a conversation. Apply a display filter for a conversation (using `tcp.stream==x` *or* `udp.stream==x`) *and then right-click on this field and select* Apply as Column.

- **[Time since reference or first frame: 0.000000000 seconds]**
  You can right-click on any number of packets in the Packet List pane and set them as Time References. The *Time* column increments from those Time Reference packets if it is set to *Seconds Since Beginning of Capture*. Again, this is a Wireshark calculation.

- **Frame Number: 1**
  This is simply the frame number in the trace file.

- **Frame Length: 86 bytes (688 bits)**
  Frame length information is contained in the "Original Packet Length" inside the EPB container of the *.pcapng* trace file. Watch this field along with the next field, the *Capture Length* field, to determine if the capture process sliced (shortened) the packets.

- **Capture Length: 86 bytes (688 bits)**
  Also provided by the EPB container of the *.pcapng* trace file, the *Capture Length* field should be the same as the *Frame Length* (original packet length) field if the entire packet has been captured. If not, consider the capture tool in use – is it set to capture only a certain number of bytes and therefore clipping off the end of the packets? This problem is indicated in Wireshark's Expert as well.

- **[Frame is marked: False]**
  You can right-click on any packet in the Packet List pane and mark the packet. This turns the packet background black with a white foreground (text color). This is only a temporary marking of the packet, however. If you really want to call attention to a packet, right-click on the packet in the Packet List pane and add a comment to the packet.

 Packet commenting is a fabulous feature that is only available when saving trace files in the .pcapng format. If you try to save a trace file that has comments in it in the old .pcap format, a warning message appears stating that the comments will be discarded if you save in this format.

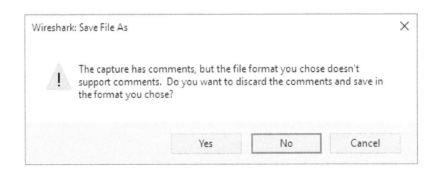

- **[Frame is ignored: False]**
  Ignoring packets hides all packet information and places *<Ignored>* in the *Info* column of the Packet List pane. When you open the trace file again, the packet information is visible again. You can use this feature to remove a packet, or set of packets, from a trace file. Simply ignore the packet(s) and select *File | Export Specified Packets* and check the *Remove Ignored packets* option.

- **[Protocols in frame: eth:ethertype:ipv6:tcp]**
  This information is based on the protocol dissectors applied to the packets by Wireshark. Most packets have more than one dissector applied.

- **[Coloring Rule Name: HTTP]**
  This field indicates the name of the coloring rule which the packet matches. The Colorize Packet List feature is enabled by default. Even if it isn't enabled, this Coloring Rule Name is still inside the *Frame* section.

- **[Coloring Rule String: http || tcp.port==80 || http2]**
  This field indicates the Coloring Rule String (based on a display filter) that the packet matches. Again, this field is visible in the *Frame* section even if the *Colorize Packet List* feature is disabled.

Now that you've looked inside the *Frame* section, click on *Statistics | Capture File Properties* or click the *Capture File Properties* button next to the *Expert Information* button on the Status Bar, as shown in the image below.

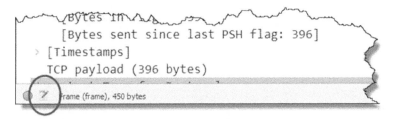

```
          Bytes in
      [Bytes sent since last PSH flag: 396]
  > [Timestamps]
    TCP payload (396 bytes)

  7  Frame (frame), 450 bytes
```

The *Capture File Properties* window displays additional information that is placed inside the *.pcapng* file during the capture-and-save process. For example, notice the OS section and the Application section. This can be important information to obtain if you are concerned about the trace file capture process.

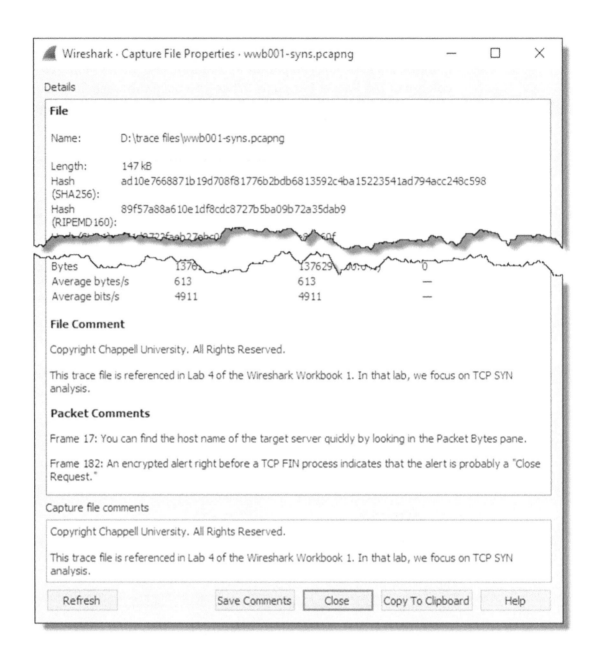

 The Capture File Properties window is very useful if you need to build an analysis report to explain what you have detected in a trace file.

Consider adding trace file comments in this window and packet comments (right-click on a packet in the Packet List pane and select Packet Comment...).

Select Copy to Clipboard in the Capture File Properties window and paste all the information (including the statistics, packet and trace file comments) into your word processing program.

You must save your trace file after adding comments. In addition, commenting is only supported with .pcapng format trace files.

Lab 4 - A5.   **Six TCP conversations support Window Scaling.**

Since this is a short trace file, you could apply a filter for SYN packets and then look at the *Info* column to see where a "WS=" value is missing. There is, however, a better way to find this information. Apply a filter for SYN/ACK packets that contain the Window Scaling option.

This filter consists of the following elements:

> The SYN bit is set to 1. (tcp.flags.syn==1)
> The ACK bit is set to 1. (tcp.flags.ack==1)
> The TCP Option Kind 3 (Window Scaling) exists. (tcp.option_kind==3)[12]

Why are we just looking at the SYN/ACK packets and not the SYN packets? Well, if the client sends a SYN and does not indicate that it supports Window Scaling, the server will not respond with the Window Scaling option. When we see a SYN/ACK with the Window Scaling option included, we can assume the client supports Window Scaling. Packets that match this filter will be from servers that support Window Scaling as well.

In the following image, we can see the *Window Scale* field in the TCP options area of the TCP header in a SYN/ACK packet.

The display filter we used was (tcp.flags.syn==1) && (tcp.flags.ack==1) && (tcp.option_kind==3).

---

[12]   Alternately, you could use && tcp.options.wscale.

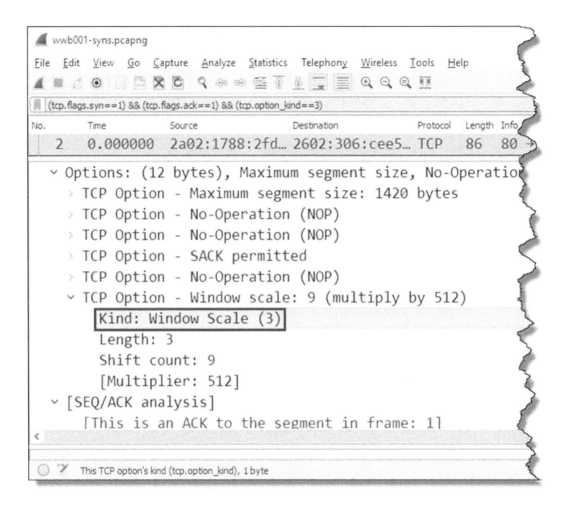

We could just count the conversations that match this filter, but what if this is a large trace file with hundreds or even thousands of TCP conversations. Instead, open the *Statistics | Conversations* window and select *Limit to display filter*.

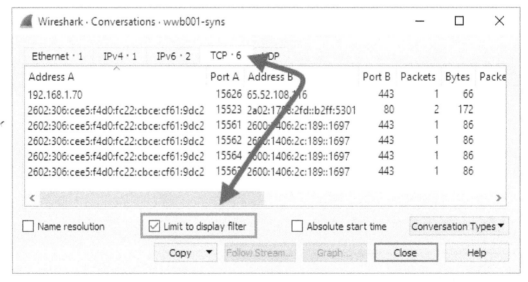

Wireshark counts the number of TCP conversations that match your filter and provides this information on the *TCP* tab.

Another great feature of the *Statistics | Conversations* window is the *Graph* button. Select a TCP conversation and click the *Graph* button.

Wireshark launches the TCP Time-Sequence (tcptrace) window.

There is almost always a better way to find packets that match a specific characteristic than scrolling through a trace file. Learn display filtering in depth.

Don't forget that you can always save those hot display filters as buttons. Just click the + on the display filter toolbar and name your button.

Lab 4 - A6. **Six TCP conversations support Selective Acknowledgment (SACK).**

Using a similar technique as Lab 4 - A5, we applied a filter for SYN/ACK packets that have the Selective acknowledgment option enabled (SACK Permitted). This is TCP option Kind 4. When we open the TCP *Conversations* window and limit the window to the display filter, we see that six conversations match our filter.

Just like Window Scaling, SACK must be supported by both sides of a TCP connection to be used. Therefore, we only need to look at the SYN/ACK packets again.

The display filter we used was (tcp.flags.syn==1) && (tcp.flags.ack==1) && (tcp.option_kind==4).[13]

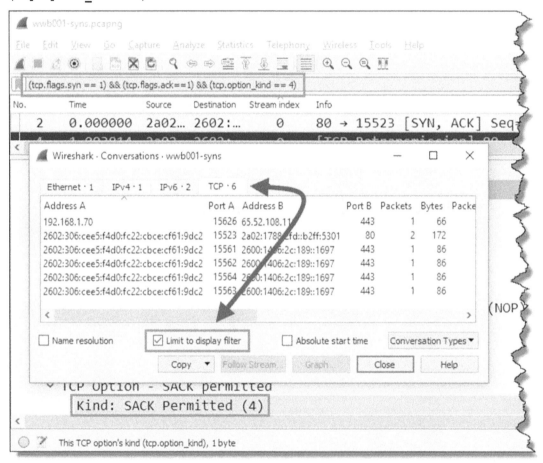

---

[13] You could replace && (tcp.option.kind==4) with && (tcp.options.sack_perm), if desired.

Lab 4 - A7.   No TCP conversations support TCP Timestamps.

Again, we are looking at SYN/ACK packets. This time, we are interested in TCP Option Kind 8, TCP Timestamps.

This time, the display filter is (tcp.flags.syn==1) && (tcp.flags.ack==1) && (tcp.option_kind==8).

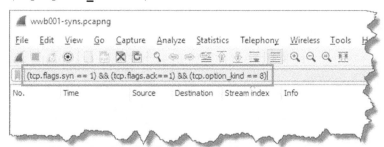

What if you don't have a packet to look at to determine the TCP Timestamps option Kind value? Check out *https://www.iana.org/assignments/tcp-parameters/tcp-parameters.xhtml* to view the entire list of assigned TCP options.

Lab 4 - A8.   Two SYN/ACK packets do not contain a Maximum Segment Size (MSS) value – frame 138 and frame 139.

In this case, we only need to look at the SYN bit and the absence of the Maximum Segment Size value. Now we are interested in both the SYN and SYN/ACK packets. The *Maximum Segment Size (MSS)* field is defined by TCP option Kind 2.

The display filter is (tcp.flags.syn==1) && !(tcp.option_kind==2).

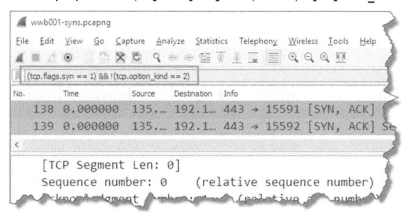

Lab 4 - A9. **Each side of a TCP connection states the maximum amount of data it can receive in a TCP packet as defined by the MSS value.**

If we look at Frames 1 and 2 of this trace file, we see the client sent a SYN packet with an MSS of 1412 and the server send a SYN/ACK packet with an MSS of 1420. These two values do not need to match. The handshake is not a negotiation.

The client is stating that the server must not send the client more than 1412 bytes of data in a TCP packet.

The server is stating that the client must not send the server more than 1420 bytes of data in a TCP packet.

```
No.        Info
  1    15523 → 80 [SYN] Seq=0 Win=8192 Len=0 MSS=1412 WS=256 SACK_PER
  2    80 → 15523 [SYN, ACK] Seq=0 Ack=1 Win=14200 Len=0 MSS=1420 SACK
```

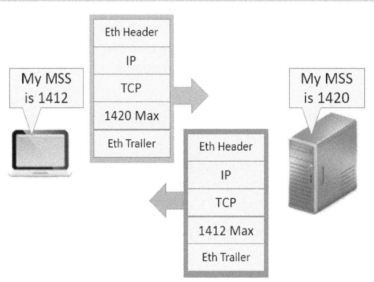

It's important to remember that the TCP handshake is not a negotiation.

Each side simply states their capabilities.

There is one interesting side note to that depiction, however.

If the client does not support a TCP option such as Selective acknowledgment, the server will not indicate it supports the option – even if it is configured to do so.

There is no reason for a server to send information regarding Selective Acknowledgment support if the client wouldn't understand it.

Lab 4 - A10.   If a TCP SYN or SYN/ACK packet does not contain a Maximum Segment Size (MSS) option, an MSS value of 536 will be used by default.

You could use the `tcp.flags.syn==1 && !tcp.options.mss_val` display filter to find the two SYN/ACK packets that do not contain the MSS option.

When working on a trace file that has numerous intertwined conversations, add a column for the stream index number so you can differentiate the conversations easily. Wireshark numbers each UDP conversation and TCP conversation separately. The numbering starts at 0. Rather than make two columns – one for the `tcp.stream` value and another for the `udp.stream` value, create a single column and change the Fields area to `tcp.stream || udp.stream`, as shown in the following image.

When you add this column, you will notice that Frames 138 and 139 are part of TCP streams 5 and 6.

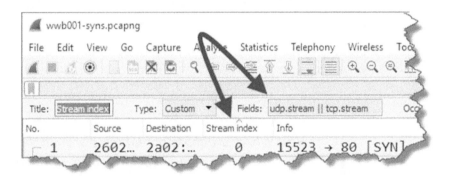

Now add a column for the *TCP Segment Len* field in the TCP header. You will notice that the client never sends a packet with more than 536-bytes of data.

This is not an optimal TCP connection if the client needs to upload lots of data to the server! Whose fault is it that this is a lousy connection? It is the server's fault (unless an internetworking device, such as a router, is changing the MSS value along the path[14]).

---

[14]   This would be very bad behavior, indeed! Unfortunately, we've seen this time and time again on networks. I'd recommend that you also capture traffic as close as possible to the server (if the server is yours) to check what the server is actually sending.

Lab 4 - A11. **Five SYN packets were sent over IPv6.**

Using a similar technique to what we used earlier in this lab, we applied a display filter for the SYN bit set on, the ACK bit set off, and IPv6.

The display filter we used was `tcp.flags.syn==1 && tcp.flags.ack==0 && ipv6`.

Unlike earlier in this lab, we don't need to open a statistics window to obtain the answer. In this case, we can simply look at the Status Bar to see the number of packets that matched our filter.

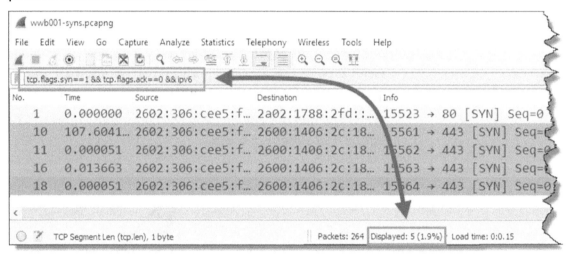

Hey! Where are those parentheses around the sections of the display filter? Isn't that going to be a problem? No, not if you are only using "and" or only using "or" in your filter. If you mix them together in a single display filter, you MUST use parentheses to explicitly state for what you are looking. If you neglect to put in parentheses when mixing operators, Wireshark turns the display filter background yellow and offers a warning in the lower left corner of the status bar, "suggest parentheses around '&&' within '||' – may have unexpected results".

Lab 4 - A12. **Frames 215 and 216 are the SYN packets that have the highest *true* TCP sequence number.**

Two packets have the highest true sequence number because one is a retransmission of the other.

Our first step is to turn off Wireshark's relative sequence number feature. Right-click on a TCP header in the Packet Details pane, select *Protocol Preferences*, and click *Relative sequence numbers* to disable this feature.

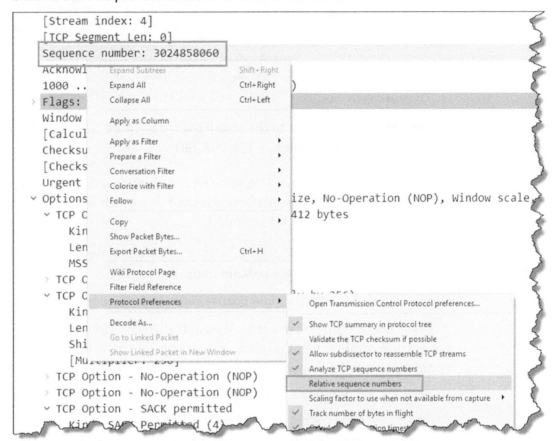

We added a column for the *Sequence number* field by right-clicking on the field and selecting *Apply as Column*.

 Whenever you are looking for the highest or lowest value of a field (such as the TCP Sequence number *field in this case), add a column for the field and sort the column.*

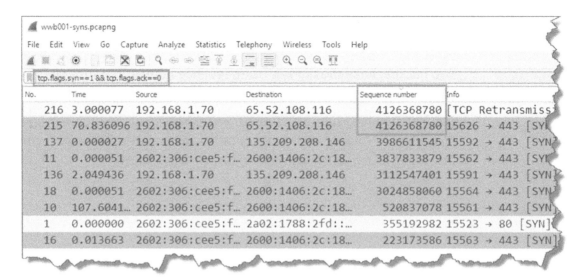

Frames 216 and 215 jump to the top of the list because they both have the highest TCP sequence number value, 4,126,368,780.

 I highly recommend that you enable relative sequence numbers again after you've answered this question. It is much simpler to use sequence number values that start at 0.

Lab 4 - A13. **No SYN or SYN/ACK packets contain data.**

We can check this with a simple display filter: `tcp.flags.syn==1 && tcp.len > 0`

It is very unusual to see data contained in the SYN or SYN/ACK packets of the TCP connection-establishment process at this time. You may, however, see data contained in the final packet of the three-way handshake, the ACK packet.

Section 3.4, Establishing a Connection, of RFC 793, Transmission Control Protocol, allows for data in these packets as seen below:

```
"Several examples of connection initiation follow.  Although
these examples do not show connection synchronization using
data-carrying segments, this is perfectly legitimate, so long
as the receiving TCP doesn't deliver the data to the user
until it is clear the data is valid (i.e., the data must be
buffered at the receiver until the connection reaches the
ESTABLISHED state)."
```

 You may have heard of TCP Fast Open, defined in RFC 7413. In TCP Fast Open, you may see data contained in the TCP SYN packets. This data is actually a cookie field. The TCP Fast Open Cookie option Kind is 34. To detect if anyone is using TCP Fast Open, use the display filter `(tcp.flags.syn==1) && (tcp.option_kind==34)`.

Lab 4 - A14.   The largest Window Scaling Shift Count is 9 (multiply the sender's Window Size value by 512).

The Window Scaling Shift Count is contained in SYN and SYN/ACK packets during the establishment of Window Scaling. This Shift Count is used to define the multiplier that the sender will apply to the advertised *Window Size Value* field.

To determine the largest Window Scaling Shift Count, added a column for the *Shift Count* field (seen in TCP SYN and SYN/ACK packets that contain the Window Scaling option). Sorting that column from high to low, we see the maximum Shift Count value of 9.

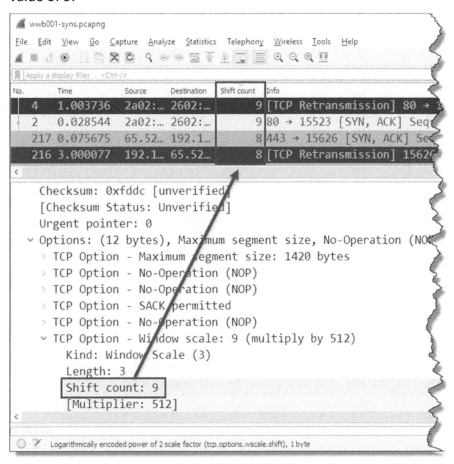

The following table shows how this Shift Count value affects the interpretation of the *Calculated window size* field.

Shift Count	Multiply the Window Size field by...
0	1
1	2
2	4
3	8
4	16
5	32
6	64
7	128
8	256
9	512
10	1,024
11	2,048
12	4,096
13	8,192
14	16,385

A shift count of 14 is defined as the maximum possible in Section 2.3 of RFC 7323, *TCP Extensions for High Performance*.

If you consider that the *Window Size* field is a 2-byte field, the maximum value in that field can be 65,535.

Multiply 65,535 by the multiplier 16,385 for a maximum *Calculated window size* field of 1,073,790,975 bytes. That should be enough to last for a while, we hope.

If a host advertises a shift count greater than 14, the receiver will simply use 14 and log an error. The TCP connection should still be established.

Lab 4 - A15. The largest Initial Round-trip Time (iRTT) seen between TCP peers is 0.075875 seconds.

Except for SYN packets, every TCP packet contains an Initial Round-trip Time (*iRTT*) field in the *[SEQ/ACK analysis]* section of the TCP header.

To measure the largest iRTT value, add this field as a column and sort the column from high to low.

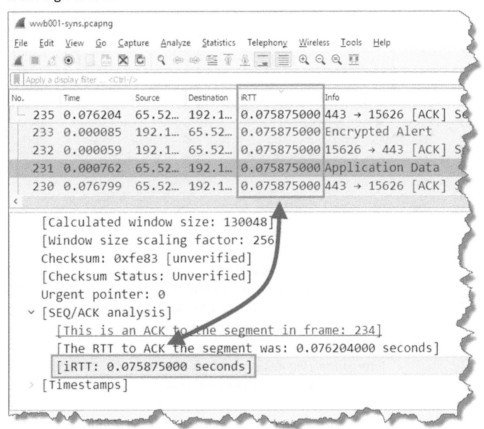

The *iRTT* field calculates the time from the first packet (SYN) to the third packet (ACK) of each TCP handshake in the trace file. The iRTT value remains the same for the entire TCP connection since it is calculated during the handshake only.

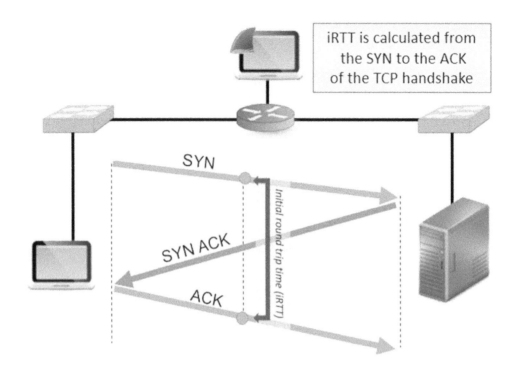

iRTT is calculated from
the SYN to the ACK
of the TCP handshake

SYN

SYN ACK

ACK

Initial round trip time (iRTT)

! *This field is very useful for troubleshooting. When analyzing delays within a TCP connection, refer to the* iRTT *field value to get an idea of the path latency between the hosts. Look for any large gaps in time between packets in a TCP stream and compare the times to the iRTT value. If there is a large difference in time values, then the delay is either caused by an interconnecting device (such as a queuing device along a path) or processing delays at the client or server.*

Lab 4 - A16. **One-half of the TCP connections were terminated using FIN and one-half of the TCP connections were terminated using Reset.**

It takes several steps to get this information. First, we apply a display filter for tcp.flags.fin==1 || tcp.flags.reset==1. If you look at the TCP flag settings shown in the *Info* column, frame 231 does not display any flags information. That is because frame 231 has data in it. Wireshark is giving us the highest-layer summary possible – and in the case of frame 231, there is data in the packet.

Simply add the *[TCP Flags]* summary line as a column. This summary line is at the bottom of the *Flags* section of the TCP header.

Finally, add and sort a *Stream index* column.

tcp.flags.fin==1 || tcp.flags.reset==1

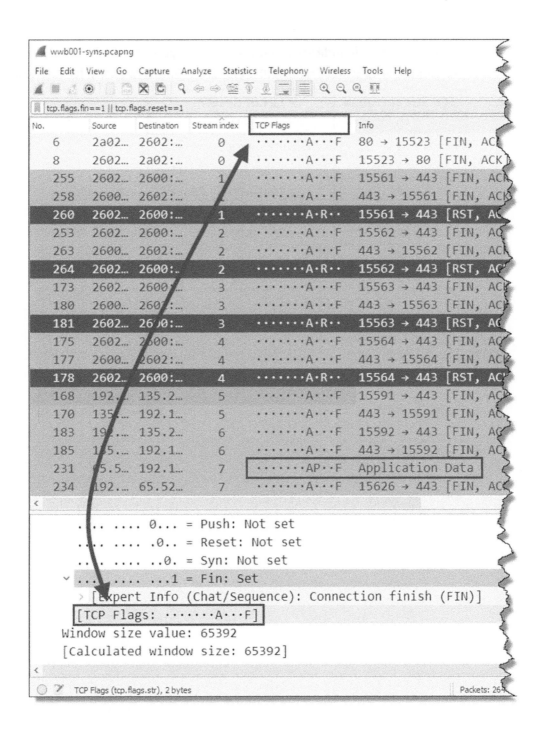

The following table indicates that there is an even split. The connections that exchanged FIN packets before Resets were ultimately closed by the Reset packets.

TCP Stream Index	FIN or Reset?
0	FIN
1	FIN, followed by Reset
2	FIN, followed by Reset
3	FIN, followed by Reset
4	FIN, followed by Reset
5	FIN
6	FIN
7	FIN

Lab 5: TCP SEQ/ACK Analysis

Objective: Examine and analyze TCP sequence and acknowledgment numbering and Wireshark's interpretation of non-sequential numbering patterns.

Trace Files:	wwb001-seqack1.pcapng
	wwb001-seqack2.pcapng

Skills Covered in this Lab

In this lab, you will have a chance to work with many key functions in Wireshark. The answers to this lab demonstrate how to use functions, including, but not limited to:

- Identify HTTP request packets
- Use DNS flags to filter on all DNS responses
- Count the TCP streams in a trace file
- Filter properly on DNS name values
- Learn how DNS name fields are constructed
- Learn when Wireshark's TCP relative sequence number starts at 0 vs. 1
- Follow TCP relative sequence numbers
- Learn how *Sequence/Acknowledgment number* fields increment during the TCP handshake
- Differentiate client services from server services
- Determine which direction data is flowing in a TCP conversation
- Learn to identify retransmissions based on sequence numbers
- Identify retransmissions triggered by the Retransmission Time Out (RTO) timer
- Learn how the RTO counter is calculated
- Learn how to locate a Wireshark bug in Bugzilla
- Examine frame size differences caused by Selective Acknowledgment (SACK) information
- Set and measure time using Time Reference frames

Use wwb001-seqack1.pcapng to answer Lab 5 - Q1 – Q10.

Note: The questions should be answered with the TCP preference *Relative sequence numbers* on.

Lab 5 - Q1. What is the IP address of the HTTP client?

_____

Lab 5 - Q2. What are the IP addresses of the DNS servers?

_____

Lab 5 - Q3. How many TCP streams are in this trace file?

_____

Lab 5 - Q4. What is the IP address of *wiresharkbook.com*?

_____

Lab 5 - Q5. Why is the sequence number set at 0 by default on frame 9?

_____

Lab 5 - Q6. Why is the Acknowledgment number set at 0 on frame 9?

_____

Lab 5 - Q7. Why is the sequence number set at 0 on frame 19?

_____

Lab 5 - Q8. Why is the Acknowledgment number set at 1 on frame 19?

_____

Lab 5 - Q9.   **Why did the sequence number increment to 1 in frame 22?**

_____

Lab 5 - Q10.   **How did Wireshark calculate the next sequence number value of 313 in frame 23?**

_____

┌──┐

Use wwb001-seqack2.pcapng to answer Lab 5 - Q11 – Q19.
This capture contains only a portion of an HTTPS session.

└──┘

Lab 5 - Q11.   **How many TCP conversations are contained in this trace file?**

_____

Lab 5 - Q12.   **Towards which direction is most of the data flowing in this trace file?**

_____

Lab 5 - Q13.   **What starting sequence number has Wireshark assigned to the TCP peers?**

_____

Lab 5 - Q14.   **How many times did the 192.168.0.12 host transmit the packet with sequence number 405 and why did it transmit this sequence number more than once?**

_____

Lab 5 - Q15.   **Which frames contain the ACK for the 192.168.0.12 host's sequence number 405 packet?**

_____

Lab 5 - Q16. How many times did the 162.125.17.131 host transmit the packets with sequence number 669 and why did it transmit this sequence number more than once?

_____

Lab 5 - Q17. If frame 10 is a duplicate of frame 9, why did the packet size change?

_____

Lab 5 - Q18. How much time elapsed from 192.168.0.12's first data packet with sequence number 405 and its data packet with sequence number 809?

_____

Lab 5 - Q19. This capture contains only a portion of an HTTPS session. What should the next sequence number be from the 192.168.0.12 host?

_____

Lab 5 Solutions

Trace Files:	wwb001-seqack1.pcapng
	wwb001-seqack2.pcapng

Use wwb001-seqack1.pcapng to answer Lab 5 - Q1 – Q10.

Lab 5 - A1.   **The IP address of the HTTP client is 10.2.2.2.**

We can apply an `http` display filter to quickly view all HTTP requests and responses. This provides us with the IP address of the client. Alternately, we can use an `http.request` filter so we only see traffic from the client.

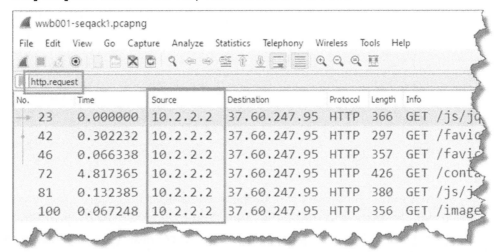

 Do you wonder why we keep asking you to identify the client and the server in these Labs?

Knowing the general purpose of each host is an important step to getting your bearings in a trace file.

When I open a new trace file, my first step is to identify the clients versus the servers.

Lab 5 - A2. **The IP addresses of the DNS servers are 10.223.68.206 and 3fdb:f7d7:fef7:f6fc:7404:d495:7718:3c87.**

The display filter `dns.flags.response==1` shows all DNS responses in the trace file. Since there are only 39 DNS responses, you could simply look at the *Source* field for the answer.

Alternately, you could look at the *Statistics | Endpoints | UDP* window, select *Limit to display filter*, and sort on the *Port* column. DNS is expected to run over port 53, so the first two items list the DNS servers' addresses.

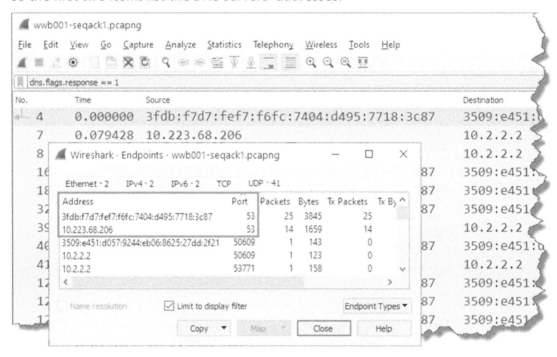

Earlier in this *Wireshark Workbook*, it was noted that there are often many ways to obtain an answer to these questions. You could have used a port filter (`udp.port==53 || tcp.port==53`), or a protocol filter (`dns`). Just avoid the dreaded "scrolling to find answers." Make Wireshark work for *you*.

Lab 5 - A3.   There are 12 TCP streams in this trace file.

A TCP "stream" can also be referred to as a conversation or connection. Open the *Statistics | Conversations* window and look at the *TCP* tab for the TCP stream count.

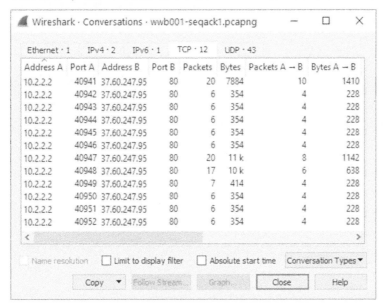

Lab 5 - A4.   The IP address of *wiresharkbook.com* is 37.60.247.95.

There are so many ways to get this answer! Let's look at the concept of "casting a wide net." We could build a very specific display filter that gives us just the packet(s) we are interested in or we could save ourselves a bit of time by "casting a wide net," or applying a general filter and then enhancing it if there are too many unrelated responses.

For example, you could start with a filter for just `dns`. That displays 82 packets. If this trace file were a lot larger, you might have just too many unrelated packets through which to wade. Let's tighten up this display filter a bit.

Since the IP address would be in a DNS response packet, we could use a `dns.flags.response==1` filter. This only displays 39 packets. We could do better, however.

To specify that we are interested in the *wiresharkbook.com* name resolution, let's try `dns contains "wiresharkbook"` as our filter. Now we are down to 16 packets.

That's not too bad, but can we get even more specific?

DNS responses that provide an A (IPv4) address place that address in a `dns.a` field. DNS responses that provide an AAAA (IPv6) address contain a `dns.aaaa` field value. Let's add these fields to our filter.

```
dns contains "wiresharkbook" && (dns.a || dns.aaaa)
```

Now you are down to four packets. Each of those four packets has the IP address for *wiresharkbook.com*.

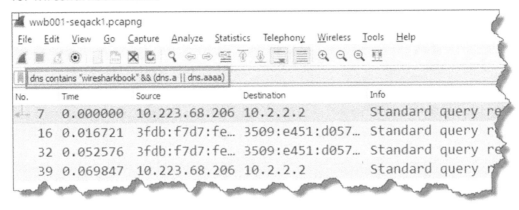

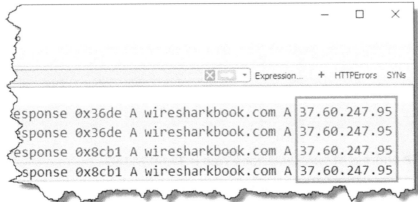

I'm sure someone reading this *Wireshark Workbook* tried the following display filter:

```
dns contains "wiresharkbook.com"
```

Try it. Go ahead. It makes sense, right? Shouldn't we see 16 packets like we did earlier? Hmmmm.... Unfortunately, no packets match this filter. To understand why, we need to look inside the DNS response packet.

```
    Questions: 1
    Answer RRs: 1
    Authority RRs: 0
    Additional RRs: 0
  v Queries
    v wiresharkbook.com: type A, class IN
        Name: wiresharkbook.com
<

0000   f2 38 89 33 be 95 f2 73   19 c0 93 39 08 00 45 00    .8.3...s ...9..E.
0010   00 4f d7 5a 40 00 40 11   07 93 0a df 44 ce 0a 02    .O.Z@.@. ....D...
0020   02 02 00 35 de 89 00 3b   f6 d9 36 de 81 80 00 01    ...5...; ..6.....
0030   00 01 00 00 00 00 0d 77   69 72 65 73 68 61 72 6b    .......w ireshark
0040   62 6f 6f 6b 03 63 6f 6d   00 00 01 00 01 c0 0c 00    book.com ........
0050   01 00 01 00 00 38 40 00   04 25 3c f7 5f             .....8@. .%<._
```

In the preceding image, we clicked on the *Name* field inside the *Queries* area of the DNS packet of frame 7. We then opened the hex window to see how this field is constructed.

Notice that the "dots" are not dots – they are length values. They are only represented as dots on the right side of the Packet Bytes window because Wireshark displays the raw packet bytes as ASCII characters. Any byte that is not in the ASCII displayable range is displayed as a dot.

The literal interpretation of this field is:

> [13]wiresharkbook[3]com[0]

If you are filtering on *wiresharkbook.com*, you won't get a hit on this. It doesn't have a "dot." An ASCII dot is 0x2E. Instead, the dot is 0x03, which does not have an ASCII equivalent.

Interestingly, `dns.qry.name=="wiresharkbook.com"` does work because Wireshark automatically accounts for the dot in the dissection process.

Creating a `dns contains "www.wiresharkbook.com"` filter would be a very common mistake.

It seems logical that it should work and that's why so many students try this out in classes.

We will look more closely at DNS filtering in Lab 8: DNS Warm-up.

Lab 5 - A5. **The sequence number of frame 9 is set to 0 by default because we are using a relative sequence number value. Wireshark starts counting at 0 on SYN and SYN/ACK packets.**

The image below shows the top of the TCP header on frame 9. Look at the hex window when you click on the *Sequence number* field. This sequence number isn't 0 – it's 2,002,189,533 (0x7756fcdd).

```
> Frame 9: 66 bytes on wire (528 bits), 66 bytes captured
> Ethernet II, Src: f2:38:89:33:be:95 (f2:38:89:33:be:95)
> Internet Protocol Version 4, Src: 10.2.2.2 (10.2.2.2),
v Transmission Control Protocol, Src Port: 40941, Dst Por
    Source Port: 40941
    Destination Port: 80
    [Stream index: 0]
    [TCP Segment Len: 0]
    Sequence number: 0       (relative sequence number)
    Acknowledgment number: 0
<

0000   f2 73 19 c0 93 39 f2 38   89 33 be 95 08 00 45 00
0010   00 34 28 7d 40 00 80 06   00 00 0a 02 02 02 95 22
0020   7a ae 9f ed 00 50 77 56   fc dd 00 00 00 00 80 02
0030   20 00 de b0 00 00 02 04   05 b4 01 03 03 08 01 01
0040   04 02
```

Relative sequence numbering is the default setting in Wireshark. When relative sequence numbering is on, so is relative acknowledgment numbering. The relative sequence numbers don't always start at 0, however.

If a trace file does not contain the SYN or SYN/ACK packets of the TCP handshake, Wireshark assigns 1 as the first relative sequence number. The relative sequence number only starts at 0 on SYN and SYN/ACK packets.

You can turn off Wireshark's relative sequence numbering feature, if desired.

When would you want to disable relative sequence numbering?

Consider if you were capturing at multiple points on a network. If there is no guarantee that the TCP handshake was captured at each location on the network, you must use the true sequence number value to match up a packet at each capture location.

To disable the relative sequence numbering feature, right-click on a TCP header in the Packet Details pane, select Protocol Preferences, and deselect Relative sequence numbers.

Lab 5 - A6.   **The acknowledgment number is set at 0 on frame 9 because it is the first packet of the handshake.**

This field would represent the next expected sequence number from the TCP peer, but no packets have been received from that peer yet. We don't know the sequence number that it will use. The Acknowledgment number should always be set at 0 in the SYN packet.

```
> Frame 9: 66 bytes on wire (528 bits), 66 bytes captured
> Ethernet II, Src: f2:38:89:33:be:95 (f2:38:89:33:be:95),
> Internet Protocol Version 4, Src: 10.2.2.2 (10.2.2.2), D
v Transmission Control Protocol, Src Port: 40941, Dst Por
     Source Port: 40941
     Destination Port: 80
     [Stream index: 0]
     [TCP Segment Len: 0]
     Sequence number: 0     (relative sequence number)
     Acknowledgment number: 0
<

0000   f2 73 19 c0 93 3  f2 38  89 33 be 95 08 00 45 00
0010   00 34 28 7d 40 0  80 06  00 00 0a 02 02 02 95 22
0020   7a ae 9f ed 00 50 77 56  fe 4d 00 00 00 00 80 02
0030   20 00 de b0 00 00 02 04  05 b4 01 03 03 08 01 01
0040   04 02
```

As mentioned earlier, if a trace file does not contain the SYN or SYN/ACK packets of a TCP handshake, Wireshark assigns 1 as the first relative sequence number. In that case, Wireshark will also assign 1 as the first relative acknowledgment number. The relative acknowledgment number is the other peer's next expected sequence number. Wireshark's relative sequence number mechanism treats sequence numbers and acknowledgment numbers the same way. The relative acknowledgment number only starts at 0 on SYN and SYN/ACK packets.

 Want to analyze TCP Sequence/Acknowledgment numbers faster? First, get more than one monitor! You cannot analyze efficiently with a single monitor. You need two at the least. Next, right-click on and add the following columns to the Packet List pane:

> Sequence number *field (consider naming it SEQ+)*
> [TCP Segment Len(gth)] *field (consider naming it LEN=)*
> Next sequence number field *(consider naming it NextSEQ)*
> Acknowledgment number field *(consider naming it ACKNUM)*

The first three columns provide the formula for TCP sequence numbering – current Sequence Number + data bytes = next Sequence number.

Lab 5 - A7.   **The sequence number is set at 0 on frame 19 because this is a SYN/ACK packet and we are using relative sequence numbers.**

Just as Wireshark sets the sequence number to 0 on SYN packets, it also sets the sequence number to 0 on SYN/ACK packets. It's a lot easier to count from 0 than 1,333,639,158.

```
> Frame 19: 66 bytes on wire (528 bits), 66 bytes captur
> Ethernet II, Src: f2:73:19:c0:93:39 (f2:73:19:c0:93:39
> Internet Protocol Version 4, Src: 37.60.247.95, Dst: 10
∨ Transmission Control Protocol, Src Port: 80, Dst Port:
    Source Port: 80
    Destination Port: 40941
    [Stream index: 0]
    [TCP Segment Len: 0]
    Sequence number: 0     (relative sequence number)
    [Next sequence number: 0     (relative sequence numbe
    Acknowledgment number: 1     (relative ack number)
0000  f2 33 89 33 be 95 f2 73  19 c0 93 39 08 00 45 00
0010  00 34 04 6e 40 00 32 06  1b b7 25 3c f7 5f 0a 02
0020  02 02 00 50 9f ed 4f 7d  b7 f6 77 56 fc de 80 12
0030  72 10 02 80 00 00 02 04  05 b4 01 03 03 07 01 01
0040  04 02
```

You really do need to know how TCP sequence numbering works.

It may feel like a tedious process, but go through a trace file and follow the Sequence number *field from a host as it sends data to a peer.*

Watch how the Sequence number *field increments by the number of data bytes sent.*

Watch how the Acknowledgment number *field indicates the next sequence number expected from a peer.*

Practice, practice, practice!

Lab 5 - A8.   **The acknowledgment number is set at 1 on frame 19 because it is a *relative* acknowledgment number and the next expected relative sequence number from the other TCP peer is 1. The TCP peer's sequence number is incrementing by the "phantom byte".**

Frame 19 is a SYN/ACK to the SYN in frame 9. When relative sequence numbering is on, so is relative acknowledgment numbering.

```
> Frame 19: 66 bytes on wire (528 bits), 66 bytes captur
> Ethernet II, Src: f2:73:19:c0:93:39 (f2:73:19:c0:93:39
> Internet Protocol Version 4, Src: 37.60.247.95, Dst: 1
v Transmission Control Protocol, Src Port: 80, Dst Port:
    Source Port: 80
    Destination Port: 40941
    [Stream index: 0]
    [TCP Segment Len: 0]
    Sequence number: 0      (relative sequence number)
    [Next sequence number: 0      (relative sequence numb
    Acknowledgment number: 1      (relative ack number)

0000  f2 38 89 33 be 95 f2 73  19 c0 93 39 08 00 45 00
0010  00 34 04 6e 40 00 32 06  1b b7 25 3c f7 5f 0a 02
0020  02 02 00 50 9f ed 4f 7d  b7 66 77 56 fc de 80 12
0030  72 10 02 80 00 00 02 04  05 b4 01 03 03 07 01 01
0040  04 02
```

During the TCP handshake, each packet that has the SYN bit on will have a "phantom byte" of data in the packet. It's not really there, but we pretend it is. This causes the *Acknowledgment number* field of the SYN/ACK packet to increment to 1.

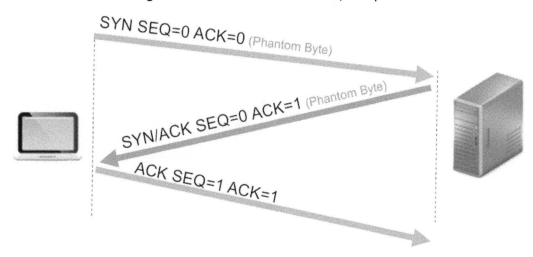

Lab 5 - A9. **The sequence number incremented to 1 in frame 22 because of the "phantom byte" in the SYN packet (frame 9).**

Even though we really didn't see a single byte of data in the TCP SYN packet, we must always assume there was one "phantom byte" sent in the packet. Since the *Sequence number* field increments for every data byte sent, the sequence number value in the final ACK of the TCP handshake will be 1.

```
> Ethernet II, Src: f2:38:89:33:be:95 (f2:38:89:33:be:95)
> Internet Protocol Version 4, Src: 10.2.2.2 (10.2.2.2), D
v Transmission Control Protocol, Src Port: 40941, Dst Port
    Source Port: 40941
    Destination Port: 80
    [Stream index: 0]
    [TCP Segment Len: 0]
    Sequence number: 1    (relative sequence number)
    Acknowledgment number: 1    (relative ack number)
    0101 .... = Header Length: 20 bytes (5)
  v Flags: 0x010 (ACK)
```

Lab 5 - A10. **Wireshark added frame 23's sequence number value (1) and TCP Segment Length value (312) to determine that this host will send sequence number 313 next.**

The sequence/acknowledgment equation is "current sequence number plus data bytes in this packet equal the next sequence number to use."

The *Next sequence number* field is not an actual TCP field—it is placed in the packets by Wireshark (hence the square brackets around the field).

```
> Frame 23: 366 bytes on wire (2928 bits), 366 bytes captured (
> Ethernet II, Src: f2:38:89:33:be:95 (f2:38:89:33:be:95), Dst:
> Internet Protocol Version 4, Src: 10.2.2.2 (10.2.2.2), Dst: 1
v Transmission Control Protocol, Src Port: 40941, Dst Port: 80,
    Source Port: 40941
    Destination Port: 80
    [Stream index: 0]
    [TCP Segment Len: 312]
    Sequence number: 1    (relative sequence number)
    [Next sequence number: 313    (relative sequence number)]
    Acknowledgment number: 1    (relative ack number)
    0101 .... = Header Length: 20 bytes (5)
  v Flags: 0x018 (PSH, ACK)
        000. .... .... = Reserved: Not set
        ...0 .... .... = Nonce: Not set
```

When you analyze the sequence/acknowledgment numbers, sometimes it helps to add the Sequence number, TCP Segment Len(gth), Next sequence number, *and* Acknowledgment number *fields as columns in the Packet List pane. Simply right-click on these fields in any TCP header and select* Apply as Column.

Use wwb001-seqack2.pcapng to answer Lab 5 questions A11 – A19.
This capture contains only a portion of an HTTPS session.

Lab 5 - A11.   There is 1 TCP conversation in this trace file.

We can obtain this information from the *Statistics | Conversations* window or we could even add a `tcp.stream` column and sort it to see that there is only one TCP conversation in this trace file (TCP stream 0).

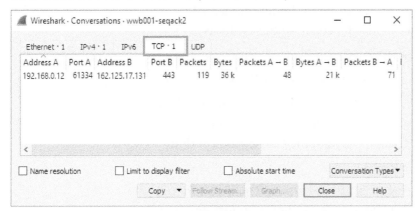

Note that you can perform TCP analysis on encrypted traffic because the TCP header is not encrypted. This enables you to rule out many network issues when you are troubleshooting. If everything looks good up to the TCP layer, then the focus must be on the application.

Lab 5 - A12. **Most data is flowing from 192.168.0.12 towards 162.125.17.131 in this trace file.**

The *Statistics | Conversations | TCP* window provides this information. Focusing on the directional *Bytes* columns, we see that 21k was transferred from Address A (192.168.0.12) towards Address B (162.125.17.131). Only 14k was transferred in the opposite direction.

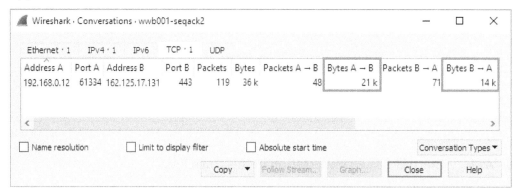

You don't have to keep the default set of conversation tabs active in this window.

Click on the *Conversation Types* button to select/deselect the tabs you would like displayed.

As of Wireshark v3 early releases, this window does not automatically detect the conversations in the trace file and apply tabs based on that information.

In other words, if you remove the IPv6 tab and there are IPv6 conversations, you just won't see them in the *Conversations* window any more.

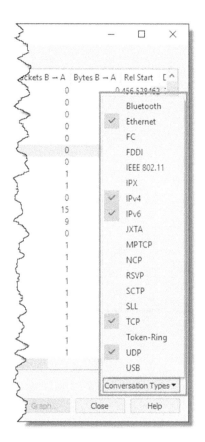

Lab 5 - A13.   Wireshark assigned 1 as the starting sequence number for each of the TCP peers.

The starting sequence number is visible in frames 1 and 2. Note that Wireshark only assigns a starting sequence number of 0 to packets with the SYN bit set. If a packet with the SYN bit is not seen, Wireshark assigns sequence number 1 to the first packet from each side of a TCP conversation.

```
> Frame 1: 388 bytes on wire (3104 bits), 388 bytes captured (3104
> Ethernet II, Src: ArrisGro_cc:c8:07 (14:ab:f0:cc:c8:07), Dst: Inte
> Internet Protocol Version 4, Src: 162.125.17.131 (162.125.17.131)
v Transmission Control Protocol, Src Port: 443, Dst Port: 61334, S
     Source Port: 443
     Destination Port: 61334
     [Stream index: 0]
     [TCP Segment Len: 334]
     Sequence number: 1       (relative sequence number)
     [Next sequence number: 335      (relative sequence number)]
     Acknowledgment number: 1     (relative ack number)
```

```
> Frame 2  458 bytes on wire (3664 bits), 458 bytes captured (3664
> Ethernet II, Src: IntelCor_06:e2:8f (4c:80:93:06:e2:8f), Dst: Arr
> Internet Protocol Version 4, Src: 192.168.0.12 (192.168.0.12), Ds
v Transmission Control Protocol, Src Port: 61334, Dst Port: 443, Se
     Source Port: 61334
     Destination Port: 443
     [Stream index: 0]
     [TCP Segment Len: 404]
     Sequence number: 1       (relative sequence number)
     [Next sequence number: 405      (relative sequence number)]
     Acknowledgment number: 335     (relative ack number)
```

Now might be an interesting time to look at the Wireshark code to see where this behavior is defined.

Visit *www.wireshark.org* and select *Develop | Browse the Code*. The Wireshark code is managed in the GIT repository.

We are looking for the TCP dissector file (*packet-tcp.c*). This resides in the */epan/dissectors* directory. When you open the *packet-tcp.c* file, look for the phrase "Start relative seq" until you reach the section explaining the use of "TCP_S_SAW_SYN/SYNACK."

```
1768   /* if this is the first segment for this list we need to store the
1769    * base_seq
1770    * We use TCP_S_SAW_SYN/SYNACK to distinguish between client and server
1771    *
1772    * Start relative seq and ack numbers at 1 if this
1773    * is not a SYN packet. This makes the relative
1774    * seq/ack numbers to be displayed correctly in the
1775    * event that the SYN or SYN/ACK packet is not seen
1776    * (this solves bug 1542)
1777    */
```

Notice that this section of the *packet-tcp.c* code refers to bug 1542. Wireshark bugs are managed by Bugzilla.

If you visit *https://bugs.wireshark.org/bugzilla/* and search on "1542," you can read all about this bug.

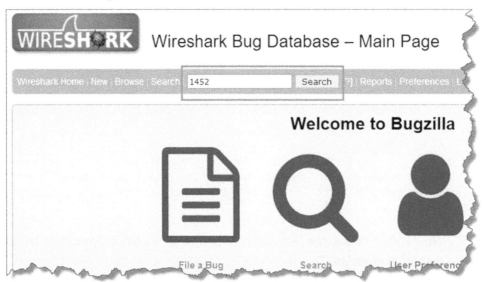

It's a good idea to learn how to read the bugs in Bugzilla. Sometimes you might find some unusual Wireshark behavior that you believe is a bug. You can look up the characteristics in Bugzilla using Search.

We won't spend time looking into this bug since it was resolved all the way back in 2007. Try it yourself. Search for "DNS response time" and see what comes up.

Lab 5 - A14. **The 192.168.0.12 host transmitted the packet with sequence number 405 a total of four times. The sender's Retransmission Time Out (RTO) timer must have expired, causing it to retransmit sequence 405 again and again.**

To quickly determine how many times this sequence number has been transmitted, you can apply a `tcp.seq==405` display filter. This does not consider the sender's IP address, of course. If you want to expand this to ensure you are only looking at packets transmitted by 192.168.0.12, edit this filter to include the address information:

`tcp.seq==405 && ip.src==192.168.0.12`

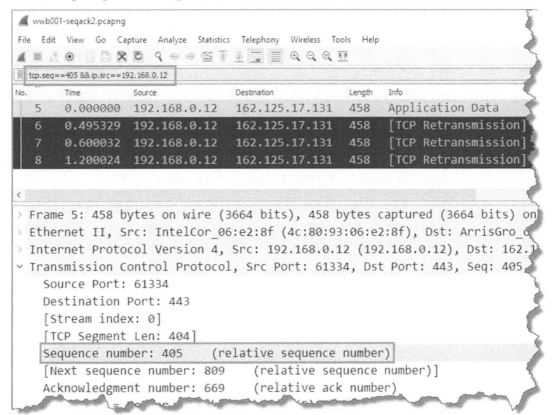

> You may have noticed that I do not use spaces on either side of the ==.
> You do not need spaces on either side of a display filter operator when
> using symbols (such as ==) rather than characters (such as eq).

Let's examine the three retransmissions of this sequence number 405 in frames 6, 7, and 8. These retransmissions must have been triggered by the expiration of the TCP Retransmission Time Out (RTO) timer. We can't be certain whether the sequence number 405 packet was lost on its way to 162.125.17.131 or the ACK to that packet was lost on its way back.

Until TCP peers know the round-trip time between them, the value of 1 second is used as the RTO. As the round-trip times are learned, the RTO value changes and adjusts. The minimum RTO is 1 second.

Calculation of the RTO timer is defined in *RFC 6298, Computing TCP's Retransmission Timer*.

Lab 5 - A15. **Frames 9, 10, 11, and 12 contain the ACK (and Duplicate ACKs) for the 192.168.0.12 host's sequence number 405 packet.**

To identify these packets, we need to determine what the *Next sequence number* field value is in the sequence number 405 packet. When we apply a filter for `tcp.seq==405`, Frames 5, 6, 7, and 8 are displayed.

Frame 5 is the original frame with sequence number 405 in it. Frames 6, 7, and 8 are retransmissions. Each of these packets indicate that the next sequence number should be 809.

We can now apply a simple `tcp.ack==809` filter to locate the packets acknowledging sequence number 405. If you want to be a bit more specific with your filter, consider using `ip.dst==192.168.0.12 && tcp.ack==809`.

The acknowledgment frames 9, 10, 11, and 12, contain an *Acknowledgment number* field value of 809. Essentially, this is acknowledging all sequence numbers from 192.168.0.12 up to, but not including, sequence number 809.

Why do we see Duplicate ACKs? That will be addressed in the next answer.

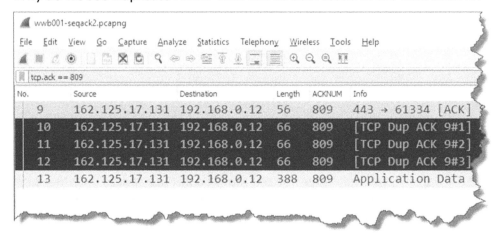

Lab 5 - A16. **The host 162. 125.17.131 transmitted packets with sequence number 669 five times. The first packet is a standard ACK, while Frames 10, 11, and 12 are Duplicate ACKs. Frame 13 is a data packet.**

The filter `ip.src==162.125.17.131 && tcp.seq==669` displays five frames.

Frame 9 acknowledges every sequence number from 192.168.0.12 up to, but not including, sequence number 809.

Why are there Duplicate ACKs?

Clear your filter and look at frames 5-8. Frames 6-8 are retransmissions of sequence number 405. The four ACKs in frames 9-12 acknowledge those four identical frames.

Frame 10 is the first Duplicate ACK – it is a duplicate of frame 9, but it contains Selective Acknowledgments for incoming sequence numbers 405 up to, but not including 809.

Frames 11 and 12 are the second and third Duplicate ACKs, respectively.

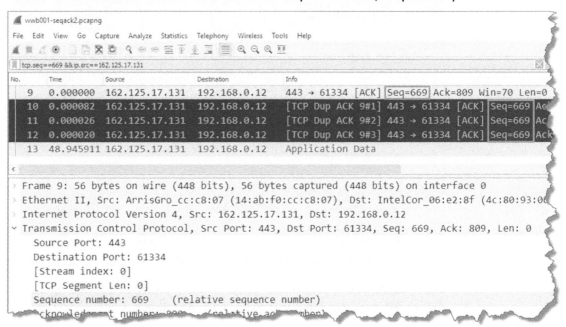

Lab 5 - A17. **Frame 10 is larger than frame 9 because it contains the SACK Left Edge and Right Edge information.**

You can detect the difference in size by looking at the *Length* column (a default column in Wireshark). Frame 9 is 56 bytes long and frame 10 is 66 bytes long. If you look inside the TCP portion of frames 9 and 10, you'll notice that frame 10 includes the SACK option.

In the next image, we added a column based on the IP header *Total Length* field. The IP header *Total Length* field includes the byte count of the IP header and any valid data.

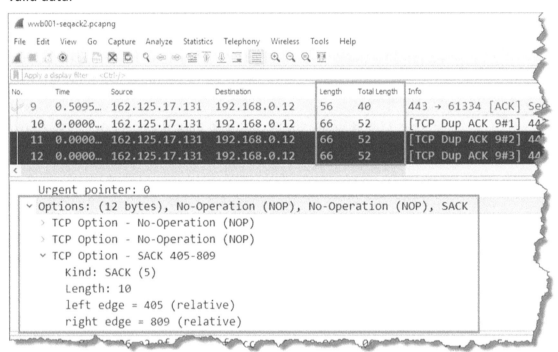

These numbers may not seem quite right. If frame 10 has an additional 12 bytes and frame 9 is 56 bytes, why isn't frame 10 showing 68 bytes in the *Length* column?

Look inside frame 9. Frame 9 contains a 2-byte VSS-Monitoring Ethernet trailer[15]. Frame 10 does not have this extra 2-byte trailer.

In this case, it is more accurate to compare the lengths using the IP header *Total Length* field values. Therefore, we added a column based on the IP header *Total Length* field.

---

[15] This is likely a false positive caused by Wireshark Bug #8997 in which Wireshark incorrectly identifies padding as a VSS-Monitoring trailer. When this bug gets fixed, you shouldn't see the VSS-Monitoring trailer information.

Lab 5 - A18.   51.761236 seconds elapsed from 192.168.0.12's first data packet with sequence number 405 and its data packet with sequence number 809.

Obtain this measurement by setting a Time Reference on frame 5 (the data packet with sequence number 405). Right-click on frame 5 and select *Set/Unset Time Reference*.

If your *Time* column is set to the default, *Seconds Since Beginning of Capture*, you can look at the Time value for frame 14 (the data packet with sequence number 809) to find the 51+ second difference.

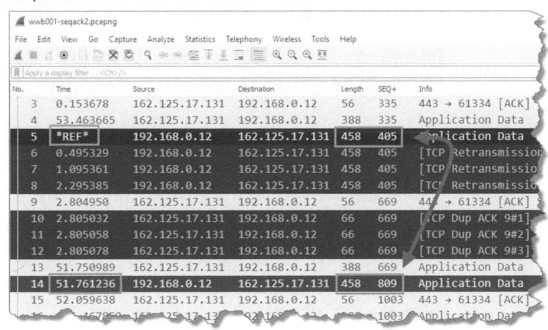

To determine the time difference between Frames 5 and 14, we set the Time Reference on frame 5 and then examined the *Frame* section in frame 14. The *Time since reference or first frame* field provides the time difference from the end of the receipt of the Time Reference frame, frame 5, and the end of the receipt of the current frame, frame 14.

In the image that follows, we set the *Time* column to *Seconds Since Previous Displayed Packet*.

```
wwb001-seqack2.pcapng

File   Edit   View   Go   Capture   Analyze   Statistics   Telephony   Wireless   Tools   Help

Apply a display filter   <Ctrl-/>
```

No.	Time	Source	Destination	Length	SEQ+	Info
3	0.145285	162.125.17.131	192.168.0.12	56	335	443 → 61334 [A
4	53.309987	162.125.17.131	192.168.0.12	388	335	Application Dat
5	*REF*	192.168.0.12	162.125.17.131	458	405	plication Dat
6	0.495329	192.168.0.12	162.125.17.131	458	405	[TCP Retransmis
7	0.600032	192.168.0.12	162.125.17.131	458	405	[TCP Retransmis
8	1.200024	192.168.0.12	162.125.17.131	458	405	[TC Retransmiss
9	0.509565	162.125.17.131	192.168.0.12	56	669	44 → 61334 [A
10	0.000082	162.125.17.131	192.168.0.12	66	669	CP Dup ACK 9#
11	0.000026	162.125.17.131	192.168.0.12	66	669	TCP Dup ACK 9#
12	0.000020	162.125.17.131	192.168.0.12	66	669	[TCP Dup ACK 9#
13	48.945911	162.125.17.131	192.168.0.12	388	669	Application Da
14	0.010247	192.168.0.12	162.125.17.131	458	809	Application Da

```
∨ Frame 14: 458 bytes on wire (3664 bits), 458 bytes captured (3664 bits) o
  › Interface id: 0 (\Device\NPF_{B0F69F5E-CEFD-4198-848B-21957F5FF508})
    Encapsulation type: Ethernet (1)
    Arrival Time: Jun  2, 2016 23:36:47.506242000 Venezuela Standard Time
    [Time shift for this packet: 0.000000000 seconds]
    Epoch Time: 1464925007.506242000 seconds
    [Time delta from previous captured frame: 0.010247000 seconds]
    [Time delta from previous displayed frame: 0.010247000 seconds]
    [Time since reference or first frame: 51.761236000 seconds]
    Frame Number: 14
```

 In earlier versions of Wireshark, the Time *column would automatically change to* Seconds Since Beginning of Capture, *but there was some buggy behavior. Wireshark does not automatically change the* Time *column settings when you set a Time Reference in the 3.x version used in the writing of this book. Of course, this column may return to its previous behavior in the future.*

Lab 5 - A19.   The next sequence number from 192.168.0.12 should be 12,525.

Simply looking at the *Next sequence number* field in the TCP header of the last packet sent from 192.168.0.12 gives us the answer.

If you had added the *Next sequence number* field as a column in the Packet List pane, you wouldn't even have to look inside the Packet Details window for the answer.

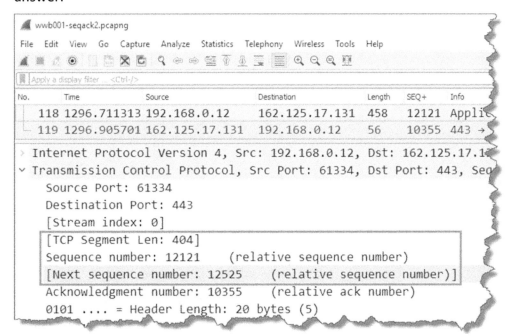

[This page intentionally left blank.]

Lab 6: You're Out of Order!

Objective: Examine Wireshark's process of distinguishing between out-of-order packets and retransmissions and identify mis-identifications.

Trace Files:	wwb001-0001.pcapng
	wwb001-0002.pcapng

Skills Covered in this Lab

In this lab, you will have a chance to work with many key functions in Wireshark. The answers to this lab demonstrate how to use functions, including, but not limited to:

- Determine the conversation counts in a trace file
- Identify a client using a display filter
- Identify a server using a display filter
- Determine the out-of-order packet count using the *Expert Information* window
- Determine the out-of-order packet count using a display filter
- Determine TCP Initial Round-Trip Time (iRTT) values
- Learn how TCP adjusts the Retransmission Time Out (RTO) timer after TCP handshake issues
- Learn how Wireshark uses time to differentiate between an out-of-order packet and a retransmission
- Filter out a stream based on the *Stream index* field value
- Identify frames defined incorrectly as out-of-order packets
- Use tcp.time_delta to locate delays
- Configure your profile's *hosts* file for name resolution use
- Find initial conversation packets based on sequence and acknowledgment number values
- Identify where out-of-order and retransmission packets should have arrived in a trace file
- Identify out-of-order packets on the TCP *Time-Sequence* graph (*tcptrace*)

Use wwb001-ooo1.pcapng to answer Lab 6 questions Q1 – Q12.

Lab 6 - Q1. How many TCP conversations are in this trace file?

_____

Lab 6 - Q2. What is the client's IP address?

_____

Lab 6 - Q3. What is the server's IP address?

_____

Lab 6 - Q4. How many out-of-order packets are detected in this trace file?

_____

Lab 6 - Q5. What is Wireshark's calculated Initial Round-trip Time (iRTT) between the TCP peers?

_____

Lab 6 - Q6. How will the iRTT affect the determination of an out-of-order packet?

_____

Lab 6 - Q7. Frame 6 is defined as an out-of-order frame. Was this frame seen earlier in the trace file?

_____

Lab 6 - Q8. Is frame 6 an out-of-order frame or a retransmission?

_____

Lab 6 - Q9.   Frame 8 is defined as an out-of-order frame. Was this frame seen earlier in the trace file?

_____

Lab 6 - Q10.   Is frame 8 an out-of-order frame or a retransmission?

_____

Lab 6 - Q11.   Frame 31 is defined as an out-of-order frame. Was this frame seen earlier in the trace file?

_____

Lab 6 - Q12.   Is frame 31 an out-of-order frame or a retransmission?

_____

Use wwb001-ooo2.pcapng to answer Lab 6 questions Q13 – Q23.

Lab 6 - Q13.   How many TCP conversations are in this trace file?

_____

Lab 6 - Q14.   What is the client's IP address?

_____

Lab 6 - Q15.   What is the server's IP address?

_____

Lab 6 - Q16.   How many out-of-order packets are detected in this trace file?

_____

Lab 6 - Q17. What is the Initial Round-trip Time (iRTT) between the TCP peers?

_____

Lab 6 - Q18. Frame is 343 defined as an out-of-order frame. When should this frame have arrived?

_____

Lab 6 - Q19. Why did Wireshark mark frame 343 as an out-of-order frame rather than a retransmission?

_____

Lab 6 - Q20. Frame is 349 defined as an out-of-order frame. When should this frame have arrived?

_____

Lab 6 - Q21. Frame 351 defined as an out-of-order frame. When should this frame have arrived?

_____

Lab 6 - Q22. Explain how these out-of-order frames are depicted on the TCP _Time-Sequence (tcptrace)_ graph.

_____

Lab 6 - Q23. Do you think it is more likely that out-of-orders are defined as Retransmissions, or that Retransmissions are defined as Out-of-Orders? Explain your answer.

_____

Lab 6 Solutions

Trace Files: wwb001-ooo1.pcapng
                wwb001-ooo2.pcapng

Use wwb001-ooo1.pcapng to answer Lab 6 questions Q1– Q12.

Lab 6 - A1.   There is one TCP conversation in this trace file.

The fastest way to know how many conversations are in a trace file is to select *Statistics | Conversations*. The conversation count is on the *TCP* tab.

There are several cool features available in the *Conversations* window.

Name resolution	This option is only active if you have name resolution enabled in the *Edit	Preferences* area. You can choose to pull name resolution information from within the trace file, a separate *hosts* file, or external name resolution server.
Limit to display filter	If you only want to know which conversations match a certain characteristic (such as a Zero Window condition), consider applying a display filter and then opening the *Conversations* window. Click Limit to Display Filter to just view conversations that match the filter.
Absolute start time	Toggle the *Rel. Start* (Relative Start) column to *Abs Start* (Absolute Start) to see the exact time of day that a conversation began.

Conversation Types	Use this drop-down list to enable/disable specific conversation types to be displayed on the *Conversation* window tabs.
Copy	Select to copy the data in the visible *Conversations* tab in either CSV (comma-separated values) or YAML (Yaml Ain't Markup Language) format.
Follow Stream (TCP and UDP only)	After selecting a conversation, you can follow the stream and see the application-layer communications between the hosts.
Graph (TCP only)	After selecting a conversation, you can quickly launch the *TCP Sequence Numbers (tcptrace)* graph.
Close	Closes the *Conversations* window.
Help	Launches the Wireshark *Conversations* window manual page.

Lab 6 - A2.   The client's IP address is 10.1.64.192.

This information is visible in the first packet of the trace file. Now that you know there is only one TCP conversation, you only need to see that one SYN packet to obtain the address of the client.

If you had a large trace file and wanted to find all the client processes, you could create and apply a filter for the SYN packets and look at the *Source* column. The display filter syntax would be tcp.flags.syn==1 && tcp.flags.ack==0.

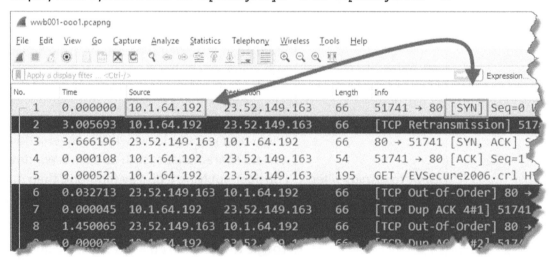

Lab 6 - A3.   **The server's IP address is 23.52.149.163.**

This information is also visible in the first packet of the trace file. If you had a large trace file and wanted to find all servers, you could use the same filter mentioned in the previous answer and just look at the *Destination* column to get this information.

You could also find servers based on their SYN/ACK packets by creating and applying a be `tcp.flags.syn==1 && tcp.flags.ack==1` display filter and looking at the *Source* column.

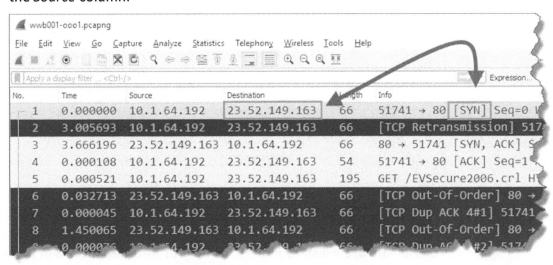

Quick Test 1

Let's see where you are on the filters at this point. Write in the display filter for each of the desired traffic. Check your answers against the table on page 152.

Traffic to View	Display Filter
SYN packets only	
SYN/ACK packets only	
SYN or SYN/ACK packets	
DNS responses	
TCP Resets	
SACK option in the TCP handshake packets	
DNS queries over IPv6	

Lab 6 - A4.   **There are seven out-of-order packets in this trace file.**

Click the *Expert Information* button to quickly get the count of out-of-order packets in this trace file. Click on any of the 7 out-of-order packets listed to jump to those packets in the trace file.

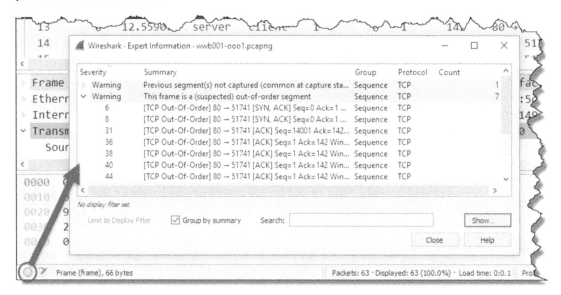

You can also use a display filter to list the out-of-order packets in the trace file. All TCP analysis items that can be listed in the *Expert Information* window have a display filter value starting with `tcp.analysis`. Type this into the display filter area and examine the drop-down list. The display filter syntax for out-of-order packets is `tcp.analysis.out_of_order`.

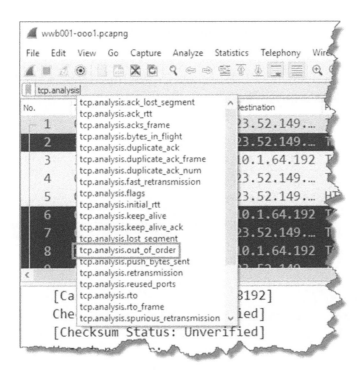

After you apply a display filter, don't count the packets in the Packet List pane! Look down at the Status Bar to see how many packets (and what percentage of packets) match your display filter, as shown in the following image.

Note that the *Load time* indicator is disabled by default. If you want to see the trace file load times again, select *Edit | Preferences | Advanced* and type in *load time* in the search area. Double-click the *Value* column to toggle the setting to TRUE.

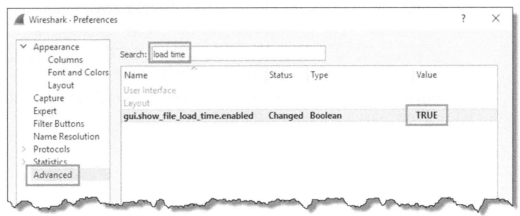

Lab 6 - A5. **Wireshark's calculated Initial Round-trip Time (iRTT) between the TCP peers is 3.666304 seconds.**

The iRTT value is contained in all TCP packets *except* the SYN packets. Expand the TCP header's *[SEQ/ACK analysis]* section to see this field.

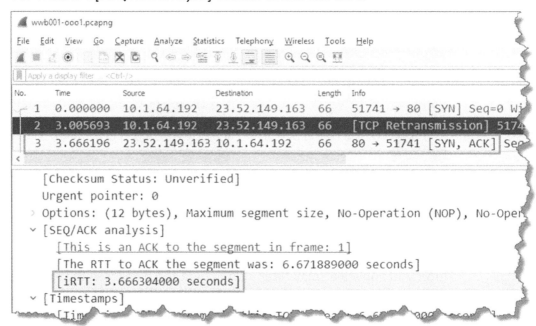

This is a pretty high iRTT value. If we look at what happened just before this, we can see why. There wasn't an answer to the initial SYN packet within the client's RTO value.

The iRTT is calculated differently than the RTT. The iRTT is only calculated once, from the first to the third packet of the TCP handshake. The RTT is calculated continuously on data packets and their related ACKs.

We don't have a valid RTT time to use yet in the RTO equation, so we will have to use a default RTO value. This value was originally defined as 3 seconds (RFC 1988), but updated in RFC 6298 to 1 second with the following exception:

```
(5.7) If the timer expires awaiting the ACK of a SYN segment and the
      TCP implementation is using an RTO less than 3 seconds, the RTO
      MUST be re-initialized to 3 seconds when data transmission
      begins (i.e., after the three-way handshake completes).
```

Why do we care so much about the iRTT value when talking about out-of-order packets? That is explained in the next answer.

Lab 6 - A6.   **The iRTT, if seen, is used to determine whether a packet is a standard retransmission or out-of-order.**

An out-of-order is defined in Wireshark's *packet-tcp.c* code as follows:

"If the segment came relatively close since the segment with the highest seen sequence number and it doesn't look like a retransmission then it is an OUT-OF-ORDER segment."

If the iRTT value is not known, we use an arbitrary value of 3 ms.

```
2038    /* If the segment came relatively close since the segment with the
        highest
2039    * seen sequence number and it doesn't look like a retransmission
2040    * then it is an OUT-OF-ORDER segment.
2041    */
2042    t=(pinfo->abs_ts.secs-tcpd->fwd->tcp_analyze_seq_info
        ->nextseqtime.secs)*1000000000;
2043    t=t+(pinfo->abs_ts.nsecs)-tcpd->fwd->
        tcp_analyze_seq_info->nextseqtime.nsecs;
2044    if (tcpd->ts_first_rtt.nsecs == 0 && tcpd->ts_first_rtt.secs == 0) {
2045        ooo_thres = 3000000;
2046    } else {
2047        ooo_thres = tcpd->ts_first_rtt.nsecs +
            tcpd->ts_first_rtt.secs*1000000000;
2048    }
```

If the TCP handshake was seen, Wireshark uses the iRTT to determine if a segment came "relatively close" to the segment with the highest sequence number. If the iRTT was not seen, Wireshark uses an arbitrary value of 3 ms.

When the iRTT value is artificially high (such as in the case of *wwb001-ooo1.pcapng*), most likely a number of retransmissions will be defined as Out-of-Order.

Consider the following flow chart when trying to figure out why Wireshark defined a packet as a Fast Retransmission, Out-of-Order, or Retransmission.

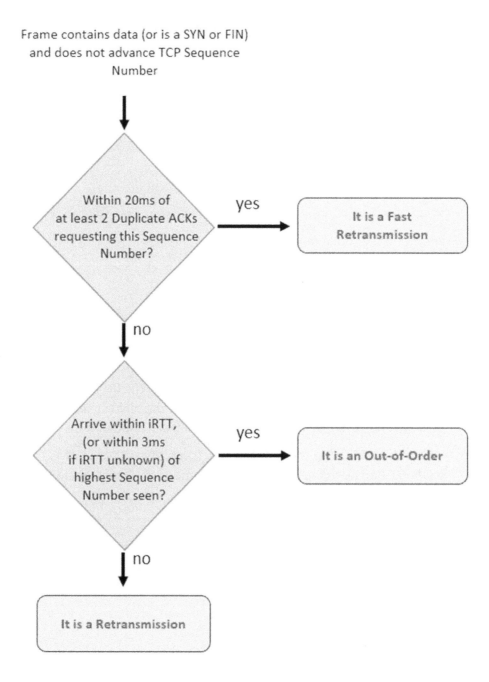

Lab 6 - A7.   Frame 6 is a SYN/ACK that was already seen in frame 3.

Since this is a small trace file, it is easy to see the previous SYN/ACK. If you were working with a very large file with lots of conversations, you would probably want to set a display filter based on the TCP *Stream index* field. In this case, tcp.stream==0.

Lab 6 - A8.   Frame 6 is retransmission, not an out-of-order.

To determine if this frame is a retransmission or an out-of-order, Wireshark looks at whether this frame arrived within the iRTT value (if known) or 3 ms (if iRTT is not known) of the previous frame from the host.

Consider making changes to your Wireshark profile when answering this question.

I suggest you add an *iRTT* as a column. The iRTT can be found in any TCP packet other than the SYN packet. You can also set frame 3 as a Time Reference and change the *View | Time Display Format* to *Seconds Since Beginning of Capture*.

I created a *hosts* file in my profile's directory and set up Wireshark to refer to that *hosts* file for the network addresses (as explained on the next pages). My *hosts* file will change the Source and Destination values to "client" and "server" which makes it very clear who is the sender of each packet.

That the server did not increase *Sequence number* field value from frame 3 to frame 6. Notice that frame 6 arrived 0.033342 seconds after frame 3.

This is faster than the known iRTT value, so Wireshark marks it as an out-of-order frame. In truth, however, it is a retransmission because it is a duplicate of frame 3. Wireshark only defined it as an out-of-order because of the time information.

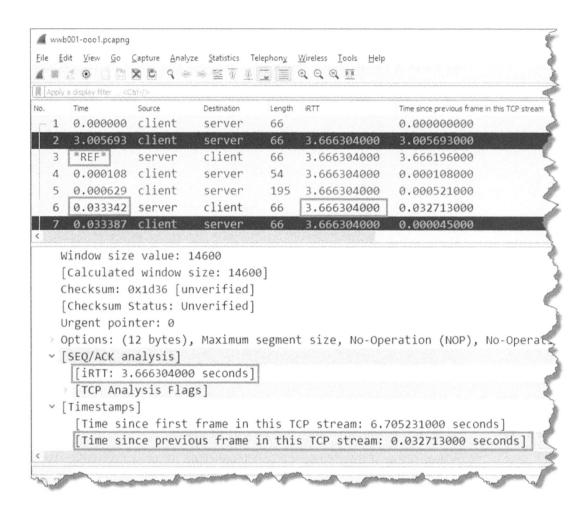

Wireshark is not correct in its definition of frame 6 as an out-of-order frame. Unfortunately, this is common with the out-of-order designation. In general, when out-of-order designations occur within the packet loss recovery process, the out-of-order packets are likely retransmissions.

 The Time since previous frame in this TCP stream *is one of my favorite fields to add as a column. This field measures from the end of one frame in a single TCP stream to the end of the next frame in that same TCP stream. When you have a trace file filled with intertwined TCP conversations, use this field to find delays in separate streams. Just add this field as a column and sort the column from high to low.*

In the previous image, I enabled name resolution to help identify packets sent from the client and server. To enable name resolution, I created a simple *hosts* file with two entries.

        10.1.64.192   client
        23.52.149.163   server

This *hosts* file must be placed in our *Wireshark Workbook 1* profile directory. To jump to the directory quickly, right-click on the *Profile* column in the Status Bar and select *Manage Profiles*. With the desired profile selected, click the hyperlink to jump to the profile directory.

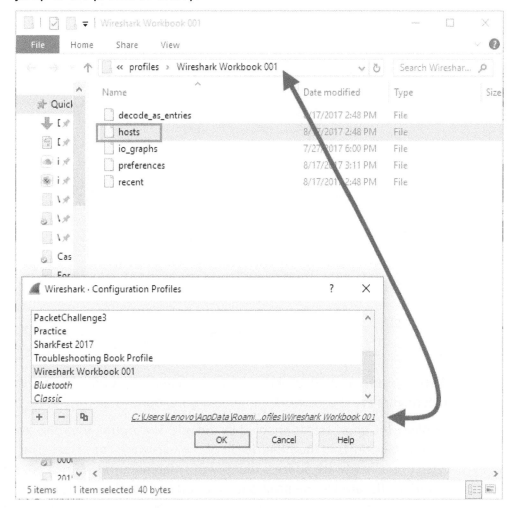

We also need to tell Wireshark that we only want to use the *hosts* file in our profile directory for name resolution. We don't want to use any other available resolution information in this case.

In the *Preferences* window, we selected *Name Resolution*. After enabling *Resolve network (IP) addresses*, we chose *Only use the profile "hosts" file*.

Wireshark has some great name resolution options. You can use the DNS information within a trace file, use an external resolver (DNS server), or only use a *hosts* file, as we did in this case. In each situation, you must enable *Resolve network (IP) addresses* to view network names.

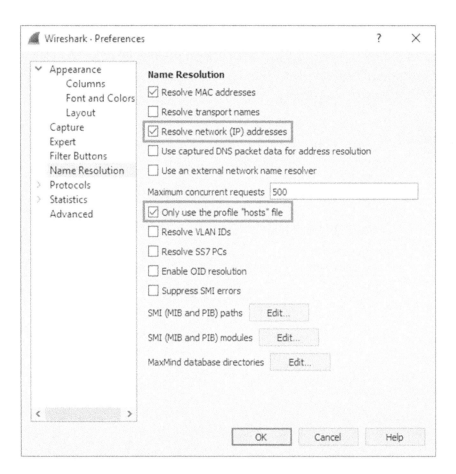

There are several configurable options for name resolution. The most common ones to configure are the network name resolution options.

Resolve MAC addresses is enabled by default. This option provides us with the Organizationally Unit Identifier (OUI) of the hardware addresses. The first three bytes of the hardware address identify the manufacturer. Wireshark references its *manuf* file (located in the program file directory) for this information.

```
∨ Ethernet II, Src: IntelCor_06:e2:8f (4c:80:93:06:e2:8f), Dst: Nomadix_00:
  > Destination: Nomadix_00:97:5d (00:50:e8:00:97:5d)
  > Source: IntelCor_06:e2:8f (4c:80:93:06:e2:8f)
    Type: IPv4 (0x0800)
```

Enabling *Resolve transport names* displays the application names associated with port numbers. Wireshark references its *services* file (also located in the program file directory) for this information.

```
No.    Source        Destination      Info
  16   10.1.64.192   23.52.149.163    51741 → http(80) [ACK]
  17   23.52.149.163 10.1.64.192      Continuation
  18      52.149.163 10.1.64.192      Continuation
```

Lab 6 - A9.   **Frame 8 is a SYN/ACK. This same SYN/ACK was seen in frame 3 and frame 6.**

This isn't a very large, complex trace file, so the answer is easy to obtain by just looking at the Packet List pane.

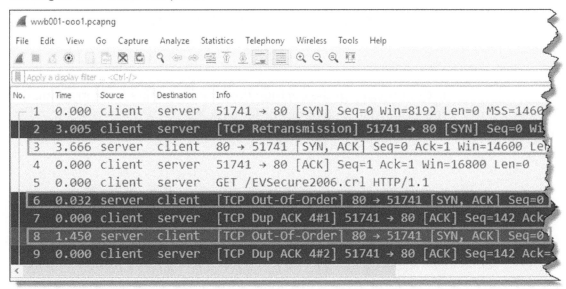

Since this is a SYN/ACK packet, we can apply a filter for tcp.flags.syn==1 && tcp.flags.ack==1 and quickly see the retransmissions. If this packet wasn't a SYN/ACK, you can build a display filter based on the *Sequence number*, *Acknowledgment number*, and *Segment Len(gth)* fields to find retransmissions.

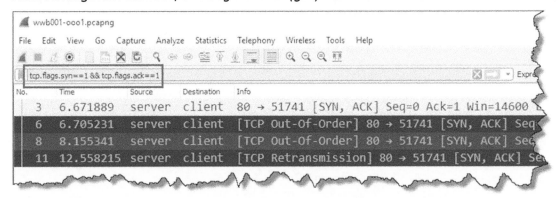

After applying this filter, we now see that this same frame was sent a total of four times. One time is defined as a standard SYN/ACK (frame 3). Twice it is defined as Out-of-Order packets (frames 3 and 6). Once it is defined as a TCP Retransmission (frame 11).

Lab 6 - A10. **Frame 8 is a retransmission.**

Even though Wireshark defined this packet as an out-of-order, we can tell it is a retransmission because this packet has been sent previously.

The last image shown indicates that this packet was sent a total of 4 times in this trace file.

Why did Wireshark mark this packet as an out-of-order?

Let's look again at the decision flow used to define fast retransmission, retransmission, and out-of-order packets.

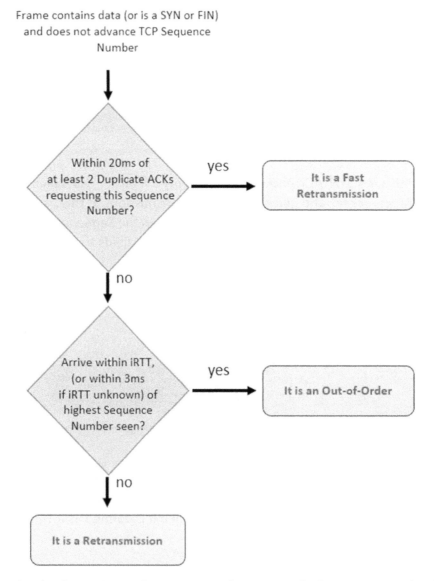

Wireshark requires at least two Duplicate ACKs before it can mark a frame as a Fast Retransmission. Since we didn't see at least two Duplicate ACKs from the client yet, frame 8 can't be defined as a Fast Retransmission.

By adding the *iRTT* and *Time since previous frame in this TCP stream* columns, we can see that frame 8 arrived well within the iRTT value. The iRTT is 3.666304 seconds and this duplicate arrived 1.450110 seconds after the previous frame from the server.

That is why Wireshark defined frame 8 as an out-of-order packet, even though it is actually a retransmission.

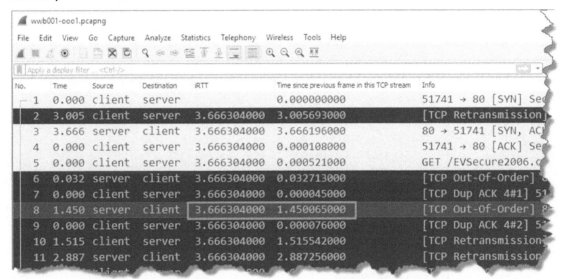

    Does it seem like you're having to look at the iRTT a lot so far in these labs?

It's one of the settings that you always want to pay attention to when troubleshooting poor network performance.

If the iRTT value is high, then applications that need to make many service requests will never be fast.

You always need to check for artificial inflation of the iRTT, as in the wwb001-ooo1.pcapng trace file. In this trace file, the iRTT has been artificially inflated because of packet loss during the TCP handshake process.

Lab 6 - A11.   **Frame 31 has not been seen earlier in the trace file.**

To determine if we've seen this frame before, we could apply a display filter that is as simple as tcp.seq==14001.

In the following image, we used a more exact filter - tcp.seq==14001 && tcp.ack==142 && tcp.len==1400. This packet is only seen once in the trace file.

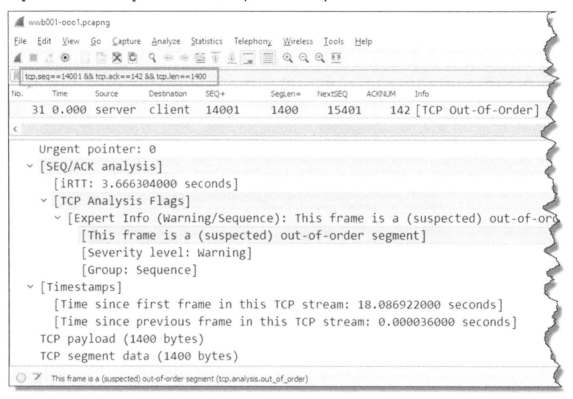

Lab 6 - A12.   **Frame 31 is an out-of-order frame.**

These are the characteristics of the traffic and frame 31:

1. The frame contains data.

2. The frame does not advance the TCP sequence number.

3. There are no Duplicate ACKs requesting this sequence number.

4. The frame arrived within the iRTT (3.666304 seconds) of the highest sequence number seen from the host.

These four characteristics cause Wireshark to mark frame 31 as an out-of-order packet.

> ## Use wwb001-ooo2.pcapng to answer Lab 6 questions Q13 – Q25.

Lab 6 - A13.   There is one TCP conversation in this trace file.

This is visible in the *Statistics | Conversations | TCP* window.

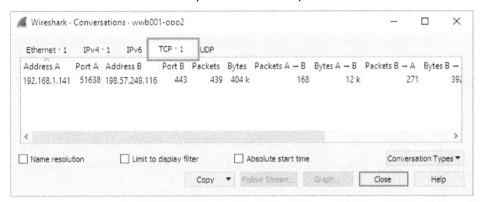

Lab 6 - A14.   The client's IP address is 192.168.1.141.

This is visible by just looking in the Packet List pane or from within the *Statistics | Conversations | TCP* window. The client is using TCP port 51638, and the server is using TCP port 443.

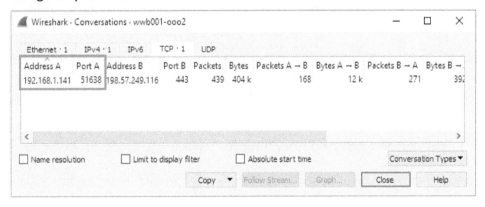

Lab 6 - A15. **The server's IP address is 198.57.249.116.**

Again, this is visible by just looking in the Packet List pane or from within the *Statistics | Conversations | TCP* window.

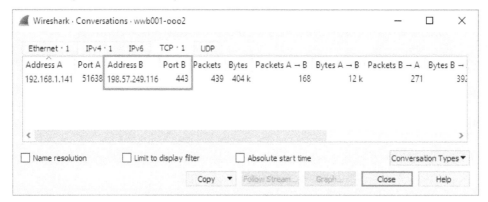

Lab 6 - A16. **There are 5 packets defined as Out-of-Order in this trace file.**

This information is obtained through the *Expert Information* window, as shown below.

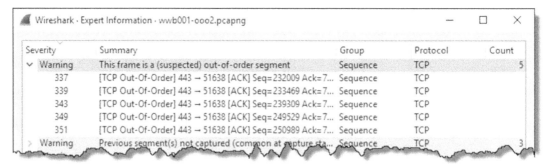

You can also apply a display filter for `tcp.analysis.out_of_order`, as shown in the next image.

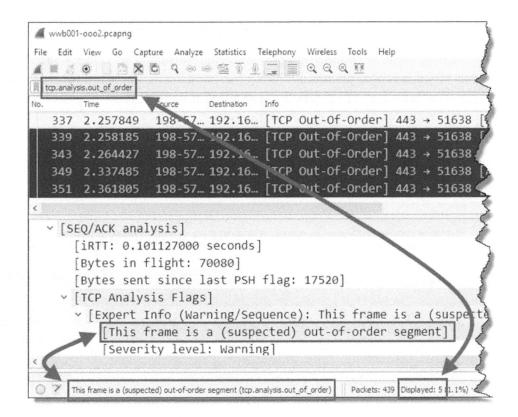

 Since TCP analysis flagged packets are pretty interesting in trace files, I recommend that you create a "TCPAnalysis" display filter button. Simply type the display filter `tcp.analysis.flags,` *click the "+" on the display filter toolbar, and name your button "TCPAnalysis."*

You can also see all this information in the Expert Information window. Simply click the Expert Information button on the left side of the Status Bar.

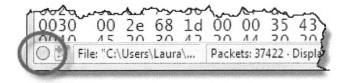

Lab 6 - A17. **The Initial Round-trip Time (iRTT) between the TCP peers is 0.101127 seconds.**

Adding our *iRTT* column makes it easy to determine this value. Remember that the iRTT value is only calculated during the handshake, but listed for reference in each packet within a TCP stream throughout that conversation. The iRTT value does not change because it is only calculated once.

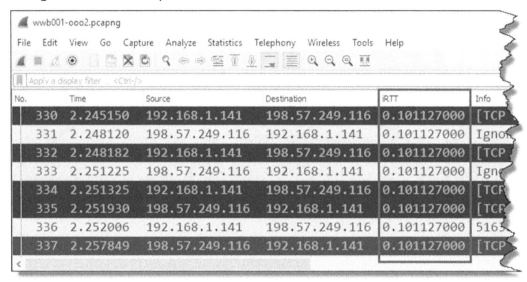

 Things to Do:

Sign up for my newsletter at https://www.chappell-university.com/newsletter.

*Check out my **Laura's Lab blog** over at https://www.chappell-university.com/lauras-lab.*

Lab 6 - A18.   Frame 343 should have arrived after frame 253 and before frame 255.

By adding columns for the *Sequence number* and *Next sequence number* fields, we can match up frame 343's sequence number value with the *Next sequence number* field value in frame 253.

Alternately, we could have applied a display filter for `tcp.nxtseq==239309`.

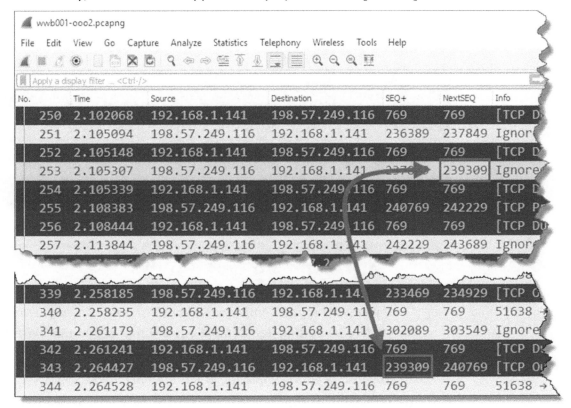

 I hope you didn't scroll to get to frame 343! To jump quickly to a packet in a trace file, use the Go To *button ≣ on the main toolbar.*

Lab 6 - A19. **Wireshark defined frame 343 as an out-of-order frame rather than a retransmission because it arrived within the iRTT of the previous frame from this host.**

We see the iRTT of this TCP conversation is 0.101127. The host 198.57.249.116 sent frame 343 just 0.003248 seconds after its previous frame.

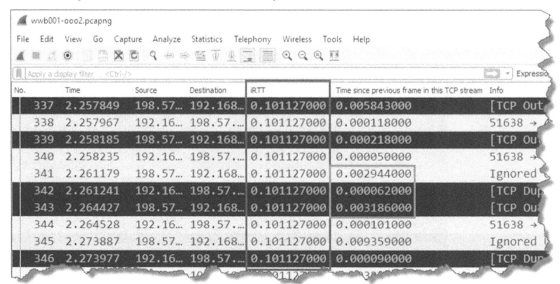

No.	Time	Source	Destination	iRTT	Time since previous frame in this TCP stream	Info
337	2.257849	198.57...	192.168...	0.101127000	0.005843000	[TCP Out
338	2.257967	192.16...	198.57...	0.101127000	0.000118000	51638 →
339	2.258185	198.57...	192.168...	0.101127000	0.000218000	[TCP Ou
340	2.258235	192.16...	198.57...	0.101127000	0.000050000	51638 →
341	2.261179	198.57...	192.168...	0.101127000	0.002944000	Ignored
342	2.261241	192.16...	198.57...	0.101127000	0.000062000	[TCP Dup
343	2.264427	198.57...	192.168...	0.101127000	0.003186000	[TCP Ou
344	2.264528	192.16...	198.57...	0.101127000	0.000101000	51638 →
345	2.273887	198.57...	192.168...	0.101127000	0.009359000	Ignored
346	2.273977	192.16...	198.57...	0.101127000	0.000090000	[TCP Dup

> **!** *If you want to reassemble out-of-order segments, enable the TCP preference setting* Reassemble out-of-order segments *(Wireshark v3 and later).*
>
> *You also need to enable the TCP preference* Allow subdissector to reassemble TCP streams *to use the out-of-order reassembly feature.*
>
> *The best way to perform reassembly of a TCP conversation is still to right-click on a packet in the Packet List pane and select* Follow | TCP Stream.

Lab 6 - A20.   Frame 349 should have arrived after frame 265.

In the image shown below, I applied a display filter to find out when this frame was expected. The display filter was `tcp.nxtseq==249529`. Based on this filter, it appears that the sequence number of frame 349 (sequence number 249,529) was expected after frame 265.

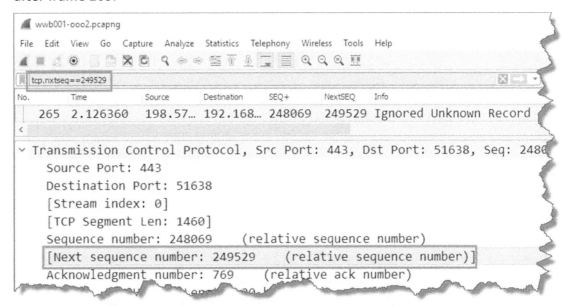

Quick Test 2

Let's see how you are doing with the TCP Sequence/Acknowledgment numbering process. Enter the missing number for the image below. Check your answers against the answers on page 152.

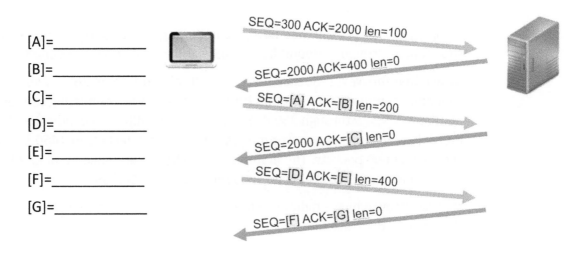

Lab 6 - A21.   **Frame 351 should have arrived after frame 265 and before frame 267.**

If you used the same technique that we used to answer the last question, you would have an unusual result. As shown below, I applied a filter for `tcp.nxtseq==250989` and frame 349 appeared. This would indicate that frame 351 should have arrived after frame 349, the previous frame from this host. That doesn't make sense. We know this should have arrived much sooner in the trace file.

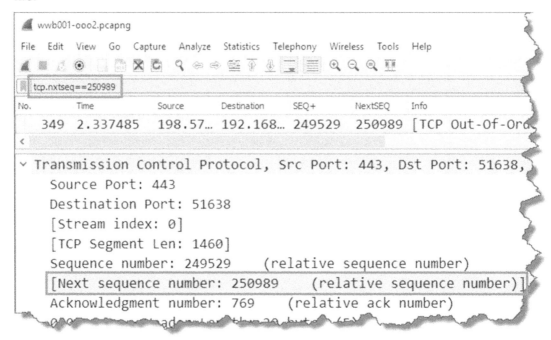

Why didn't this display filter technique work this time? Notice that frame 349 is also defined as out-of-order.

To figure out what happened here, we need to go back to the spot when frame 349 should have arrived – around frame 265 – and look at what happened.

Notice that the *Next sequence number* field value on frame 265 is 249,529. The next sequence number seen from that host is 252,449. We are missing sequence numbers 249,529 through 252,448. That large of a difference indicates that we lost more than one packet at that time. Based on typical packets of 1460 bytes, it looks like we lost two packets. The first missing packet is sequence number 249,529 and the second missing packet used sequence number 250,989.

Now we know why we didn't see a *Next sequence number* field value of 250,989 at this point in the trace file.

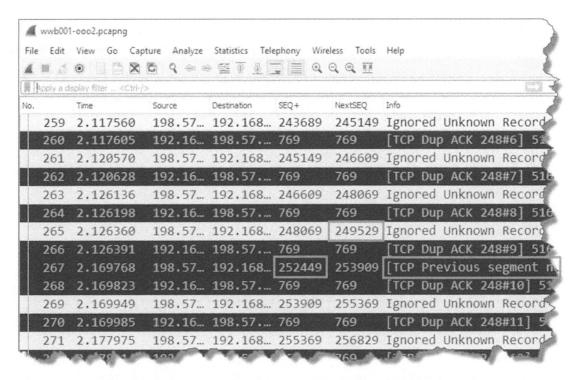

The following illustration shows what happened in a bit cleaner, clearer format. We can see the *Sequence number* field and *Next sequence number* field values of the two missing packets.

When you are trying to sort out the sequence number information at the time of missing packets, sometimes you must go back farther in the trace file and do a bit of math to figure out how many packets were lost at a single time.

Lab 6 - A22.   **These out-of-order frames appear later in time along the TCP *Time-Sequence (tcptrace)* graph, rather than close to their nearest sequence numbers.**

In the TCP *Time-Sequence (tcptrace)* graph shown (*Statistics | TCP Stream Graphs | Time-Sequence (tcptrace)*) shown below, we zoomed in to point out the out-of-order frames.

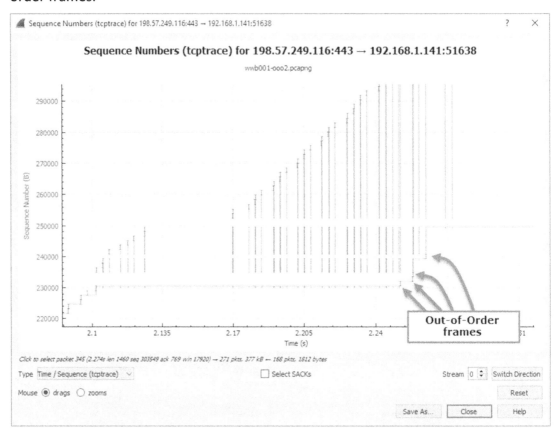

 The TCP Time-Sequence (tcptrace) *graph is one of my favorite graphs. It really does paint a picture. Notice the red lines that appear when you graph this trace file. Those are Selective ACKs indicating that we are still seeing acknowledgments for data packets, even though we are missing some segments at times. If those out-of-order frames had actually been retransmissions and we captured upstream from the point of packet loss, we may have seen each of them in two places — once in their proper spot along the Sequence Number (Y axis) group, and again later in time.*

Lab 6 - A23. **More often, retransmissions are defined as out-of-orders simply because they arrive soon after other packets sent from the same host.**

The Wireshark developers had to figure out how to differentiate these two types of issues. Using the iRTT (or 3 ms if the iRTT is not known) is a great idea. Unfortunately, if you are in the middle of a packet loss recovery operation, you may see other recovery packets in the trace file very close to the time of your retransmission. That will cause Wireshark to mark your retransmissions as out-of-order packets.

We know from looking at *wwb001-ooo1.pcapng* that problems with the TCP handshake can set an artificially high iRTT. This can also cause numerous retransmissions to be defined as Out-of-Orders.

Quick Test 1 Answers

The following table contains the answers to the Quick Test on page 127.

Traffic to View	Display Filter
SYN packets only	`tcp.flags.syn==1 && tcp.flags.ack==0`
SYN/ACK packets only	`tcp.flags.syn==1 && tcp.flags.ack==1`
SYN or SYN/ACK packets	`tcp.flags.syn==1`
DNS responses	`dns.flags.response==1`
TCP Resets	`tcp.flags.reset==1`
SACK option in the TCP handshake packets	`tcp.option_kind==4` or `tcp.options.sack_perm`
DNS queries over IPv6	`dns.flags.response==0 && ipv6`

Quick Test 2 Answers

The following image contains the answers to the Quick Test 2 on page 147.

How did you do? This is a skill you must master!

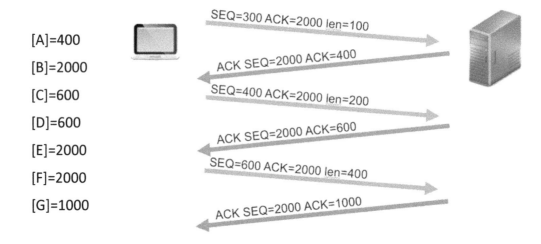

[A]=400

[B]=2000

[C]=600

[D]=600

[E]=2000

[F]=2000

[G]=1000

SEQ=300 ACK=2000 len=100

ACK SEQ=2000 ACK=400

SEQ=400 ACK=2000 len=200

ACK SEQ=2000 ACK=600

SEQ=600 ACK=2000 len=400

ACK SEQ=2000 ACK=1000

Lab 7: Sky High

Objective: Examine and analyze traffic captured as a host was redirected to a malicious site.

Trace File: wwb001-skyhigh.pcapng

Skills Covered in this Lab

In this lab, you will have a chance to work with many key functions in Wireshark. The answers to this lab demonstrate how to use functions, including, but not limited to:

- Examine arrival time metadata inside individual frames
- Use MAC address information to identify vendor products on the network
- Create a single filter to locate multiple MAC addresses
- Use DHCP to identify the name of network devices
- Locate the most active client for a specific protocol or application
- Identify IPv4/IPv6 addresses used by DNS servers
- Locate DNS errors
- Find the percentage of DNS error responses in a trace file
- Identify the client operating system based on HTTP User-Agent information
- Determine what search phrase is being used by a host
- Measure the time required to execute a search term
- Detect a malicious HTTP redirection process
- Identify when server responds to multiple host names
- Reassemble HTTP objects
- Determine what virus detection tool was running when a host was compromised

Lab 7 - Q1. **On what date was this trace file captured?**

_____

Lab 7 - Q2. **How many HTTP responses are in this trace file?**

_____

Lab 7 - Q3. **Are there any Apple products located on, and communicating onto, the local network?**

_____

Lab 7 - Q4. **What IP addresses are used by the most active HTTP client (based on byte count) in this trace file?**

_____

Lab 7 - Q5. **What IP addresses are used by the DNS servers in this trace file?**

_____

Lab 7 - Q6. **How many DNS queries are in this trace file?**

_____

Lab 7 - Q7. **How many DNS error responses are in this trace file?**

_____

Lab 7 - Q8. **What operating system is the client using?**

_____

Lab 7 - Q9. What search engine is the client using?

_____

Lab 7 - Q10. What is the user looking up in the search engine?

_____

Lab 7 - Q11. How long does it take the user to type the search term?

_____

Lab 7 - Q12. To what server does the client make the first HTTP GET request after the search process?

_____

Lab 7 - Q13. What host names are associated with 66.84.12.75?

_____

Lab 7 - Q14. To where is the user redirected after clicking the radar view?

_____

Lab 7 - Q15. What image files were downloaded from the suspicious server?

_____

Lab 7 - Q16. What audio files play on the user's machine?

_____

Lab 7 - Q17. **What defense tool is supposedly launched in the background on the user's system?**

_____

Lab 7 - Q18. **What virus detection tool is loaded on the user's machine?**

_____

Lab 7 Solutions

Lab 7 - A1.   This trace file was captured on February 17, 2017.

There are three places that you can see the date in this trace file:

- in the *Frame* section of the packets
- in the HTTP responses (which provides the HTTP server date information)
- in the *Capture File Properties* window (left side of the Status Bar)

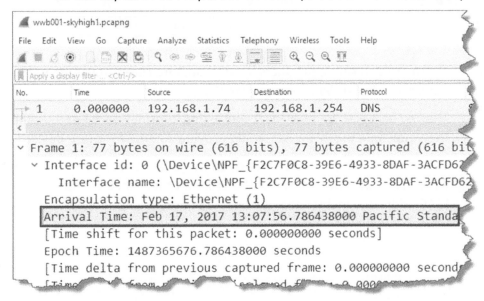

 Another field you may see in the Frame *section would be the* Packet Comments *field. The field shows up with a bright green background. Wonder if a trace has comments? Try a* frame.comment *filter, apply a* frame.comment.expert *column, or look at the* Capture File Properties *window.*

Lab 7 - A2. **There are 73 HTTP responses in this trace file.**

To locate HTTP response packets, simply apply a display filter for `http.response`.

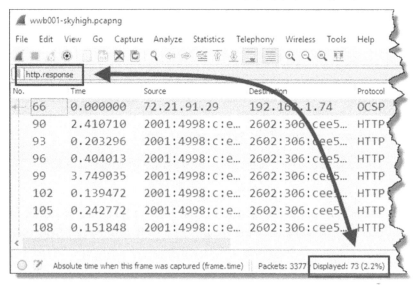

Lab 7 - A3. **There are two Apple products located on, and communicating onto, the local network – *jillos-iPhone* and *Lauras-iPad*.**

The key here is to look for local addressing information related to Apple. You can then look for a protocol that would provide a name for these devices.

To identify Apple products that are on the local network, we will open the *Statistics | Endpoints* window and select the *Ethernet* tab. Since we don't have all the Apple MAC addresses memorized, we enabled name resolution inside the *Endpoints* window, as shown below.

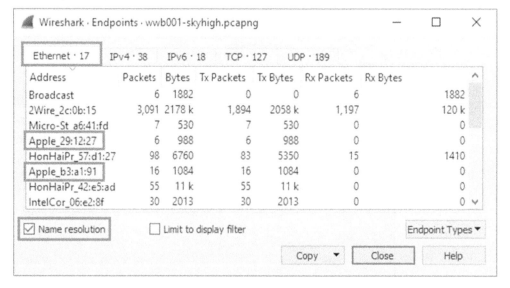

Using the right-click method, we created a display filter to show traffic to or from these two MAC addresses. We right-clicked on *Apple_29:12:27* and selected *Prepare a Filter | Selected*.

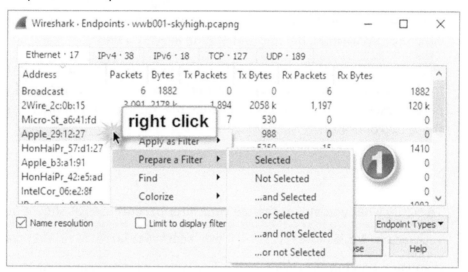

Next, we right-clicked on *Apple_b3:a1:91* and selected *Prepare a Filter | ...or Selected*.

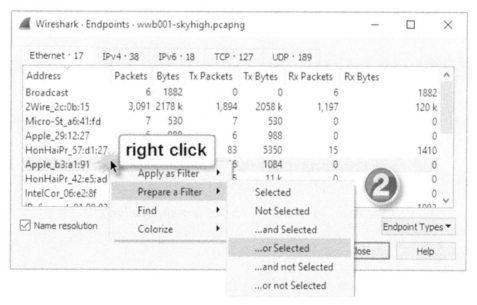

Wireshark created the following display filter:

`(eth.addr==9c:35:eb:29:12:27) || (eth.addr==64:9a:be:b3:a1:91)`

If you are following along, click the *Apply* button 🔲 to see traffic to or from these two MAC addresses.

Out of the 22 packets displayed, the DHCP packets are the most interesting because they contain a *Host Name* field. In order to add DHCP to your filter, you must add `&& dhcp` (if you are working with Wireshark v3 or later).

If you are working with Wireshark v1 or v2, you will need to use `&& bootp`. Earlier versions of Wireshark did not understand `dhcp` as a filter.

Your display filter area will turn yellow because Wireshark detected that you are mixing `&&` with `||` (and with or). Wireshark wants you to be careful of your parentheses as their location can change the meaning of the filter when you mix these two operators[16].

To clarify what you mean, change your filter parentheses as shown below:

`(eth.addr==9c:35:eb:29:12:27 || eth.addr==64:9a:be:b3:a1:91) && dhcp`[17]

If you are working with Wireshark v3 or later, you also may want to add a *Host Name* column (`dhcp.option.hostname` from inside the DHCP requests) as we did in the image below. If you are working on Wireshark v1 or v2, you can add a `bootp.option.hostname` column instead.

Interestingly, the NEWS.txt *file for Wireshark v3 and later indicates that the* bootp *filter may go away someday.*

It is great to have a dhcp *filter now, but* bootp *should still stick around. Why?*

All DHCP packets are BOOTP packets over IPv4. Not all BOOTP packets are DHCP packets, however.

We really need both filters to remain available.

---

[16] When you use Wireshark's right-click method and select *Apply as Filter* or *Prepare a Filter* with any of the "..." selections, Wireshark places parentheses around everything that is in the current display filter field, adds the operator, and adds the new term in parentheses. The parentheses we end up with are not necessarily the way we would have placed the parentheses if we had just typed the filter term. Wireshark does this to force left-to-right evaluation of the display filter expression.

[17] Or use `&& bootp` if you are working with Wireshark v1 or v2.

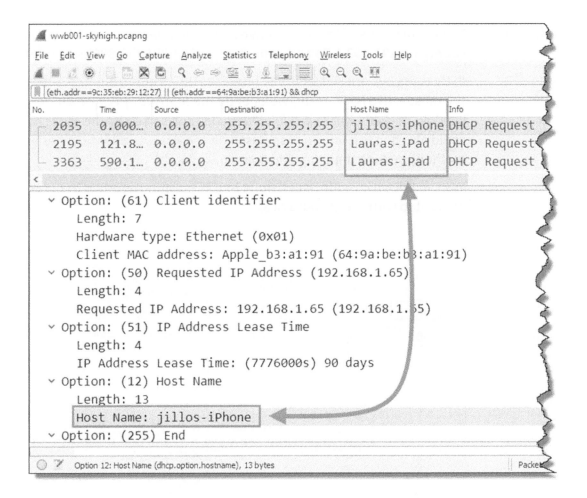

 It is always fascinating to see what mobile devices are blasting the name of the owner onto the network.

In some cases, you can detect the name of companies or even the most recent WLAN SSIDs to which devices have connected.

Lab 7 - A4.   **The IP addresses of the most active HTTP client in this trace file (based on byte count) are 192.168.1.74 and 2602:306:cee5:f4d0:5db5:805e:bf47:deda.**

In this case, we applied a display filter for HTTP traffic using `tcp.port==80`. To find the most active HTTP client, we opened the *Statistics | Conversations | TCP* window, clicked *Limit to display filter*, and then sorted by the *Bytes* column. You could also find this information based on the *Packets* column, if desired. Both methods provide the same information.

We can tell which addresses belong to HTTP clients based on the port numbers associated with the IP addresses.

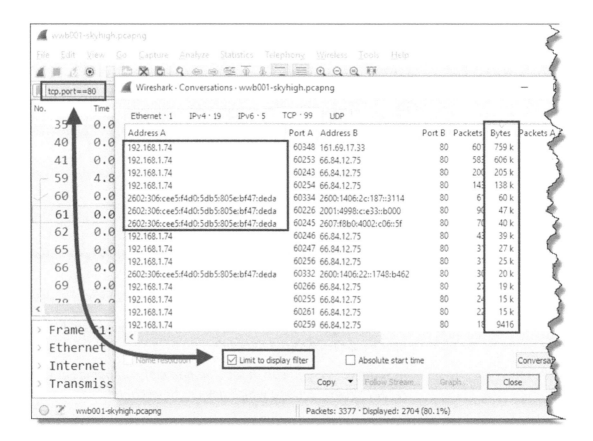

 When you are asked to identify the "most active" host, it is good to clarify if someone is interested in the activity level based on the byte/bit count or the packet count. In this situation, you would have come up with the same answer regardless of whether you sorted on the Bytes *column or the* Packets *column.*

Lab 7 - A5.   **The IPv4 and IPv6 addresses used by the DNS servers in this trace file are 192.168.1.254 and 2602:306:cee5:f4d0::1.**

There are several ways to get this answer.

This time I filtered on DNS responses using the *Response* flag in a DNS frame.

After expanding the *Flags* section in a DNS response packet, I right-clicked on the *Response* field and selected *Apply as Filter | Selected*.

The resulting filter is dns.flags.response==1.

If you want to use a very basic filter first, you can start with just dns.

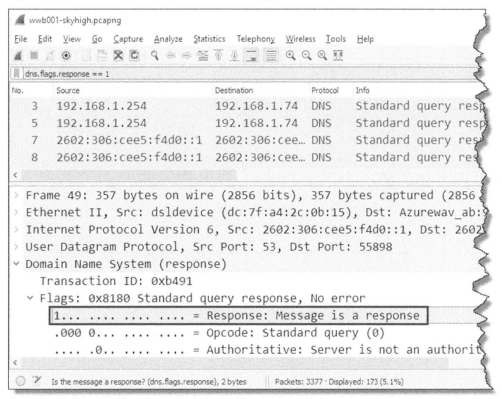

 No one wants to write down IPv6 addresses! IPv6 addresses are long and cumbersome. Here's a nice hint… rather than try to write down the address correctly, right-click on the IPv6 address in the IPv6 header and select Copy | Value. *Paste the information into another program and voila! No typos, no hassle!*

Lab 7 - A6. **There are 197 DNS queries in this trace file.**

It would be great if you could just type `dns.request` or `dns.query` to get this answer. Unfortunately, both of those filters are invalid[18].

Just as we filtered on the DNS *Flags* bit set to 1 for the last answer, we filtered on the DNS *Flags* bit set to 0 this time to detect DNS queries.

The filter is `dns.flags.response==0`.

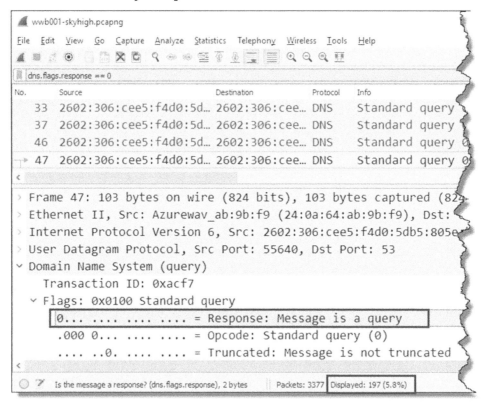

 Remember that if you ever want to learn the display filter syntax of a field, click on the field in the Packet Details window and look at the Status Bar.

The display filter field value will appear to the right of the Capture File Properties *button (on the left side of the Status Bar).*

---

18 Maybe this will change in a later version of Wireshark. That would be nice.

Lab 7 - A7. **There are fourteen DNS error responses in this trace file.**

Again, we need to go into a DNS packet to find out what makes a packet a DNS error response. You will need to expand the DNS *Flags* field to find the *Reply code* field. Any value other than a 0 indicates a DNS error.

We applied a filter for `dns.flags.rcode > 0`. The Status Bar indicates there are 14 (0.4%) DNS errors in this trace file.

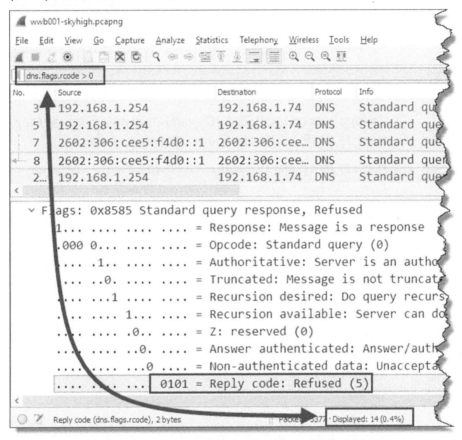

We could also have used a negative filter: `dns.flags.rcode != 0`, but the use of the != will cause Wireshark to display a yellow warning background. I just didn't want to see that background color, so I decided to use the > instead.

The != *operator causes a lot of confusion in Wireshark. The only time to avoid this operator is when you are using a "combo field name" – a field name that represents more than one field.*

Examples of combo field names include tcp.port, udp.port, eth.addr, *and* ip.addr. *Each of these field names represents source and destination fields.*

For example, ip.addr != 192.168.1.10 *expands and is evaluated as if it were written:*

ip.src != 192.168.1.10 || ip.dst != 192.168.1.10

*Packets sent **to** 192.168.1.10 would be shown because they wouldn't have 192.168.1.10 in the source IP address field.*

*Packets sent **from** 192.168.1.10 would be shown because they wouldn't have 192.168.1.10 in the destination IP address field.*

That is why ip.src != 192.168.1.10 || ip.dst != 192.168.1.10 *does not remove any packets from view.*

The display filter !ip.addr==192.168.1.10 *expands and is evaluated as if it were written:*

!(ip.src == 192.168.1.10 || ip.dst == 192.168.1.10)

This filter will remove any packets from view that have 192.168.1.10 in either the source or destination IP address field. Since you are likely using a negative filter to remove something from view, this is the proper syntax.

It's ok to use != *when you are looking at a field name that only represents a single field, such as the* dns.flags.rcode *field.*

Lab 7 - A8. **The HTTP client is using Microsoft Windows 10.**

This information is contained in the *User-Agent* field of the client's HTTP requests. To find this information quickly, we applied a filter for `http.request.method== GET`[19] and then looked inside the HTTP section of some of the GET packets. We see the reference to Windows NT in the User-Agent value.

A quick Internet search for "Windows NT 10.0" indicates that this client is using Windows 10.

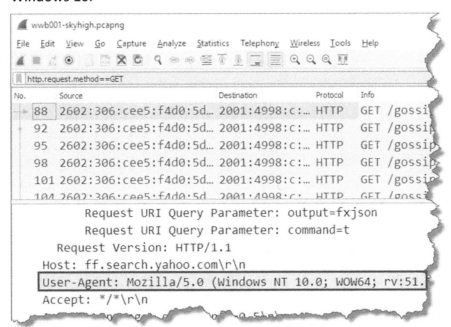

The *User-Agent* field is interesting! You can find out about a lot of background processes by looking at this field. We added a column based on the *User-Agent* field and then sorted this column to see what other User-Agent values might be in the trace file.

There are three different values in the *User-Agent* field. We know the first one is generated by the browser (Firefox) and indicates the client is running Windows 10.

We also see Microsoft-WNS/10.0 and Microsoft BITS/7.8 in the *User-Agent* field of other frames.

Microsoft-WNS/10.0

Used in the background to fetch *Live Tiles* for the Windows 10's *Start* Menu. Frame 1989 contains a GET request with this User-Agent value. Notice the Request

---

[19] You don't need to put quotes around your search term if it is only one word.

URI (Uniform Resource Identifier) and the *Host* fields. We can see this is related to a *Live Tiles* update.

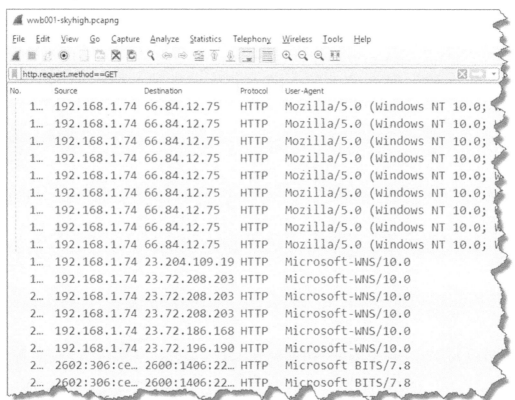

Microsoft BITS/7.8

According to Microsoft, BITS stands for Background Intelligent Transfer Service (BITS). This technology is used to transfer files between a client and server and provide progress information related to the transfers. Frame 2324 is a GET using the Microsoft BITS User-Agent value. When we examine the *Request URI* and the *Host* fields, this traffic appears to be related to the Microsoft *Live Tiles* ("tilesize'") and the information is coming from an Akamai server.

   Semicolons separate the individual elements of the User-Agent string. You can learn more about the elements of various User-Agent strings at http://www.useragentstring.com.

Lab 7 - A9. **The client is using Yahoo as its search engine.**

You can add to the existing `http.request.method==GET` filter to focus on requests made by the browser (not the WNS or BITS traffic). Rather than type that looooong User-Agent value for the Firefox browser requests, right-click on the *User-Agent* field in a Firefox request and select *Apply as Filter | ...and Selected*. This only displays 44 packets. Inside the first displayed packet, notice the *Host* field indicates *ff.search.yahoo.com*. That's the search engine in use.

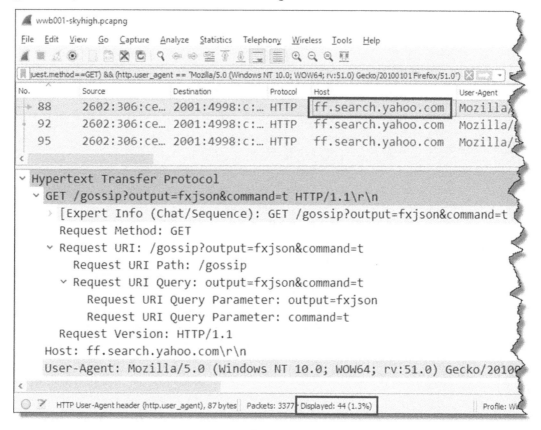

Lab 7 - A10. **The user is searching for "tahoe weather forecast."**

We could have just kept the same display filter used for the last question. It's a pretty long display filter, however.

We tried a simpler filter, `http.request`.

Looking in the *Info* column, you'll see the search process echoing back the user's search term.

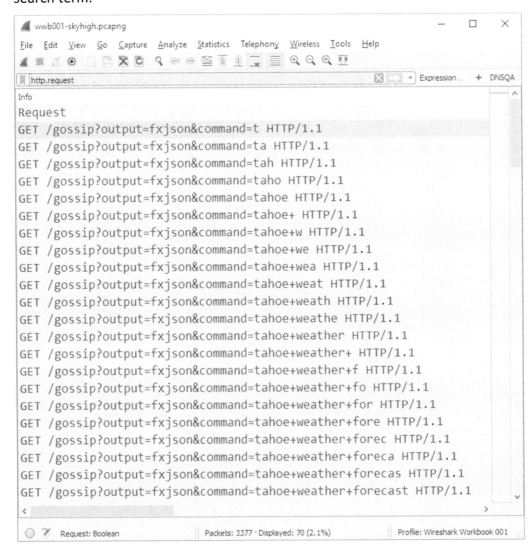

Lab 7 - A11. **It takes the user 7.690452 seconds to type the search term "tahoe weather forecast."**

By setting a Time Reference on the first GET of the search and then changing the *Time* column setting to *Seconds Since Beginning of Capture*, we can measure the time from the beginning to the end of the search submission.

To set a Time Reference, right-click on the frame in the Packet List pane and select *Set/Unset Time Reference*.

If you have changed the *Time* column so it is not set at the default value, you must change it back. Select *View | Time Display Format | Seconds Since Beginning of Capture*.

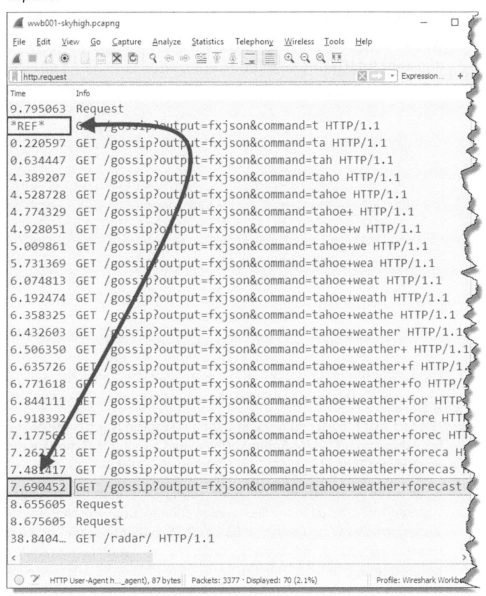

> ⓘ *Rather than change the* Time *column setting, you could add another column that contains this delta time value and leave the* Time *column at the default settings.*
>
> *To add another column with this setting, expand the Frame section in the Packet Details pane. You will see several lines containing time information.*
>
> *Right-click on the* [Time delta from previous displayed frame: x.x seconds] *line and select* Apply as column.

Lab 7 - A12. **After the search process, the client sends an HTTP GET to *weathermaps006.ga*.**

We can find this information using the display filter `http contains "GET"` and displaying the HTTP *Host* field.

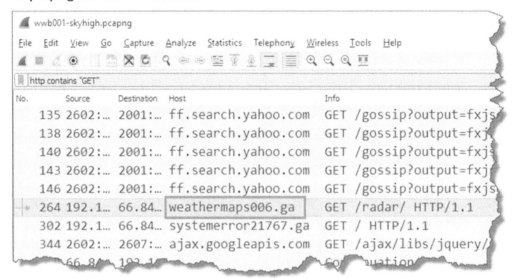

On the user's screen, the search result showed a Weather Underground site as a result. That is the link upon which the user clicked.

The fact that the user hit a site in Gabon is suspicious (*ga* is the country code top-level domain (ccTLD) for Gabon). Why would a server in Gabon be providing weather for Tahoe?

Note: If you enable Wireshark's name resolution preference setting, you will see *systemerror21767.ga* in the Destination column. Both *weathermaps006.ga* and *systemerror21767.ga* resolve to 66.84.12.75, but at this point in the trace file, only *weathermaps006.ga* has been resolved. The resolution for *systemerror21767.ga* occurs later and will override the previous resolution to *weathermaps006.ga* when the name resolution preference is enabled.

Spamhaus maintains statistics on the "10 Most Abused Top Level Domains.[20] Some of the domains that seem to consistently appear in this list include the following:

.loan   .ga (Gabon)
.gq (Equatorial Guinea)   .ml (Mali)
.gdn (Global Domain Name)   .tk (Tokelau)
.ltd (Limited, as in Limited Liability Company)   .world
.shop   .organic
.work   .date
.cf (Central African Republic)

---

[20]   See *https://www.spamhaus.org/statistics/tlds/*.

Lab 7 - A13. **Both *weathermaps006.ga* and *systemerror21767.ga* are associated with 66.84.12.75.**

There is a lot of DNS traffic in this trace file, so there's a good chance that we'll see this IP address show up as part of the resolution process. If you look inside any DNS response that contains an A record, you can find the field upon which to build a display filter.

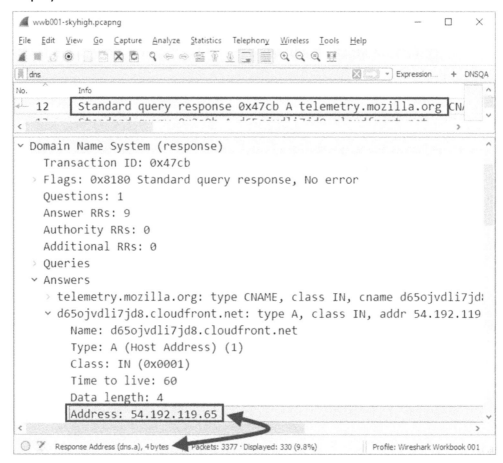

Using the DNS response *Address* field, we can filter on dns.a==66.84.12.75.

The results are shown in the following image.

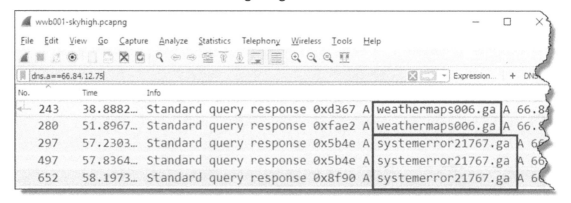

Lab 7 - A14.   **After clicking the radar view, the user was redirected to *systemerror21767.ga*.**

We can easily see this if we remove all filters and look at what occurs after frame 264 (the GET request).

We see an HTTP response code *302 Moved Temporarily* in frame 270. When you look inside frame 270, you can see the *Location* field pointing the client to *http://systemerror21767.ga*.

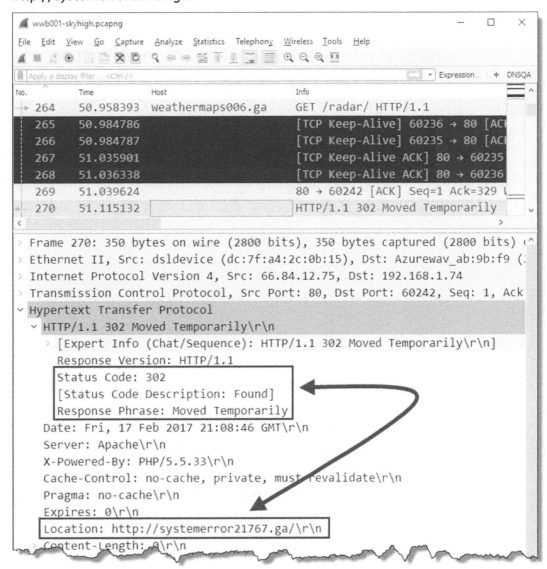

The \r\n is an end-of-line marker defined by the HTTP specification. It denotes a carriage return[21] line feed (CRLF).

---

[21]   For those of you who do NOT have gray hairs, a carriage return is what you used to do on a typewriter to get to a new line. The "carriage" was the roller that your paper would drape over and your keys would hit. Now I feel old.

Lab 7 - A15.   **Ten image files were downloaded from the suspicious server: *1.png, 2.png, 3.png, 4.png, 5.png, alert-1.png, alert-5.png, defender.png, fatal.png, and heading.png.***

There are a few ways we can obtain this answer. If we just look at the HTTP GET requests using `http contains "GET"`, we see a request for *alert-1.png* and *heading.png*.

There are many other images requested by the client, however.

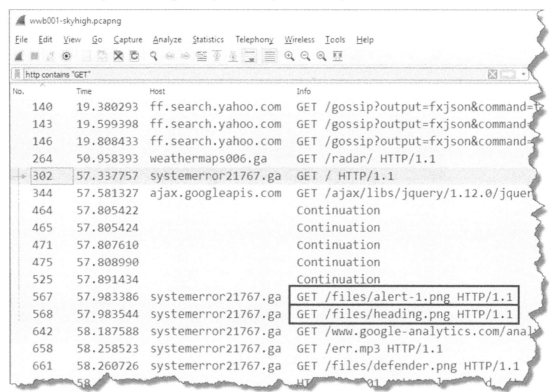

Ensure your TCP preference setting *Allow subdissector to reassemble TCP streams* is enabled and then select *File | Export Objects | HTTP*.

Sorting the *Content Type* column in the *HTTP Object List* window enables us to see the image/png files that were downloaded from the *systemerror21767.ga* server.

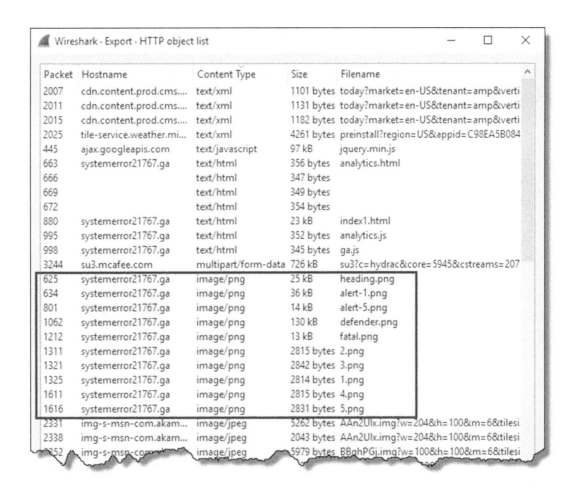

If you export the objects to a directory, look at the *alert-5.png* file. The following image was displayed on the client's screen.

The *alert-1.png* file is shown below.

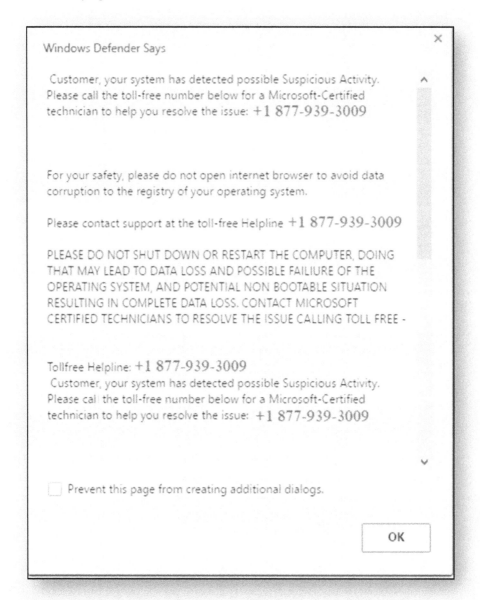

Lab 7 - A16. **Two *err.mp3* audio files play on the user's machine.**

Following the same steps of sorting the *HTTP Object List* window, we see the client downloaded two audio files from *systemerror21767.ga*. Both files are named *err.mp3*, but they are not the same file.

We can see that one file is 574 kB and the other file is only 17 kB.

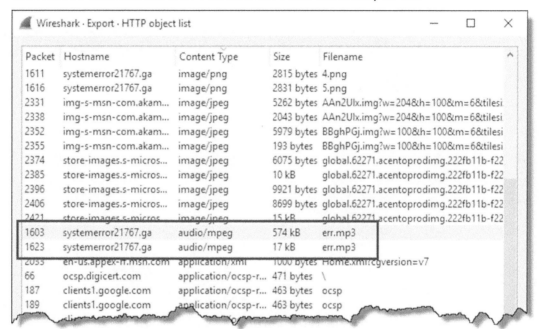

Apply the filter `http request && frame contains "mp3"` to the trace file.

You will notice that one of the files is contained in the *error_extra* directory.

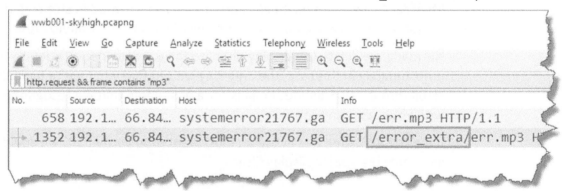

If you choose to *Save All* the HTTP objects, Wireshark saves all the files into the same directory. When Wireshark sees two files with the same name, it will append (1) to the second file. You will see *err.mp3* and *err(1).mp3* in your directory of saved files.

Lab 7 - A17. **Windows Defender is supposedly launched in the background on the user's system.**

The file *defender.png* displays on the user's screen. This image is opened from *systemerror21767.ga*, not from the local Windows Defender application.

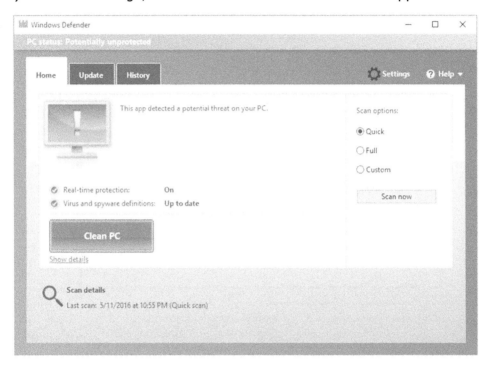

Lab 7 - A18. **The McAfee virus detection tool is loaded on the user's machine.**

A simple `dns` filter indicates that the user's system is resolving the address for McAfee. As you can see, it didn't do this user much good in stopping the redirection to *systemerror21767.ga* or the launching of the image or audio files.

Normally, we like to use display filters to focus on the packets of interest, but unfortunately in this case, the only way we can find what we're looking for is to just scroll through DNS queries looking for a host name that we recognize is associated with virus detection software.

If we knew McAfee was in use and just wanted to verify that, we could apply a `dns contains mcafee` display filter.

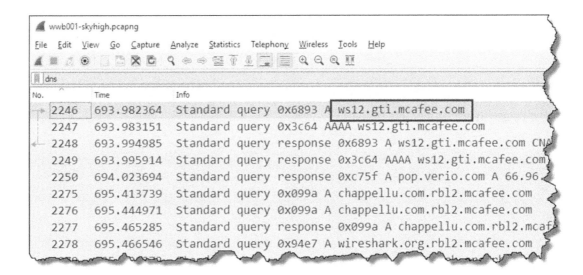

[This page intentionally left blank.]

Lab 8: DNS Warm-Up

Objective: Examine and analyze DNS name resolution traffic that contains canonical name and multiple IP address responses.

`Trace File: wwb001-dnswarmup.pcapng`

Skills Covered in this Lab

In this lab, you will have a chance to work with many key functions in Wireshark. The answers to this lab demonstrate how to use functions, including, but not limited to:

- Determine the number of DNS packets in a trace file
- Measure DNS response time
- Identify multiple IP addresses associated with a single host name
- Detect DNS errors in a trace file
- Identify which IP address a client uses when multiple addresses are returned
- Determine how long a DNS client can cache DNS information
- Determine if recursive or iterative DNS queries are in use
- Identify the canonical name for a host

Lab 8 - Q1. How many DNS packets are in this trace file?

_____

Lab 8 - Q2. How long did it take to resolve the IP address for _blog.wireshark.org_?

_____

Lab 8 - Q3. How long did it take to resolve the IP address for _np.lexity.com_?

_____

Lab 8 - Q4. What IP addresses were provided for _np.lexity.com_?

_____

Lab 8 - Q5. Are there any DNS errors in this trace file?

_____

Lab 8 - Q6. What IP addresses were provided for _wireshark.org_ and _www.wireshark.org_?

_____

Lab 8 - Q7. What IP address did the client use for _www.wireshark.org_?

_____

Lab 8 - Q8. How long can the client cache the DNS information received for _www.wireshark.org_?

_____

Lab 8 - Q9. Is the client requesting recursive or iterative DNS queries?

_____

Lab 8 - Q10.   **What IP address was provided for *www.gnome.org*?**

_____

Lab 8 - Q11.   **How many DNS responses contain CNAME entries?**

_____

[This page intentionally left blank.]

Lab 8 Solutions

Trace File: wwb001-dnswarmup.pcapng

Lab 8 - A1.   **There are 58 DNS packets in this trace file.**

After applying a simple `dns` filter, we can examine the Status Bar to see the *Displayed: 58 (2.8%)* value.

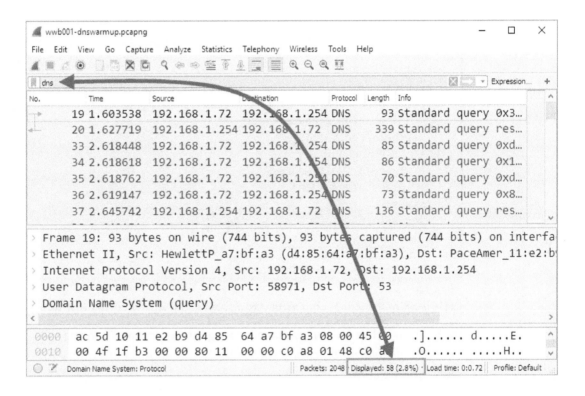

Lab 8 - A2.   **It took 0.028857 seconds to resolve the IP address for *blog.wireshark.org*.**

We can expand our simple `dns` filter to look specifically for DNS queries/responses that contain *blog.wireshark.org*. There is a trick to this one, however.

If we use `dns contains "blog.wireshark.org"`, no packets are displayed. This throws off a lot of people when they are looking for specific DNS queries or responses in a trace file.

In the image shown next, we applied a `dns matches "blog.wireshark.org"` display filter. When you use the `matches` operator, Wireshark interprets what follows as a regular expression. In regular expressions, a dot is a wildcard.

Let's look at why `dns contains "blog.wireshark.org"` does not work.

In the image that follows, we are looking inside packet 73 in the *wwb001-dnswarmup.pcapng* trace file. This is an A record query for *www.google.com*.

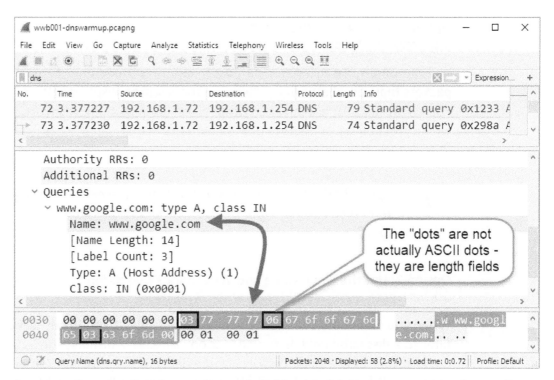

By expanding the *Queries* section and clicking on the *Name: www.google.com* line, we can see the bytes that make up this *Name* field.

Inside DNS packets, domain names are represented by a combination of length fields and labels.

What we see as "dots" inside an address such as *www.google.com*, are the length fields. They are not ASCII dots. These length fields indicate the number of characters in each label.

The first byte is 0x03 which indicates there is a 3-byte label coming up.

Length	Hex	Label
3 bytes	0x77 77 77	www

After the "www," we see the length value of 6 (0x06).

Length	Hex	Label
6 bytes	0x67 6f 6f 67 6c 65	google

The next length value is 3 (0x03) again.

Length	Hex	Label
3 bytes	0x63 6f 6d	com

The final length field value is 0 (0x00) which denotes the end of the name.

So how can we filter on DNS packets that contain a specific name? There is more than one way to do this.

Option 1: Start with a Broad Filter
```
dns contains "blog"
```

You can simply use `dns contains "blog"` as a very broad filter to start. All DNS packets that contain the value "blog" in them will be displayed. It's quick to type. You might see a lot of undesired packets, or you might not. It's worth a try. This works great on *wwb001-dnswarmup.pcapng*.

 Again, I refer to this process as "widening the net" – a fishing-related term meaning that you use a larger net and possibly get a larger variety of fish and other items to start.

Option 2: Use the Field Name and Wireshark's Dissection
```
dns.qry.name contains "blog.wireshark.org"
```

When you define the DNS *Name* field in your display filter, Wireshark applies your filter to a dissected field. In the dissection, Wireshark displays the length field as dots, so your filter works. The DNS *Name* field is `dns.qry.name`. Remember that any time you click on a field, Wireshark indicates that field's display filter name in the Status Bar, as shown in the following image.

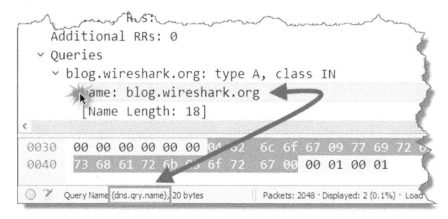

Lab 8 - A3. **It took 0.033507 seconds to resolve the IP address for *np.lexity.com*.**

Using the options listed in the previous answer, we can quickly locate the DNS query and response for *np.lexity.com* (frames 36 and 39). In this case we used `dns matches "np.lexity.com"`. We used `matches` because in regular expressions the dots are treated as wildcard characters. Since we know these are not actually dots, but length fields, this filter works.

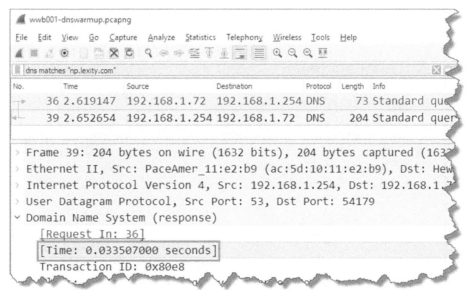

Lab 8 - A4. **The IP addresses 54.243.97.198, 23.23.89.255, 50.16.186.82, and 23.21.88.136 were provided for *np.lexity.com*.**

The previous answer required that we locate the DNS request and response for *np.lexity.com*. Packet 39 is the DNS response.

When we expand the DNS section of packet 39, we can see the resolved IP addresses for *np.lexity.com*.

In this case, a canonical name (CNAME) is listed for *np.lexity.com*. It appears that the actual host name is *lexity-pixel-prod-1637257845.us-east-1.elb.amazonaws.com*. The familiar "amazonaws" indicates the site is hosted by Amazon's AWS (Amazon Web Services).

AWS offers cloud computing and hosting services. A single site can be replicated to various locations around the world to serve content locally (edge serving). This improves browsing performance by reducing the latency between the clients and the server.

This response contains a CNAME answer and multiple IP addresses for the *lexity-pixel-prod-1637257845.us-east-1.elb.amazonaws.com* host.

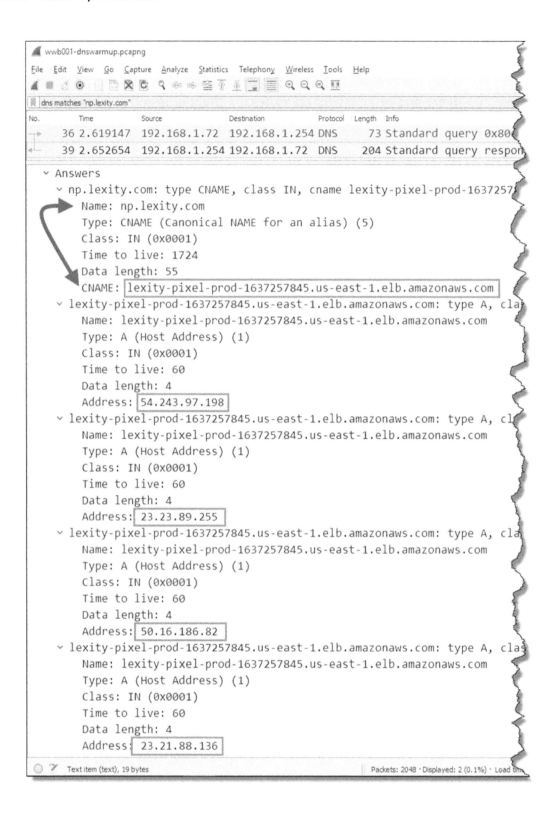

Lab 8 - A5.   **There are no DNS errors in this trace file.**

To find DNS errors quickly, we need to know (1) the *Reply code* field name and (2) the value(s) that would indicate errors.

Reply codes will only be in response packets. In the image below, we clicked on frame 20 and expanded the DNS *Flags* section. The *Reply code* field in this packet contains the binary value *0000* which indicates there are no errors in this response.

Any value greater than 0 would indicate an error. We can easily create and apply a filter for DNS error responses – dns.flags.rcode > 0.

In the image below, we applied a filter for dns just to illustrate the location of the DNS *Reply code* field.

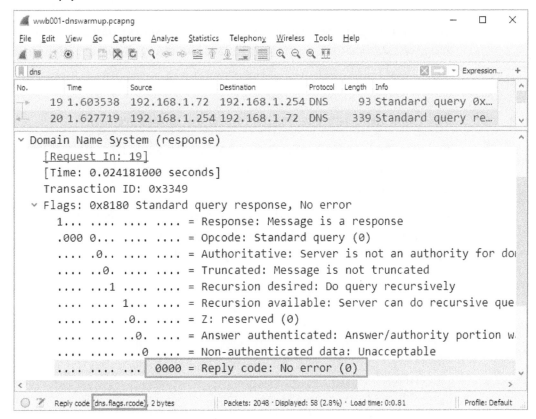

 I would turn this display filter into a display filter button so it is readily available when troubleshooting. Consider clicking the + on the display filter toolbar to create a DNSErr button.

Lab 8 - A6. **The IP addresses 162.159.241.165 and 162.159.242.165 were provided for** *wireshark.org* **and** *www.wireshark.org***.**

Here is a perfect time to cast a wide net using `dns contains "wireshark"` because we are looking for two host names that contain "wireshark."

```
Info
Standard query 0xde1d A www.wiresharktraining.com
Standard query response 0xde1d A www.wiresharktraining.com CNAME sbsfe-p10.geo.mf0.yaho
Standard query 0x787f A wireshark.org
Standard query response 0x787f A wireshark.org A 162.159.241.165 A 162.159.242.165
Standard query 0xa7cc A www.wireshark.org
Standard query response 0xa7cc A www.wireshark.org A 162.159.241.165 A 162.159.242.165
Standard query 0xa5e7 A blog.wireshark.org
Standard query response 0xa5e7 A blog.wireshark.org A 162.159.242.165 A 162.159.241.165
```

We can disregard the responses for *www.wiresharktraining.com* and *blog.wireshark.org*. If this filter displays too many unrelated DNS responses, we can use `dns.qry.name contains wireshark.org`.

Lab 8 - A7. **The client used 162.159.241.165 for** *www.wireshark.org***.**

By selecting frame 435 (the DNS response for *www.wireshark.org*) and then removing our display filter, we can see the client sending a SYN packet to 162.159.241.165 in frame 436.

Although there were two addresses offered for *www.wireshark.org*, the client used the first address provided. It is typical behavior for a host to select the first address listed when multiple addresses are provided.

```
Source          Destination     Protocol  Length  Info
192.168.1.72    162.159.241.165  TCP        54 6903 → 80 [ACK] Seq=257 Ack=702 Win=6499
162.159.241…    192.168.1.72     HTTP       60 HTTP/1.1 301 Moved Permanently  (text/htm
192.168.1.72    162.159.241.165  TCP        54 6903 → 80 [ACK] Seq=257 Ack=707 Win=64992
192.168.1.72    192.168.1.254    DNS        77 Standard query 0xa7cc A www.wireshark.or
192.168.1.254   192.168.1.72     DNS       109 Standard query response 0xa7cc A www.wir
192.168.1.72    162.159.241.165  TCP        66 6905 → 80 [SYN] Seq=0 Win=8192 Len=0 MSS
192.168.1.72    162.159.241.165  TCP        66 6906 → 80 [SYN] Seq=0 Win=8192 Len=0 MSS
162.159.241…    192.168.1.72     TCP        66 80 → 6905 [SYN, ACK] Seq=0 Ack=1 Win=146
162.159.241…    192.168.1.72     TCP        66 80 → 6906 [SYN, ACK] Seq=0 Ack=1 Win=146
192.168.1.72    162.159.241.165  TCP        54 6905 → 80 [ACK] Seq=1 Ack=1 Win=65700 Le
192.168.1.72    162.159.241.165  TCP        54 6906 → 80 [ACK] Seq=1 Ack=1 Win=65700 Ler
192.168.1.72    162.159.241.165  HTTP      379 GET / HTTP/1.1
162.159.241…    192.168.1.72     TCP        60 80 → 6905 [ACK] Seq=1 Ack=326 Win=16384
162.159.241…    192.168.1.72     TCP      1145 80 → 6905 [PSH, ACK] Seq=1 Ack=326 Win=1
```

Lab 8 - A8. **The client can cache the DNS information received for *www.wireshark.org* for 300 seconds.**

To find the DNS cache time for the *www.wireshark.org* IP addresses, we need to look inside the DNS response for *www.wireshark.org*.

```
> Frame 435: 109 bytes on wire (872 bits), 109 bytes captured (872
> Ethernet II, Src: PaceAmer_11:e2:b9 (ac:5d:10:11:e2:b9), Dst: He
> Internet Protocol Version 4, Src: 192.168.1.254, Dst: 192.168.1.7
> User Datagram Protocol, Src Port: 53, Dst Port: 62155
v Domain Name System (response)
    [Request In: 434]
    [Time: 0.036814000 seconds]
    Transaction ID: 0xa7cc
  > Flags: 0x8180 Standard query response, No error
    Questions: 1
    Answer RRs: 2
    Authority RRs: 0
    Additional RRs: 0
  v Queries
    > www.wireshark.org: type A, class IN
  v Answers
    v www.wireshark.org: type A, class IN, addr 162.159.241.165
        Name: www.wireshark.org
        Type: A (Host Address) (1)
        Class: IN (0x0001)
        Time to live: 300
        Data length: 4
        Address: 162.159.241.165
    v www.wireshark.org: type A, class IN, addr 162.159.242.165
        Name: www.wireshark.org
        Type: A (Host Address) (1)
        Class: IN (0x0001)
        Time to live: 300
        Data length: 4
        Address: 162.159.242.165
```

Lab 8 - A9. **All the client DNS requests are recursive DNS queries.**

We need to check all the client DNS queries to determine if these queries are recursive or iterative.

Recursive Query

When a recursive query is used, the client wants its DNS server to perform the entire resolution if it does not have the information. If that DNS server does not have the information in cache, that DNS server will begin the process of "walking the DNS tree" to resolve the address for the client. The client simply waits for the resolution to complete (hopefully successfully).

Iterative Query

When an iterative query is used, the client does not want its DNS server to perform the entire resolution if it does not have the information. Instead, the DNS server will hand the client a referral to another DNS server that might have the resolution information.

In the following image, you will see that we used a display filter based on the client's IP address in the *Source IP Address* field and added that we are looking at DNS traffic only. The display filter is `ip.src==192.168.1.72 && dns`.

This displays all the client DNS queries. In the DNS *Flags* section, we right-clicked on the *Recursion desired: Do query recursively* line and added this as a column.

How could you build a display filter that looks for iterative DNS queries from our client? We need to specify (1) the client's IP address as the source and (2) look for the value 0 in the *Recursion Desired* field (indicating that recursion is not desired – it is an iterative query).

```
ip.src==192.168.1.72 && dns.flags.recdesired==0
```

Since we determined that all the DNS queries from the client are recursive in this trace file, applying this display filter should yield no packets.

Lab 8 - A10. **The name *www.gnome.org* has a canonical name of *socket.gnome.org* which resolved to 91.189.93.3.**

Again, we can first cast a wide net by using the display filter `dns contains "gnome"`. By looking at the 8 displayed packets we can see that *www.gnome.org* resolved to 91.189.93.3.

```
Info
Standard query 0x6a00 A mail.gnome.org
Standard query response 0x6a00 A mail.gnome.org CNAME proxy.gnome.org A 209.132.180
Standard query 0x0d3a A www-old.gnome.org
Standard query 0x0455 A static.gnome.org
Standard query response 0x0d3a A www-old.gnome.org CNAME proxy.gnome.org A 209.132.
Standard query response 0x0455 A static.gnome.org CNAME proxy.gnome.org A 209.132.18
Standard query 0x1a9c A www.gnome.org
Standard query response 0x1a9c A www.gnome.org CNAME socket.gnome.org A 91.189.93.3
```

Alternately, we could have used `dns.resp.name==www.gnome.org` to view the single packet that contains the answer.

A truly lazy filter (casting a wide net) would be `frame contains "gnome"`.

If you try this filter, you will find 34 frames that match the filter. These frames include DNS queries, DNS responses, TLS Client Hello packets, TLS Server Hello packets, HTTP GET requests and HTTP responses.

Since we were specifically interested in the DNS responses, it makes more sense to filter for `dns.resp.name==www.gnome.org`.

Lab 8 - A11. **Twenty-four DNS responses contain CNAME entries.**

To obtain this answer, we can use a display filter based on the *DNS Response Type* field. The CNAME type value is 5. Our filter is dns.resp.type==5.

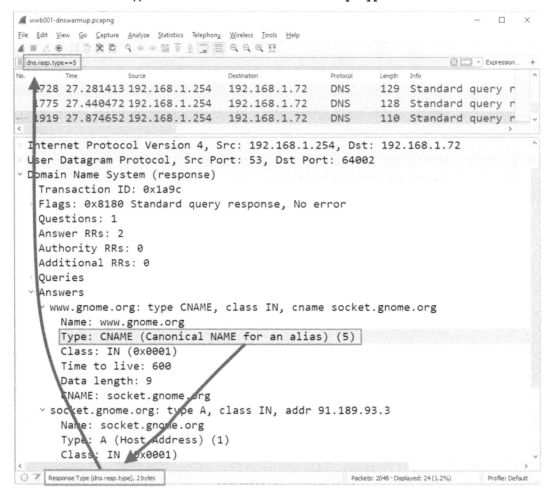

Lab 9: Hacker Watch

Objective: Analyze TCP connections and FTP command and data channels between hosts.

Trace File: wwb001-hackerwatch.pcapng

Skills Covered in this Lab

In this lab, you will work with many key functions in Wireshark including, but not limited to:

- Identify company relationships based on DNS traffic
- Determine the maximum Calculated Window Size offered by TCP peers
- Compare path latency using the Initial Round-Trip Time (iRTT) value
- Identify successful FTP logins (user names and passwords)
- Determine if Active, Passive, Extended Active, or Extended Passive mode connections are in use
- Filter on specific traffic types and list related stream index values
- Correlate packets with applications in a trace file

Lab 9 - Q1.   What company appears to be in charge of *hackerwatch.org*?

_____

Lab 9 - Q2.   What is the maximum Calculated Window Size offered by the client?

_____

Lab 9 - Q3.   What is the maximum Calculated Window Size offered by the FTP server?

_____

Lab 9 - Q4.   What is the slowest Initial Round-Trip Time (iRTT) between the client and the FTP server?

_____

Lab 9 - Q5.   What user names are provided by the FTP client?

_____

Lab 9 - Q6.   What passwords are provided by the FTP client?

_____

Lab 9 - Q7.   What user name and password combinations are accepted by the FTP server?

_____

Lab 9 - Q8.   Did the FTP client use active or passive connections for the FTP data transfer?

_____

Lab 9 - Q9. List the order in which the FTP command and data connections are established in this trace file. Use the TCP stream index number when referring to the different connections.

_____

_____

_____

_____

_____

Lab 9 - Q10. **Extra Credit:**
Explain the purpose of the _courier.push.apple.com_ traffic in this trace file.

_____

_____

_____

_____

_____

[This page intentionally left blank.]

Lab 9 Solutions

Trace File: wwb001-hackerwatch.pcapng

Lab 9 - A1.   **McAfee appears to be in charge of *hackerwatch.org*.**

A simple filter for dns contains hackerwatch displays the answer. The *Info* column of frame 12 includes "SOA ns1.mcafee.com." The primary name server and responsible authority's mailbox both include "McAfee."

This is the *Start of Authority* record. Authoritative name servers for a zone must include the SOA record of the zone in the authority section of a DNS response when reporting that no data of the requested type exists. This trace file indicates that there was no IPv6 (AAAA record) for *md5.hackerwatch.org* when this trace file was taken. This is considered a "negative answer" from an Authoritative Server. For more information on this response, read *RFC 2308, Negative Caching of DNS Queries (DNS NSCACHE)*.

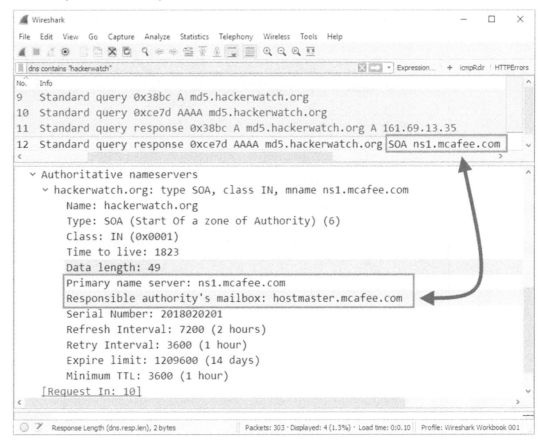

Lab 9 - A2. **The maximum Calculated Window Size offered by the client is 66,048.**

Any time you need to find out the maximum or minimum value of a field, consider placing that field in a column that can then be sorted.

In this case, we right-clicked on the *[Calculated window size]* field and added it as a column.

We are only interested in the client's calculated window size value, so I identified the client (noted by the host sending SYN packets and DNS request packets) and applied a display filter for ip.src==192.168.1.70 || ipv6.src==2600:1700:79e0:1e70:f5dd:e68a:13f2:4adc.

The last step was to sort the *Calculated window size* column from high to low and jump to the top of the sorted column.

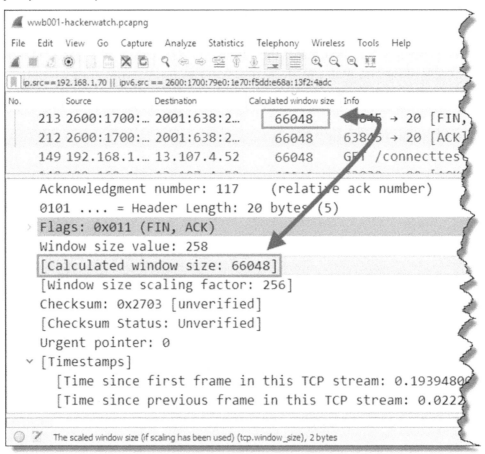

Lab 9 - A3.   **The maximum Calculated Window Size offered by the FTP server is 28,800.**

After applying a simple `ftp` filter[22], we can see the FTP server's traffic. Sorting the *Calculated window size* field indicates the maximum value offered by the server is 28,800 bytes.

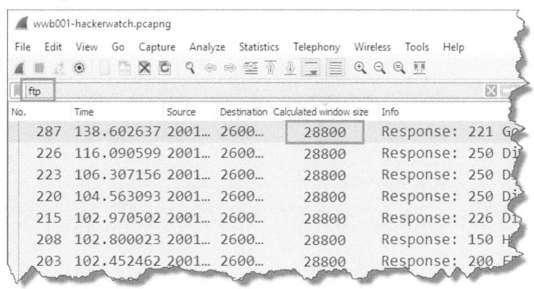

 The Calculated window size *field indicates the amount of receive buffer space available at the source of the packet.*

If a host advertises a Window Size of 0 (which also indicates a Calculated Window Size of 0), it means the sender has no available buffer space remaining. This value might be sent in SYN, FIN, and Reset packets, but Wireshark doesn't care about those packets. Wireshark cares about the Calculated Window Size value advertised in data packets and ACK packets.

Wireshark does watch for other TCP packets sent with a Window Size of 0. When Wireshark sees these packets, it marks them as [TCP Zero Window segment].

Wireshark cannot detect "low window sizes," however. For example, if a host advertises a Calculated Window Size of 500 bytes, Wireshark thinks that's just fine. If the peer has more than 500 bytes queued up to send, however, it can't send it. There isn't enough receive buffer space.

You can watch for this using your Calculated window size *column.*

---

[22]   You could also use a `tcp.srcport==21` filter or even a filter based on the FTP server's IP address, if desired.

Lab 9 - A4. **The slowest Initial Round-Trip Time (iRTT) between the client and the FTP server is 0.200035 seconds.**

We are interested in the FTP command channel traffic **and** the data channel traffic, in this case. To obtain this answer, I applied a display filter based on the source address of the FTP server and added a column based on the *iRTT* field. Sorting that field enables us to quickly find the slowest iRTT value between the client and the FTP server.

This field value is calculated during the handshake process and retained throughout each TCP conversation.

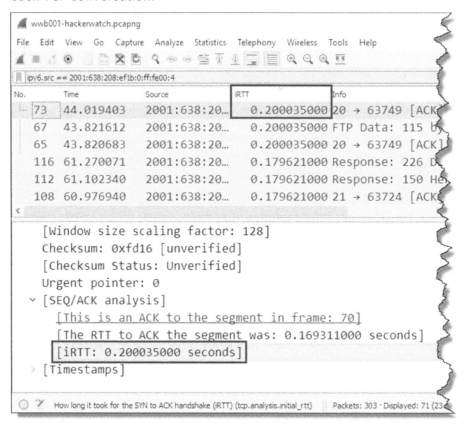

Lab 9 - A5. **The user names *markregion* and *anonymous* are provided by the FTP client.**

Using an `ftp` filter can provide this information, but you'd have to scroll through the packet list to find the USER commands.[23]

Why not just filter on the packets that contain the FTP USER command? A simple filter would be `frame contains "USER"`.

A more exact filter would be `ftp.request.command=="USER"`.

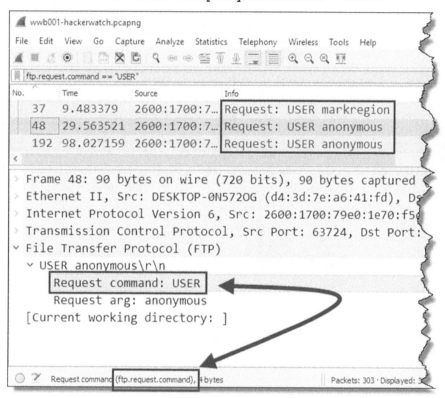

---

[23] If you've ever seen me present at a conference or private class, you know I hate scrolling. There is almost always a better way to find the packets of interest. Typically, a well-structured display filter will provide your answer.

Lab 9 - A6.   **The passwords *itstoohotoutside*, *itsstilltoohotoutside*, and *bozo* were provided by the FTP client.**

Again, you could use a simple `ftp` filter, but then you'd be scrolling through packets looking for the PASS command packets.

Why not just filter on `ftp.request.command=="PASS"`?

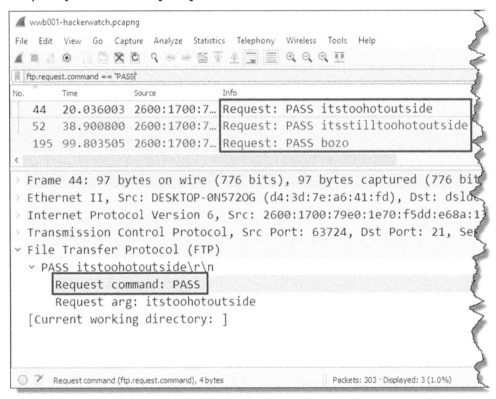

Lab 9 - A7.   **The successful FTP user name and password combinations are *anonymous/itsstilltoohotoutside* and *anonymous/bozo*.**

To find this answer, the best filter might be just `ftp`. That means scrolling, however. In this case, it isn't too bad.

If you had hundreds or even thousands of FTP connections in your trace, you might want to try filtering on the *USER* command packets, *PASS* command packets, and *530 Login Incorrect* responses to find out which login attempts succeeded, and which did not.

The filter would be `ftp.request.command=="USER"` || `ftp.request.command=="PASS"` || `ftp.response.code==530`. Try it on this trace file.

In the next image, we've added a TCP *Stream index* column to help differentiate between the various TCP connections in the trace file.

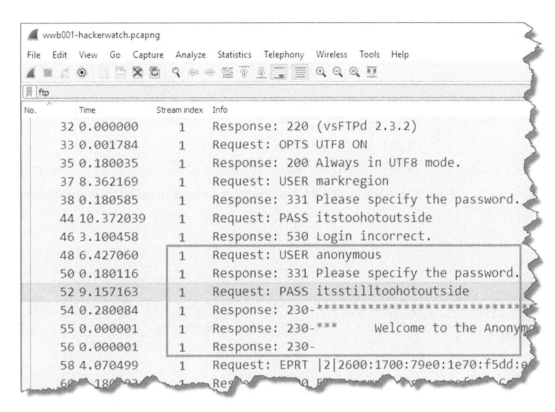

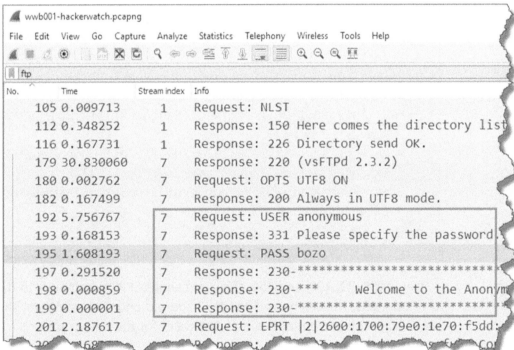

Lab 9 - A8. **The FTP client is using Extended Active Mode for IPv6 for the FTP data transfer.**

There are four FTP commands that are used to define active and passive mode data transfers:

> PORT: Active Mode
> PASV: Passive Mode
> EPRT: Extended Active Mode for IPv6
> EPSV: Extended Passive Mode for IPv6

We can use the membership operator in to display all four commands at once:

`ftp.request.command in {PORT PASV EPRT EPSV}`

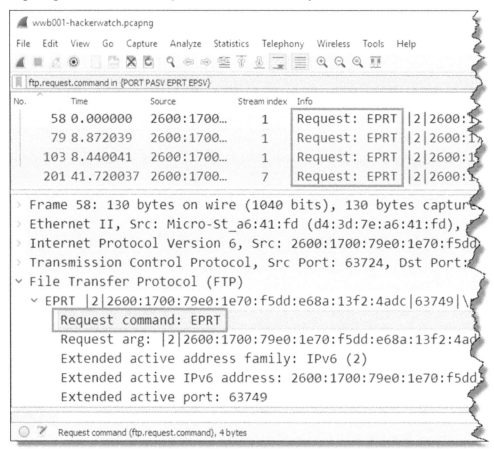

In frames 58, 79, 103, and 201, the client sends EPRT commands to the server. In these packets, the client provides its IP address and port numbers. The server establishes the TCP connections to the client for the data transfer.

These active mode connections are atypical connection types because the server sends the SYN packet to the client to establish these connections. How would you build a filter to identify the SYN packets traveling from the server towards the client?

The filter `ipv6.src==2001:638:208:ef1b:0:ff:fe00:4 && tcp.flags.syn==1 && tcp.flags.ack==0` would work.

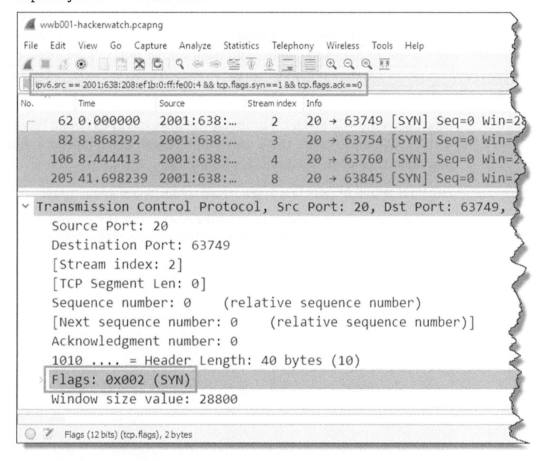

Lab 9 - A9. **The order in which the FTP command and data connections are established in this trace file are as follows:**

Stream #	Connection Type	Initiated By
1	Command (*markregion* login failed)	Client
	Command (*anonymous* login successful)	
2	Data (directory listing)	Server
3	Data (directory listing)	Server
4	Data (directory listing)	Server
7	Command (*anonymous* login successful)	Client
8	Data (directory listing)	Server

Filtering on the TCP SYN bit is probably the fastest way to obtain this information initially. When you notice there are numerous port 80 connections, however, you may want to remove those packets from view.

The filter would be `tcp.flags.syn==1 && !tcp.port==80`.

The TCP *Stream index* field does not truly exist in the TCP header. It is added by Wireshark as a counter for the different TCP conversations (connections) seen in the trace file.

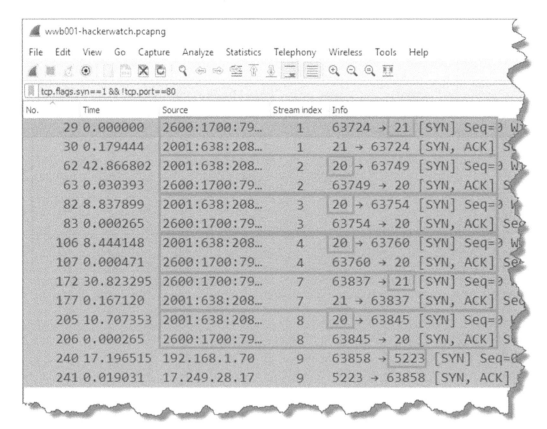

In the previous image, I placed a large box around the SYN and SYN/ACK packets of streams 1, 2, 3, 4, 7, and 8. I've placed a small box around the destination port number in the SYN packets. We see the FTP command channel connections are begun by the FTP client to the server's port 21. The FTP data channel connections are begun by the FTP server from port 20.

 When you see a field in square brackets, that field is not in the actual trace file. It is created by Wireshark. In this example, we are using the Stream index *field.*

Lab 9 - A10. **The *courier.push.apple.com* traffic in this trace file is Apple Push Notification (APN) traffic which is used by "third party application developers to send notification data to applications installed on Apple devices."**

The first step would be to locate the *courier.push.apple.com* traffic in the trace file. A simple `frame contains "courier"` filter identifies frames 235, 236, 238, 239, 243, and 245.

The first four frames are just DNS queries and responses. Frames 243 and 245 are Transport Layer Security (TLS) frames. Since the traffic is encrypted, we won't be able to see the commands and responses. Let's look up *courier.push.apple.com* on the Internet.

A bit of research on Apple Push Notification (APN) indicates that all the APN traffic will run to or from a 17.0.0.0/8 address. Apple owns the entire 17.0.0.0 address space.

Essentially, APN is used by "third party application developers to send notification data to applications installed on Apple devices." That's interesting, but the client in this case is a Windows 10 host.

Frame 267 is a GET request. The User-Agent is:

Mozilla/5.0 (Windows NT 10.0; Win64; x64; rv:61.0) Gecko/20100101 Firefox/61.0

What Apple-specific application might be running on a Windows host? This Windows host is likely using iCloud. That is the application that launched and relies on APN.

Learn more about Apple Push Notification at *https://developer.apple.com/library/archive/documentation/NetworkingInternet/Conceptual/RemoteNotificationsPG/APNSOverview.html#//apple_ref/doc/uid/TP40008194-CH8-SW1.*

[This page intentionally left blank.]

Lab 10: Timing is Everything

Objective: Analyze and compare path latency, name resolution, and server response times.

Trace File: wwb001-responsetime.pcapng

Skills Covered in this Lab

In this lab, you will have a chance to work with many key functions in Wireshark. The answers to this lab demonstrate how to use functions, including, but not limited to:

- Identify DNS retransmissions
- Analyze DNS query contents
- Detect DNS "naked domain name" resolutions[24]
- Measure DNS response time when retransmissions occurred
- Examine SOA information in unsuccessful IPv6 address resolution
- Identify the client browser in use
- Properly associate HTTP requests and responses
- Measure extreme HTTP response times
- Determine the best path latency time between a client and server
- Identify how caching can improve browsing performance

---

[24] A domain name without the *www* or other subdomain preceding it is considered a "naked domain name." Wow – that could have been something skanky, eh?

Lab 10 - Q1.   What is the IP address of the client in this trace file?

_____

Lab 10 - Q2.   What is the IP address of the DNS server?

_____

Lab 10 - Q3.   How many times did the client retransmit the DNS request for the IPv4 address of *www.africadosul.org.br*?

_____

Lab 10 - Q4.   What IPv4 address was resolved for *www.africadosul.org.br*?

_____

Lab 10 - Q5.   How long did it take to resolve the IPv4 address of *www.africadosul.org.br*?

_____

Lab 10 - Q6.   What was the result of the DNS request for the IPv6 address of *www.africadosul.org.br*?

_____

Lab 10 - Q7.   What is the iRTT time between the client and the server in TCP stream 0?

_____

Lab 10 - Q8.   What browser is being used by the HTTP client?

_____

Lab 10 - Q9. What frame number contains the HTTP response to the client's GET / HTTP 1.1 request?

_____

Lab 10 - Q10. What web server software is being used by the HTTP server?

_____

Lab 10 - Q11. What is the HTTP response time to the client's GET / HTTP 1.1 request?

_____

Lab 10 - Q12. Examine other connections between the client and the _www.africadosul.org.br_ server. What is the fastest iRTT value between the client and _www.africadosul.org.br_?

_____

Lab 10 - Q13. Would you expect a second browsing session to _www.africadosul.org.br_ to load the home page faster? Explain your answer.

_____

_____

_____

[This page intentionally left blank.]

Lab 10 Solutions

Trace File: wwb001-responsetime.pcapng

Lab 10 - A1.   The IP address of the client in this trace file is 192.168.1.70.

The first packets in the trace file provide this information. We see a series of DNS queries being made from 192.168.1.70.

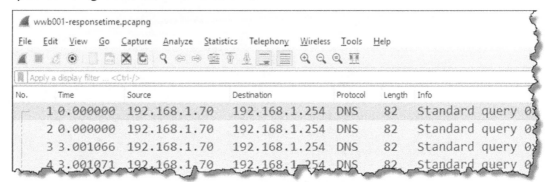

Lab 10 - A2.   The IP address of the DNS server is 192.168.1.254.

Again, we can obtain this information from the first few packets in the trace file. If we didn't see the DNS packets at the top of this trace file, we could have used a dns display filter to view the DNS traffic.

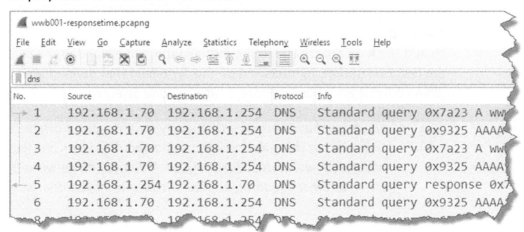

Lab 10 - A3.   **The client retransmitted the DNS request for the IPv4 address of**
www.africadosul.org.br once.

To obtain this answer we can create a filter for (1) DNS queries for (2) an A record
for (3) _www.africadosul.org.br_.

DNS Requests
The first _Flags_ field is the _Response_ field. This field is set to 0 for queries and 1 for
responses. The display filter syntax is dns.flags.response==0. To start building our
filter, we right-clicked on the _Response_ field in frame 1 and selected _Prepare a
Filter_.

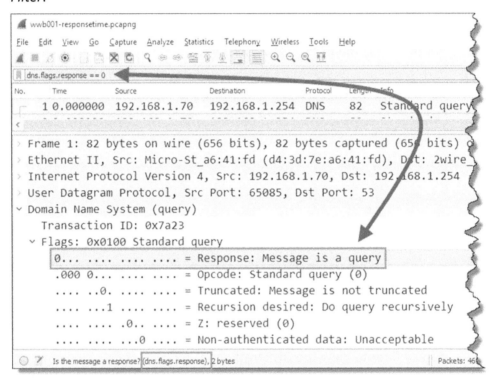

A Record
To add the A record criteria to the display filter, we expanded the _Queries_ section of
the first DNS packet, right-clicked on the _Type_ field that defined an A record
(IPv4 address) and chose _Prepare a Filter | …and Selected_.

   You might have noticed a DNS query for africadosul.org.br _(without the
"www"), but the question was asking about a retransmitted A record
request for_ www.africadosul.org.br. _A domain name without a preceding
_www, _or other subdomain value, is called a "naked domain name."_

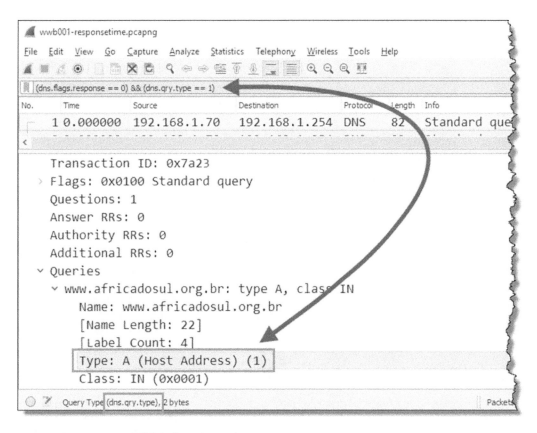

Host Name *www.africadosul.org.br*

To add the final piece to the filter, we right-clicked on the *Name* field in frame 1 and chose *Prepare a Filter | ...and Selected* again. The value *www.africadosul.org.br* is already in the field so we don't need to edit our display filter.

Using the right-click method, we created the display filter
```
((dns.flags.response==0) && (dns.qry.type==1)) &&
(dns.qry.name=="www.africadosul.org.br").
```

Applying this display filter indicates there is an initial DNS request for the IPv4 address of *www.africadosul.org.br* in frame 1 and a retransmission in frame 3.

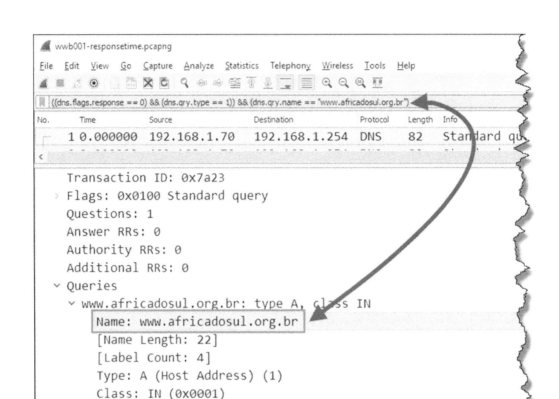

We can see the same Transaction ID (0x7a23) used for both requests – the second request is a retransmission.

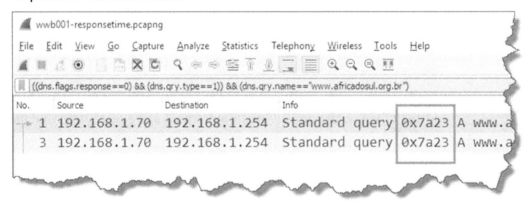

Lab 10 - A4.   The IP address 187.45.193.168 was resolved for *www.africadosul.org.br*.

You can simply apply a `dns` filter to obtain this answer in this trace file. There aren't too many DNS packets to look through.

If the file were larger, however, you may want to apply a filter for DNS responses that contain the name *www.africadosul.org.br*.

The filter `dns.flags.response==1 && dns.resp.name=="www.africadosul.org.br"` would provide the solution.

 This same IP address was resolved for africadosul.org.br *in frame 16. Throughout the trace file, however, the client places "www.africadosul.org.br" in the HTTP* Host *field in it's GET requests.*

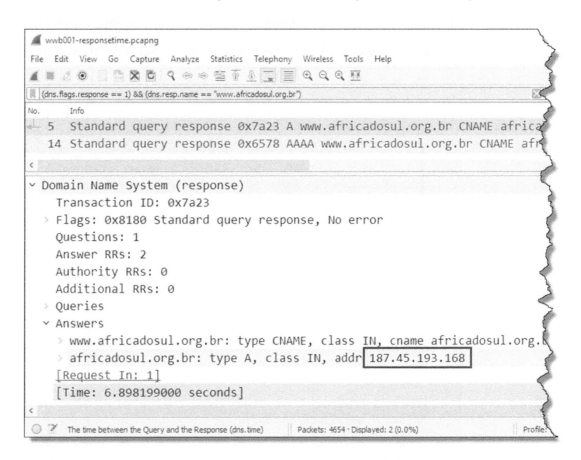

Lab 10 - A5.   **It took 6.898199 seconds to resolve the IPv4 address of *www.africadosul.org.br*.**

In Lab Answer 10-A3, we noted that there was a retransmission of the DNS query for the IPv4 address of *www.africadosul.org.br*. How did this affect Wireshark's DNS response time calculation?

To see the original A request, the retransmitted request and the response, we can use the DNS *Transaction ID* field value which will be the same for all three packets. The filter syntax is dns.id==0x7a23.

The first A record request is timestamped 0 because it is the first packet of the trace file. If it were not the first packet of the trace file, we'd have to set a Time Reference to measure the time from the A record request to the corresponding response.

The retransmitted A record request occurred approximately 3 seconds later.

The response came 6.898199 seconds after the *first* A record request.

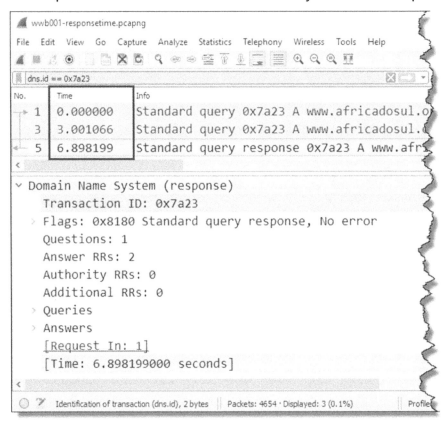

If the first A record request did not make it to the DNS server, then the actual DNS response time would be 3.897133 seconds (measured from frame 3 - that did make it to the server - to frame 5, the response).

Regardless of which response time you wish to use, we are dealing with very slow DNS resolution.

Lab 10 - A6. **The DNS request for the IPv6 address of *www.africadosul.org.br* did not provide an IPv6 address.**

Frame 14 is the DNS response to the AAAA record request in frame 8. Filtering for `dns.flags.response==1 && dns.qry.type==28 && dns.qry.name=="www.africadosul.org.br"` displays frame 14 only.

The name *www.africadosul.org.br* did not resolve to an IPv6 address. The AAAA response in frame 14, provides you with the Start of Authority (SOA), primary name server, responsible authority's mailbox, and other information. Frame 14 did not provide an IPv6 address.

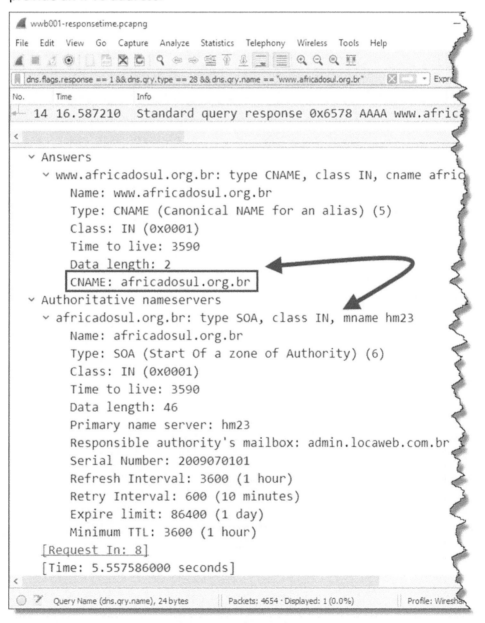

Did you note the DNS response time for the IPv6 query? A whopping 5.557586 seconds. That information was certainly not in the local DNS server's cache.

Lab 10 - A7. **The iRTT time between the client and server in TCP stream 0 is 0.186110 seconds.**

We can look inside any TCP stream 0 packet except the SYN packet, to get this information in the [SEQ/ACK analysis] section.

If you wanted to, you could apply a `tcp.stream==0` filter to view just this one TCP conversation.

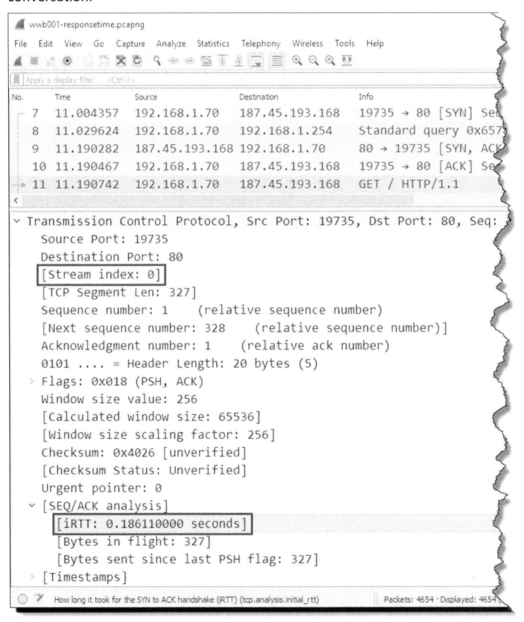

Lab 10 - A8. **The client is using Firefox.**

You can usually get the client browser information from any HTTP request packet. To find these frames, a simple `http.request` filter would work.

You could also add a *http.user_agent* column to find this information quickly.

In this trace file, we see the first client request in frame 11. The User-Agent line has been split in the following image in order to fit all the field contents.

```
> Frame 11: 381 bytes on wire (3048 bits), 381 bytes captured (3048
> Ethernet II, Src: Micro-St_a6:41:fd (d4:3d:7e:a6:41:fd), Dst: 2w
> Internet Protocol Version 4, Src: 192.168.1.70, Dst: 187.45.193.
> Transmission Control Protocol, Src Port: 19735, Dst Port: 80, Se
v Hypertext Transfer Protocol
   v GET / HTTP/1.1\r\n
      v [Expert Info (Chat/Sequence): GET / HTTP/1.1\r\n]
         [GET / HTTP/1.1\r\n]
         [Severity level: Chat]
         [Group: Sequence]
      Request Method: GET
      Request URI: /
      Request Version: HTTP/1.1
   Host: www.africadosul.org.br\r\n
   User-Agent: Mozilla/5.0 (Windows NT 10.0; WOW64; rv:54.0)
               Gecko/20100101 Firefox/54.0\r\n
   Accept: text/html,application/xhtml+xml,application/xml;q=0.9,
   Accept-Language: en-US,en;q=0.5\r\n
   Accept-Encoding: gzip, deflate\r\n
```

> **!** *The* useragentstring.com *is a great resource when analyzing User Agent string information.*

Lab 10 - A9.   Frame 23 contains the HTTP response to the client's GET / HTTP 1.1 request.

If you answered 75 to this question, you need to disable your TCP preference setting *Allow subdissector to reassemble TCP streams*.

When this TCP preference setting is enabled and the response spans multiple frames, Wireshark reassembles the frames of the response and places the response code in the *Info* column of the last packet of the reassembled set. In addition, the HTTP response time is measured from the request to the end of the reassembled set.

When this TCP preference setting is disabled, the HTTP response time is measured from the request to the actual response packet.

The fastest way to change this setting is to right-click any TCP header line in the Packet Details pane and select *Protocol Preferences*.

```
Frame 11: 381 bytes on wire (3048 bits), 381 bytes captured (3048 bit
> Ethernet II, Src: Micro-St_a6:41:fd (d4:3d:7e:a6:41:fd), Dst: 2wire_2
> Internet Protocol Version 4, Src: 192.168.1.70, Dst: 187.45.193.168
> Transmission Control Protocol, Src Port: 19735, Dst Port: 80, Seq: 1,
v Hypertext Transfer Protocol
  v GET / HTTP/1.1\r\n
    > [Expert Info (Chat/Sequence): GET / HTTP/1.1\r\n]
      Request Method: GET
      Request URI: /
      Request Version: HTTP/1.1
    Host: www.africadosul.org.br\r\n
    User-Agent: Mozilla/5.0 (Windows NT 10.0; WOW64; rv:54.0) Gecko/201
    Accept: text/html,application/xhtml+xml,application/xml;q=0.9,*/*;q
    Accept-Language: en-US,en;q=0.5\r\n
    Accept-Encoding: gzip, deflate\r\n
    Connection: keep-alive\r\n
    Upgrade-Insecure-Requests: 1\r\n
    \r\n
    [Full request URI: http://www.africadosul.org.br/]
    [HTTP request 1/1]
    [Response in frame: 23]

  Transmission Control Protocol (tcp), 20 bytes        Packets: 4654 · Displayed: 4654 (100.0%
```

Lab 10 - A10.   The HTTP server is running on Apache.

After clicking on the hyperlink to the response frame 23, we see the HTTP server is stating that it is running on Apache. There is no way to verify that information, however.[25]

```
> Frame 23: 1514 bytes on wire (12112 bits), 1514 bytes captured (12112 b
> Ethernet II, Src: 2wire_2c:0b:15 (dc:7f:a4:2c:0b:15), Dst: Micro-St_a6
> Internet Protocol Version 4, Src: 187.45.193.168, Dst: 192.168.1.70
> Transmission Control Protocol, Src Port: 80, Dst Port: 19735, Seq: 1, A
v Hypertext Transfer Protocol
   v HTTP/1.1 200 OK\r\n
      > [Expert Info (Chat/Sequence): HTTP/1.1 200 OK\r\n]
        Response Version: HTTP/1.1
        Status Code: 200
        [Status Code Description: OK]
        Response Phrase: OK
     Date: Sun, 30 Jul 2017 23:45:23 GMT\r\n
     Server: Apache\r\n
     Expires: Thu, 19 Nov 1981 08:52:00 GMT\r\n
     Cache-Control: no-store, no-cache, must-revalidate, post-check=0, pr
```

It's always interesting to see what's contained in both HTTP client request and HTTP server response packets.

One way to quickly see the information exchanged is to right-click on an HTTP packet in the Packet List pane and select Follow | TCP stream.

If the object downloaded to the client is gzipped or deflated, use Follow | HTTP stream.

---

[25]   The packets don't lie, but network devices do!

Lab 10 - A11. **The HTTP response time to the client's GET / HTTP 1.1 request is 27.582389 seconds.**

Wow! This is going to be a loooooong day if you must spend much time waiting on this server.

```
˅ HTTP/1.1 200 OK\r\n
  > [Expert Info (Chat/Sequence): HTTP/1.1 200 OK\r\n]
    Response Version: HTTP/1.1
    Status Code: 200
    [Status Code Description: OK]
    Response Phrase: OK
  Date: Sun, 30 Jul 2017 23:45:23 GMT\r\n
  Server: Apache\r\n
  Expires: Thu, 19 Nov 1981 08:52:00 GMT\r\n
  Cache-Control: no-store, no-cache, must-revalidate, post-check=0, pr
  Pragma: no-cache\r\n
  Set-Cookie: PHPSESSID=ujur41ug86fhbmv5r18l08fgc6; path=/\r\n
 > Content-Length: 25970\r\n
  Connection: close\r\n
  Content-Type: text/html\r\n
  \r\n
  [HTTP response 1/1]
  [Time since request: 27.582389000 seconds]
  [Request in frame: 11]
  File Data: 1126 bytes
> Line-based text data: text/html (21 lines)
```

If you answered 27.769840 seconds, you probably left that dreaded TCP preference setting *Allow subdissector to reassemble TCP streams* on.

The TCP preference setting Allow subdissector to reassemble TCP streams *should be on when you are reassembling objects or doing TLS/SSL analysis. The current Wireshark default configuration has this setting enabled.*

There is now (as of Wireshark v3) a No Reassembly *profile installed automatically with Wireshark. If you prefer to keep this preference setting on, you can now quickly switch to a profile where this setting is disabled.*

Lab 10 - A12. The fastest iRTT value between the client and the *www.africadosul.org.br* server is 0.184990 seconds.

Since we know the IP address of the *www.africadosul.org.br* server, we can apply a filter based on that address and then add an *iRTT* column.

The *iRTT* field filter would be `tcp.analysis.initial_rtt`, so you could make an `ip.addr==187.45.193.168 && tcp.analysis.initial_rtt` filter to only see packets to or from the server that contain an iRTT value, as shown in the next image.

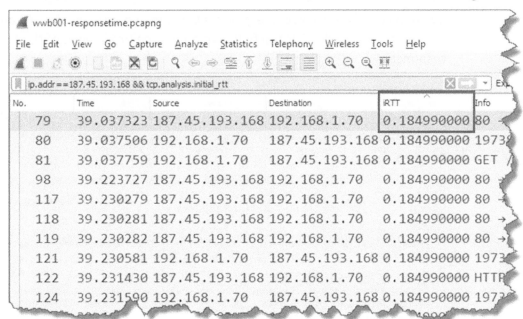

 You can right-click on a field in the Packet Details pane and select Copy | Value *when you don't want to type long numbers.*

This is a great technique to use when working with time fields and IPv6 addresses!

Lab 10 - A13. **The *www.africadosul.org.br* web server uses a "no-cache" setting in all response frames except one. The second browsing session to obtain the home page of *www.africadosul.org.br* would take the same amount of time to load.**

If the DNS information is cached by our local DNS server, we would expect the DNS resolution process to be faster as well.

Server load time, however, wouldn't be affected much because we see the "No-cache" setting in all but one of the HTTP response frames.

By applying a filter for `http.response && ip.src == 187.45.193.168` and adding a column for the Cache-Control field, we notice the prevalence of the "no-cache" responses.

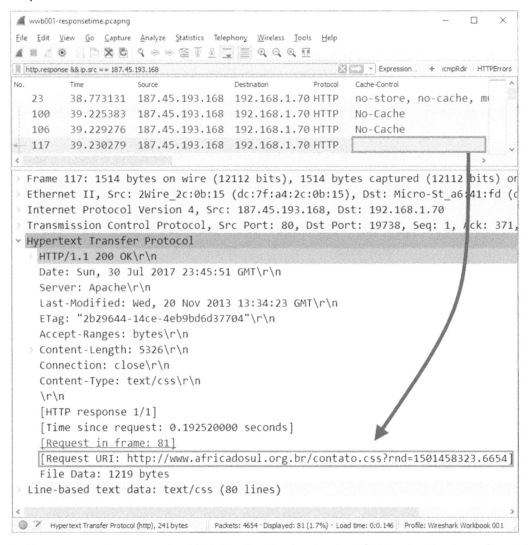

In the image above, I am highlighting the Cache-Control field value (it doesn't exist in frame 117). The arrow points towards the related URI value. It appears the client is allowed to cache this one *.css* file only.

Lab 11: The News

Objective: Analyze capture location, path latency, response times, and keep-alive intervals between an HTTP client and server.

Trace File: wwb001-thenews.pcapng

Skills Covered in this Lab

In this lab, you will have a chance to work with many key functions in Wireshark. The answers to this lab demonstrate how to use functions, including, but not limited to:

- Identify the name of an HTTP server without using DNS
- Determine if the capture was taken closer to a client or a server
- Count the connections required to load a web page
- Calculate the average Initial Round-Trip Time (iRTT) between hosts
- Calculate the average HTTP response time in a trace file
- Export filtered columns to *.csv* format
- Reassemble a stream to identify a client's interest
- Identify a content delivery service based on a server's response
- Compare the *Expert Information* results with TCP reassembly on and off
- Determine the interval of TCP keep-alives

Lab 11 - Q1. What is the IP address of the HTTP client?

_____

Lab 11 - Q2. What is the IP address of the HTTP server?

_____

Lab 11 - Q3. What domain name is associated with the HTTP server?

_____

Lab 11 - Q4. Do you think this trace file was taken closer to the HTTP client or closer to the HTTP server?

_____

Lab 11 - Q5. How many TCP connections were established to load this web page?

_____

Lab 11 - Q6. What is the average iRTT between the HTTP client and server?

_____

Lab 11 - Q7. What is the average HTTP response time in this trace file?

_____

Lab 11 - Q8. Based on this trace file, how long did it take to load the web site?

_____

Lab 11 - Q9.   In what topic is the client interested?

_____

Lab 11 - Q10.   What content delivery service is in use in this trace file?

_____

Lab 11 - Q11.   Are there significant TCP errors in this trace file?

_____

Lab 11 - Q12.   At what interval do the TCP keep-alive processes occur?

_____

[This page intentionally left blank.]

Lab 11 Solutions

Trace File: wwb001-thenews.pcapng

Lab 11 - A1.   **The IP address of the HTTP client is 10.9.9.9.**

This answer is visible at the start of the trace file. We see the initial SYN packets from the client and we see an HTTP GET request.

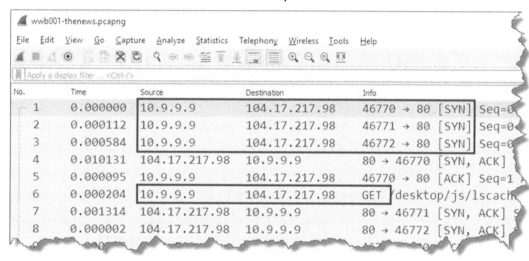

Lab 11 - A2.   **The IP address of the HTTP server is 104.17.217.98.**

Another easy question to answer. We see a SYN/ACK from the HTTP server in frame 4 and the destination address in all the packets we looked at to answer the previous question.

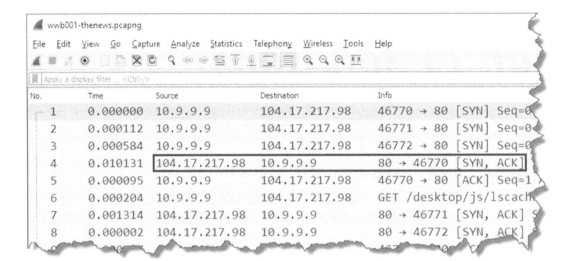

Since any service can run on any port number, we can look a bit further into the trace for the first HTTP response from the server in frame 17.

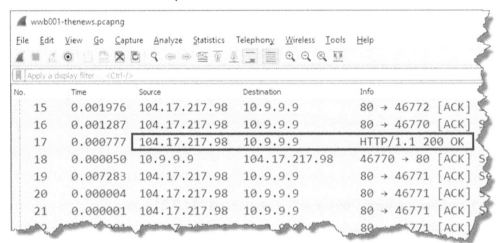

Lab 11 - A3.   **The domain name *thejournal.ie* is associated with the HTTP server.**

This is another easy question to answer. In frame 6, the *Host* field indicates the client is sending a GET request to a host name that includes the *thejournal.ie* domain name. All the GET requests in this trace file include the *thejournal.ie* domain name in the *Host* field.

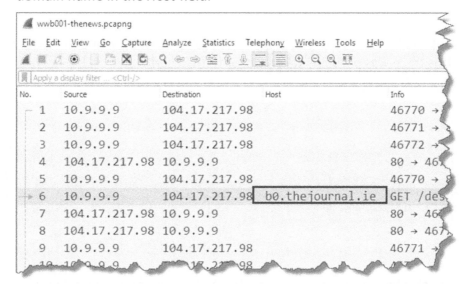

Lab 11 - A4.   **This trace file was taken closer to the HTTP client than to the HTTP server.**

To determine whether the capture was taken closer to one side of the connection or the other, we can look at delta times within individual SYN-SYN/ACK-ACK sets.

The following image illustrates how the delta times in the handshake process can be used to determine the capture proximity to the client or server.

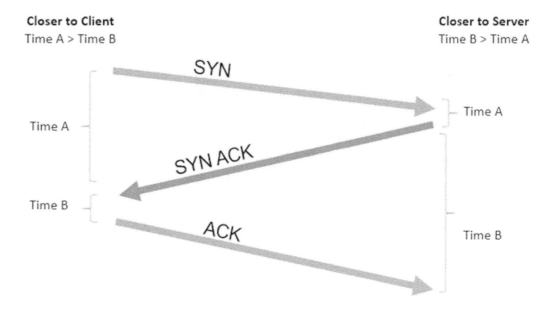

If the time from the SYN to the SYN/ACK (Time A) is larger than the time from the SYN/ACK to the ACK (Time B), then your capture was probably taken closer to the client.

If the time from the SYN to the SYN/ACK (Time A) is smaller than the time from the SYN/ACK to the ACK (Time B), then your capture was probably taken closer to the server.

Applying a display filter for `tcp.stream==0`, we see that Time A is larger than Time B. This trace was probably taken closer to the client.

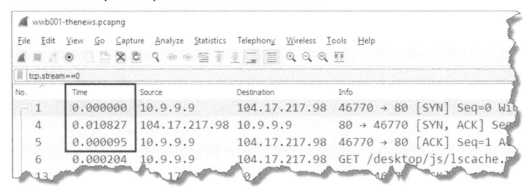

Check a few other streams in the trace file to verify the time deltas.

Lab 11 - A5.   There were 26 TCP connections established to load this web page.

The *Statistics | Conversations* window shows the number of TCP conversations in the trace file. All of these conversations were between the client at 10.9.9.9 and the server at 104.17.217.98.

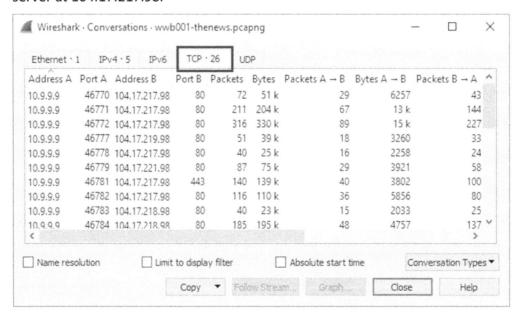

Lab 11 - A6. **The average iRTT between the client and server is 0.013767 seconds.**

To determine the average iRTT, we need to add a column based on the *iRTT* field (found in the *[SEQ/ACK analysis]* section of the TCP section of the Packet Details pane. Note that the iRTT value is not contained in SYN packets.

We will extract this column and use Excel to obtain the average.

Since we only want one iRTT value per TCP connection, we applied a `tcp.flags.syn==1 && tcp.flags.ack==1` display filter to show only the SYN/ACK packet of each TCP connection.

Now we only have 26 packets displayed – one for each connection in the trace file.

 It is important to capture from the start of a TCP connection whenever possible. If a TCP connection had already been established before we began our capture process, we would have missed the TCP handshake and, therefore, we would not have an iRTT value to use in calculating these averages.

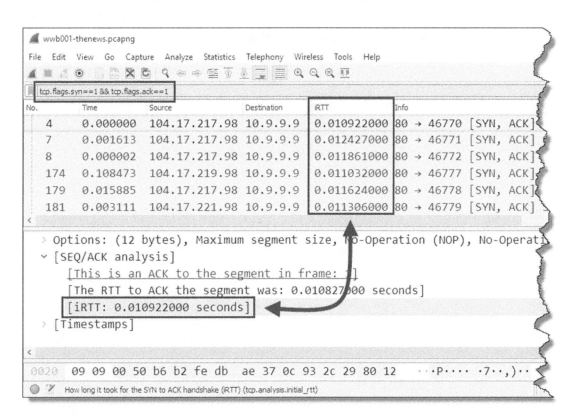

Selecting *File | Export Packet Dissections | As CSV*, we saved just the *Packet summary line* information. We unchecked the *Packet Details* option (enabled by default). We called this file *iRTTaverage.csv*.

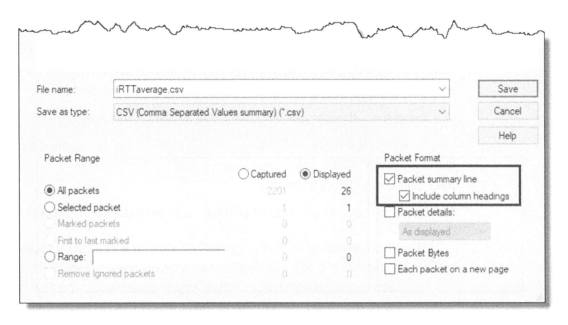

In Excel, we applied the average function to the *iRTT* column to obtain the answer. The iRTT is only measured down to the millisecond-level. Excel's calculated average only exceeds six places due to the average calculation. You may consider setting up Excel to limit the result cell to six decimal places.

	A	B	C	D	E	F	G	H
1	No.	Time	Source	Destination	iRTT	Info		
2	4	0	104.17.217.98	10.9.9.9	0.010922	80 > 46770 [SYN, ACK] Seq=0 Ack=		
3	7	0.001613	104.17.217.98	10.9.9.9	0.012427	80 > 46771 [SYN, ACK] Seq=0 Ack=		
4	8	0.000002	104.17.217.98	10.9.9.9	0.011861	80 > 46772 [SYN, ACK] Seq=0 Ack=		
5	174	0.108473	104.17.219.98	10.9.9.9	0.011032	80 > 46777 [SYN, ACK] Seq=0 Ack=		
6	179	0.015885	104.17.217.98	10.9.9.9	0.011624	80 > 46778 [SYN, ACK] Seq=0 Ack=		
7	181	0.003111	104.17.221.98	10.9.9.9	0.011306	80 > 46779 [SYN, ACK] Seq=0 Ack=1		
8	197	0.205288	104.17.217.98	10.9.9.9	0.011724	443 > 46781 [SYN, ACK] Seq=0 Ack=		
9	198	0.000002	104.17.217.98	10.9.9.9	0.011625	80 > 46782 [SYN, ACK] Seq=0 Ack=		
10	201	0.000881	104.17.218.98	10.9.9.9	0.011999	80 > 46783 [SYN, ACK] Seq=0 Ack=		
11	203	0.001574	104.17.218.98	10.9.9.9	0.013483	80 > 46784 [SYN, ACK] Seq=0 Ack=		
12	204	0	104.17.218.98	10.9.9.9	0.012808	80 > 46785 [SYN, ACK] Seq=0 Ack=1		
13	205	0.000001	104.17.218.98	10.9.9.9	0.012498	80 > 46786 [SYN, ACK] Seq=0 Ack=		
14	209	0.000886	104.17.218.98	10.9.9.9	0.013199	80 > 46787 [SYN, ACK] Seq=0 Ack=1		
15	210	0.000001	104.17.218.98	10.9.9.9	0.012649	80 > 46788 [SYN, ACK] Seq=0 Ack=		
16	353	0.060673	104.17.217.98	10.9.9.9	0.018233	80 > 46789 [SYN, ACK] Seq=0 Ack=		
17	407	0.033034	104.17.219.98	10.9.9.9	0.010526	80 > 46790 [SYN, ACK] Seq=0 Ack=		
18	551	0.06188	104.17.221.98	10.9.9.9	0.011907	80 > 46794 [SYN, ACK] Seq=0 Ack=1		
19	554	0.001627	104.17.221.98	10.9.9.9	0.013378	80 > 46795 [SYN, ACK] Seq=0 Ack=		
20	1331	4.863468	104.17.217.98	10.9.9.9	0.023157	80 > 46857 [SYN, ACK] Seq=0 Ack=		
21	1332	0	104.17.217.98	10.9.9.9	0.023076	80 > 46858 [SYN, ACK] Seq=0 Ack=		
22	1333	0.000001	104.17.217.98	10.9.9.9	0.022516	80 > 46859 [SYN, ACK] Seq=0 Ack=		
23	1548	0.110781	104.17.221.98	10.9.9.9	0.012845	443 > 46861 [SYN, ACK] Seq=0 Ack=		
24	1555	0.004442	104.17.220.98	10.9.9.9	0.014467	443 > 46862 [SYN, ACK] Seq=0 Ack		
25	1559	0.000002	104.17.220.98	10.9.9.9	0.014421	443 > 46863 [SYN, ACK] Seq=0 Ac		
26	1711	0.048518	104.17.221.98	10.9.9.9	0.013882	80 > 46864 [SYN, ACK] Seq=0 Ack		
27	1776	0.050036	104.17.219.98	10.9.9.9	0.010368	80 > 46865 [SYN, ACK] Seq=0 Ack=		
28					0.013766654			
29								

Lab 11 - A7.   The average HTTP response time in this trace file is 0.024321 seconds.

We will use the same general steps to obtain this average as we used in the previous answer.

Remember to disable the TCP preference setting *Allow subdissector to reassemble TCP streams* before starting.

First, we will add the HTTP *Time* (`http.time`) column. Next, we apply a filter to reduce the number of packets displayed to just the ones that have this `http.time` field.

Finally, we will extract the packet dissections and use Excel to obtain an average for the HTTP *Time* column.

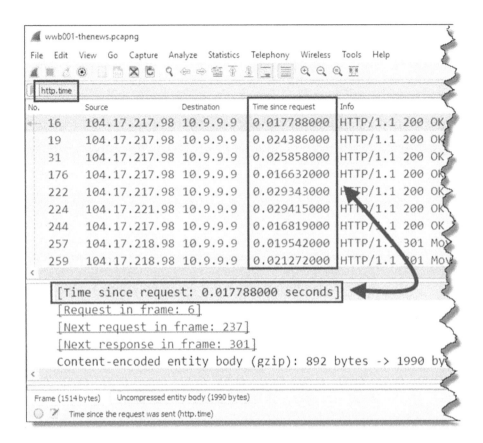

Again, selecting *File | Export Packet Dissections | As CSV*, we saved just the Packet summary line information. We called this file *HTTPResponseTime2.csv*.

In Excel, we applied the average function to the *Time since request* column to obtain the answer. Excel's calculated average only exceeds six places due to the average calculation. You may consider setting up Excel to limit the result cell to six decimal places.

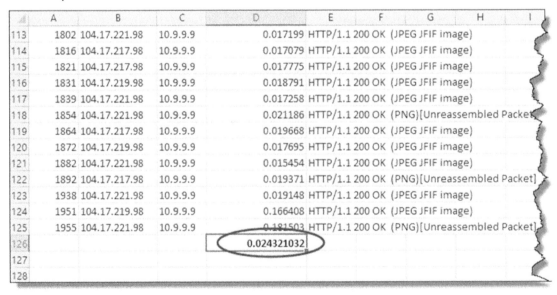

Lab 11 - A8.   **Based on this trace file, the web site loaded in 5.824737 seconds.**

The page is fully loaded once the last data packet arrives at the client. We don't want to consider time for the FIN process or any TCP keep-alive processes.

You could use a filter that removes TCP keep-alive packets and only shows data packets:

```
!tcp.analysis.keep_alive && tcp.len > 0
```

The last data packet is in frame 1963.

After setting the *Time* column to *Seconds Since Beginning of Capture*, we can see the time until the final data packet is 5.824737.

You can also see the *Time since reference or first frame* inside the *Frame* section of the last packet.

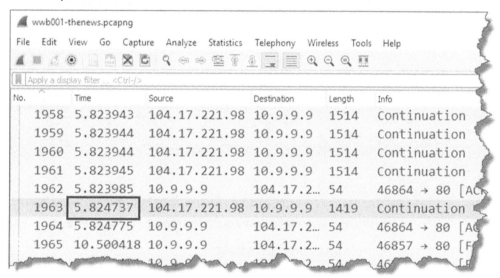

Lab 11 - A9. **The client is interested in "web sites you never knew existed."**

Reassembling the first TCP stream provides us with this answer. The HTTP *Referer*[26] field indicates the client came from the *Daily Edge* article regarding "*websites-you-never-knew-existed.*"

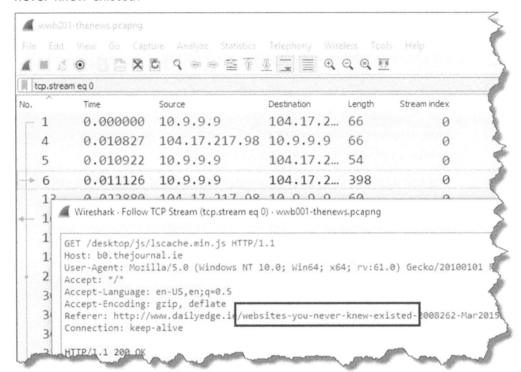

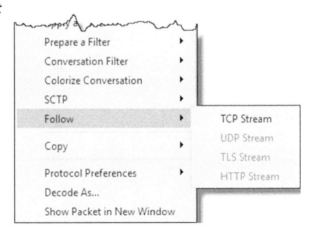

! *The ability to reassemble the application-layer communications is a great feature. You can follow more than just TCP streams:*

People often wonder about the HTTP streams option.

The HTTP option should be used when you are reassembling HTTP traffic where the object being downloaded has been gzipped. This option automatically decompresses the gzipped data.

---

[26] This word is misspelled in the RFC. Wireshark follows the RFC's spelling mistake.

Lab 11 - A10. The content delivery service in use is Cloudflare.

To answer this question, we need to look inside the HTTP responses from the server. In each of the HTTP responses, we see the server listed as Cloudflare.

In the image below, we added an `http.response.code` display filter to view HTTP responses only. We also added the *Server* field as a column.

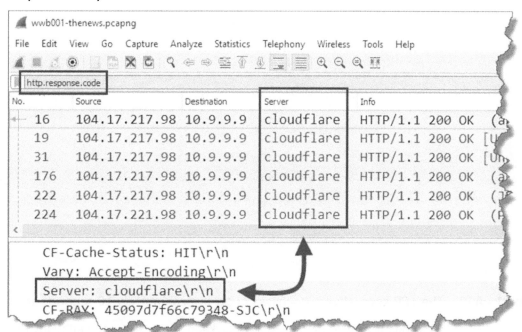

 Cloudflare is another content delivery network (CDN) provider.

Reassembly of gzip compressed data was mentioned in the previous tip.

Why not try out Wireshark's decompressing capability now.

Add a column based on the HTTP response Content-Encoding field. You will notice that several frames indicate the content is encoded using gzip.

Right-click on frame 16 and select Follow | TCP Stream. *You will notice the JavaScript (.js) objects are unreadable.*

Now try it again using Follow | HTTP Stream. *Notice you can read the JavaScript now.*

```
var lscache=function(){function l(){if(void 0!==d)return
d;try{n("__lscachetest__","__lscachetest__"),c("__lscachetest__"),d
function s(){void 0===m&&(m=null!=window.JSON);return m}function n(
{localStorage.removeItem(f+e+a);localStorage.setItem(f+e+a,b)}funct
{localStorage.removeItem(f+e+a)}function r(a,b){!t||!1 in window||"f
window.console.warn||(window.console.warn("lscache - "+a),b&&window
error was: "+b.message))}
```

Lab 11 - A11. There are no significant TCP errors in this trace file.

The fastest way to determine if there are significant TCP errors in the trace file is to open the *Expert Information* window.

We see minimal TCP issues – just four instances of packet loss and four out-of-order segments.

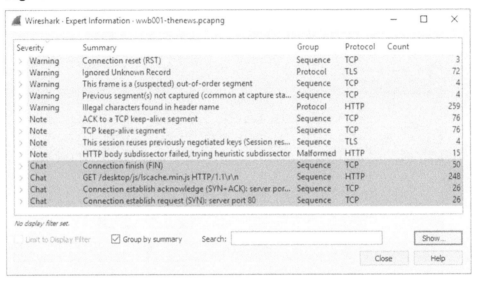

Severity	Summary	Group	Protocol	Count
> Warning	Connection reset (RST)	Sequence	TCP	3
> Warning	Ignored Unknown Record	Protocol	TLS	72
> Warning	This frame is a (suspected) out-of-order segment	Sequence	TCP	4
> Warning	Previous segment(s) not captured (common at capture sta...	Sequence	TCP	4
> Warning	Illegal characters found in header name	Protocol	HTTP	259
> Note	ACK to a TCP keep-alive segment	Sequence	TCP	76
> Note	TCP keep-alive segment	Sequence	TCP	76
> Note	This session reuses previously negotiated keys (Session res...	Sequence	TLS	4
> Note	HTTP body subdissector failed, trying heuristic subdissector	Malformed	HTTP	15
> Chat	Connection finish (FIN)	Sequence	TCP	50
> Chat	GET /desktop/js/lscache.min.js HTTP/1.1\r\n	Sequence	HTTP	248
> Chat	Connection establish acknowledge (SYN+ACK): server por...	Sequence	TCP	26
> Chat	Connection establish request (SYN): server port 80	Sequence	TCP	26

No display filter set.

Limit to Display Filter ☑ Group by summary Search: [   ] Show...

Close   Help

Lab 11 - A12. The TCP keep-alives processes occur approximately 10 seconds apart.

By applying a filter on `tcp.analysis.keep_alive`, we can see just the keep-alive packets.

In addition, consider setting the *Time* column to *Seconds Since Previous Displayed Packet* or adding a TCP delta column based on the *Time since previous frame in this TCP stream* field.

When you look at the *Time* column, you will see the process appears to occur 5 seconds apart. This is misleading, however.

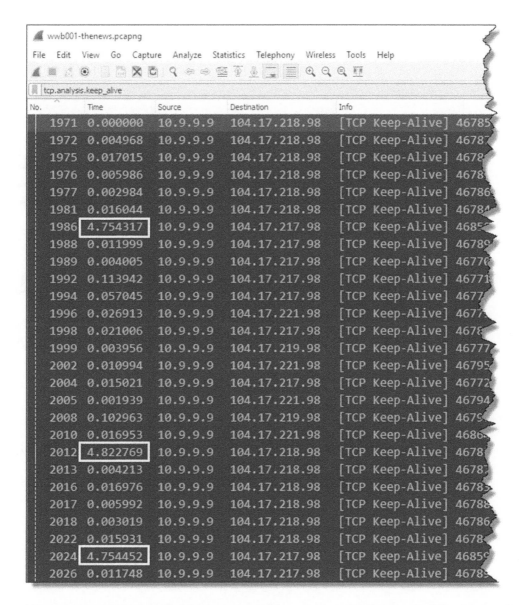

We want to look at individual conversations to see the interval of the keep-alives in the separate conversations.

Let's add a TCP delta column based on the *Time since previous frame in this TCP stream* field.

Inside the *[Timestamps]* section in any TCP header, right-click on the *Time since previous frame in this TCP stream* and select *Apply as Column*. You can also sort the *Stream index* column from low to high to group together each of the streams.

Now you will notice the keep-alive interval is 10 seconds, not 5 seconds, for each conversation.

Continue checking the individual streams – each of the connections that utilize TCP keep-alives is using a 10-second interval.

Lab 12: Selective ACKs

Objective: Analyze the process of establishing Selective acknowledgment (SACK) and using SACK during packet loss recovery.

Trace File: `wwb001-tcpslesre.pcapng`

Skills Covered in this Lab

In this lab, you will have a chance to work with many key functions in Wireshark. The answers to this lab demonstrate how to use functions, including, but not limited to:

- Identify the target server name in TLS/SSL communications
- Determine which TCP streams have transmission issues
- Differentiate the use of TCP SEQ/ACK analysis display filters
- Extract a trace file subset based on a filtered *Conversations* window
- Identify the Initial Round-trip Time (iRTT) of a TCP conversation
- Compare client and server TCP capabilities (MSS, Window Scaling, SACK)
- Locate the point at which packet loss began in a trace file
- Determine the relative sequence number at the start of packet loss
- Estimate the number of packets lost in a set
- Interpret TCP Selective Acknowledgment Left Edge/Right Edge blocks
- Use a display filter to count Duplicate ACKs
- Identify a missing segment range based on SACK Left Edge/Right Edge values
- Locate the point of packet loss recovery
- Examine how the acknowledgment number changes as packet recovery progresses
- Determine why Wireshark defined retransmissions as out-of-orders

Lab 12 - Q1.   What is the IP address of the client in this trace file?

_____

Lab 12 - Q2.   How many TCP streams are in this trace file?

_____

Lab 12 - Q3.   How many of these streams have Duplicate ACK packets?

_____

Lab 12 - Q4.   Which TCP stream number has the greatest number of Duplicate ACKs?

_____

Lab 12 - Q5.   Export the TCP stream that has the greatest number of Duplicate ACKs to a new
trace file called *dupeackSACK.pcapng*. We will examine this trace file for the
following questions.

How many packets are in your new *dupeackSACK.pcapng* trace file?

_____

On the next page, you will load this new trace file that you saved.

Trace File: dupeackSACK.pcapng (created by you)

Lab 12 - Q6. What is the IP address of the server in this TCP stream?

_____

Lab 12 - Q7. What is the iRTT value for this TCP stream?

_____

Lab 12 - Q8. What are the TCP capabilities of each TCP peer as defined in the TCP handshake?

_____

Lab 12 - Q9. On what frame number does Wireshark first indicate that a previous segment was not captured?

_____

Lab 12 - Q10. What is the relative sequence number of the first missing segment?

_____

Lab 12 - Q11. How many bytes are missing at this point in the trace file?

_____

Lab 12 - Q12. Examine TCP Dup ACK 248#1 (frame 250). Explain what the SACK Left Edge (SLE) and Right Edge (SRE) information in the TCP header indicate.

_____

Lab 12 - Q13. How is the _Acknowledgment number_ field used for this packet loss recovery process?

_____

Lab 12 - Q14. What will happen to the SACK Left Edge as the client receives additional data bytes?

_____

Lab 12 - Q15. What will happen to the SACK Right Edge as the client receives additional data bytes?

_____

Lab 12 - Q16. What are the relative sequence numbers of the second set of missing bytes in this trace file?

_____

Lab 12 - Q17. How do the _Acknowledgment number_ and _SACK Left Edge/Right Edge_ fields change after the second [TCP Previous segment not captured] indication?

_____

Lab 12 - Q18. How many times did the client send Duplicate ACKs requesting the first missing segment set?

_____

Lab 12 - Q19. When is the first missing segment received?

_____

Lab 12 - Q20. What happens to the _Acknowledgment number_ field value from the client after the first missing data segment is received?

_____

Lab 12 - Q21. Why are frames 337 and 339 defined as Out-Of-Order?

_____

Lab 12 Solutions

Trace File: wwb001-tcpslesre.pcapng

Lab 12 - A1. **The IP address of the client is 192.168.1.141.**

This is evident in the very first set of packets in the trace file. The first packet is a SYN packet going to port 443. The client is establishing a connection for HTTPS. The Client Hello packet follows the TCP handshake completion.

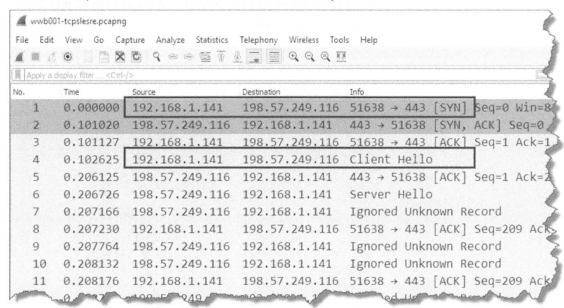

If we want to know the name of the server to whom the client is connecting, we can look inside the Client Hello packet.

You will need to expand the *Transport Layer Security* section (or *Secure Socket Layer* section if you're an using an older version of Wireshark), *TLSv1 Record Layer*, *Handshake Protocol*, and *Extension: server_name* areas to get to the name of the target server.

```
  ⌄ Extension: server_name (len=23)
      Type: server_name (0)
      Length: 23
    ⌄ Server Name Indication extension
        Server Name list length: 21
        Server Name Type: host_name (0)
        Server Name length: 18
        Server Name: www.lcuportal2.com
  › Extension: renegotiation_info (len=1)
  › Extension: supported_groups (len=8)
```

Rather than expand the contents of the TLS section of this packet to get to the *Server Name* area, consider just looking at the Packet Bytes window. The name of the target server is easy to see.

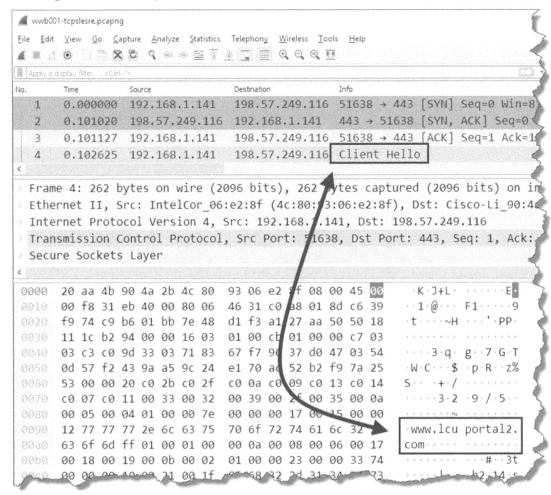

Lab 12 - A2. There are 22 TCP streams in this trace file.

Opening *Statistics | Conversations*, the number of TCP conversations is shown on the *TCP* tab. It appears that all the conversations are port 80 or port 443 traffic.

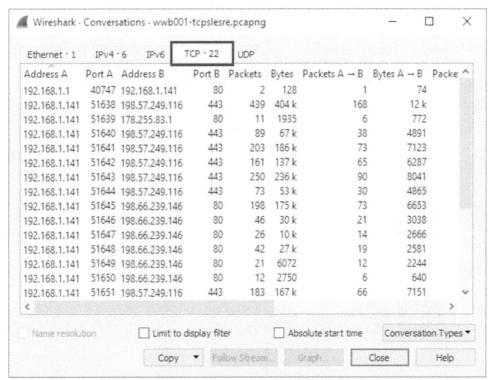

 If you are using the UDP tab in the Statistics | Conversations *window to count UDP conversations, you must be careful.*

Wireshark counts broadcast and multicast traffic as conversations.

For example, if a host boots up and broadcasts DHCP Discover packets onto the network, Wireshark will add a line under the UDP tab showing a conversation (albeit one way) between the client and the broadcast address. That's not an actual conversation between hosts.

Lab 12 - A3.   There are six TCP streams that contain duplicate ACK packets.

Apply a `tcp.analysis.duplicate_ack` display filter to the trace file and then enable *Limit to display filter* in the *Conversations* window.

This is a simple field existence filter.

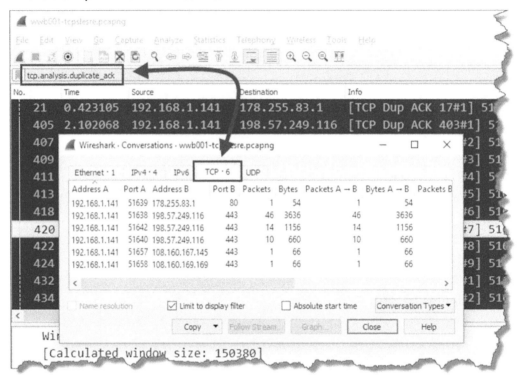

 You may have noticed that Wireshark has two similar display filters available – `tcp.analysis.duplicate_ack` *and* `tcp.analysis.duplicate_ack_frame`.

The display filter `tcp.analysis.duplicate_ack` *can only detect packets defined as duplicate ACKs.*

The display filter `tcp.analysis.duplicate_ack_frame`, *however, can be used to look for specific ACK frames that are being duplicated. For example,* `tcp.analysis.duplicate_ack_frame==403` *detects all the duplicates to the ACK of frame 403.*

The following image shows some display filters that can be used to view packets that contain a field or packets that contain a specific field value.

```
[SEQ/ACK analysis]                          tcp.analysis
  [iRTT: 0.101127000 seconds]               tcp.analysis.initial_rtt==0.101127
v [TCP Analysis Flags]                      tcp.analysis.flags
    [This is a TCP duplicate ack]           tcp.analysis.duplicate_ack
  [Duplicate ACK #: 1]                      tcp.analysis.duplicate_ack_num==1
v [Duplicate to the ACK in frame: 403]      tcp.analysis.duplicate_ack_frame==403
```

Remember the fields that are enclosed in square brackets are Wireshark interpretations; they don't actually exist in the frame.

Regardless, you can build a column or display filter on any field shown in the Packet Details pane, whether that field exists in the header or was created by Wireshark.

In the above image, each of the display filters shown are based on Wireshark interpretation lines inside of a TCP header.

Consider the following display filters that are based on Wireshark interpretation lines:

`frame.number==1`

`frame.coloring_rule.name=="TCP SYN/FIN"`

`frame.coloring_rule.string=="tcp.flags & 0x02 || tcp.flags.fin==1"`

`frame.protocols=="eth:ethertype:ip:tcp"`

`frame.time=="Mar  5, 2015 18:11:54.793298000"`

`tcp.window_size > 261340`

Lab 12 - A4. **TCP stream number 0 has the greatest number of duplicate ACKs in this trace file.**

Since we applied a display filter for `tcp.analysis.duplicate_ack` and applied this display filter to the TCP *Conversations* window, we already have this information visible.

Sorting the *Packets* column brings up a conversation that has 46 Duplicate ACKs.

Now we just need to find the TCP stream number of that conversation.

Click on the conversation at the top of the sort order, click the *Follow Stream…* button and then close the Follow Stream window. Wireshark places a `tcp.stream eq 0` in the display filter input field.

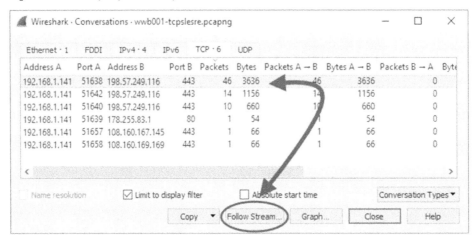

Wireshark adds the *Stream index* field inside the TCP header area. Alternately, if you created a *Stream index* column, the answer should be visible in this column.

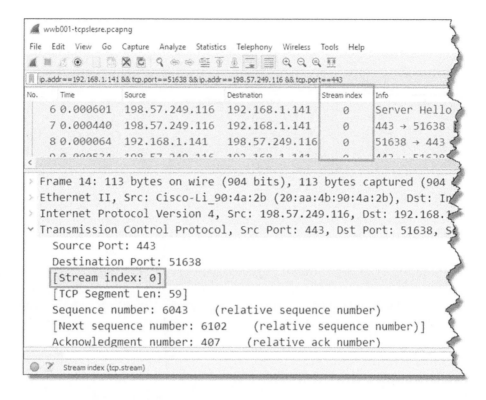

Lab 12 - A5. **After exporting TCP stream 0 to a new trace file called *dupeackSACK.pcapng*, we found the new trace file has 439 packets.**

There are two ways we could export this conversation.

1. We could use a display filter for `tcp.stream==0`,and then select *File | Export Specified Packets*.

2. We could return to the *Conversations* window, right-click on the conversation of interest, select *Apply as Filter | Selected | A ↔ B* and then select *File | Export Specified Packets*.

Since we identified the stream index number already, we used the `tcp.stream==0` display filter before exporting.

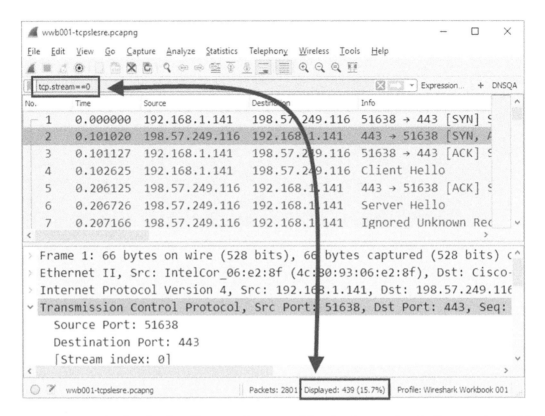

Once we apply the display filter to the trace file, the Status Bar indicates that 439 packets matched the display filter.

The next step is *File | Export Specified Packets*. Wireshark's default setting exports the displayed packets only.

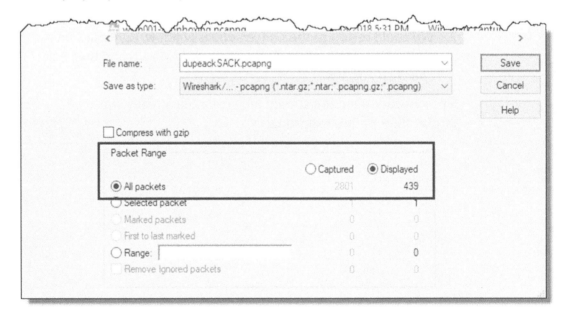

Upon opening your new *dupeackSACK.pcapng* file, you'll notice the total count of packets is 439. Perfect.

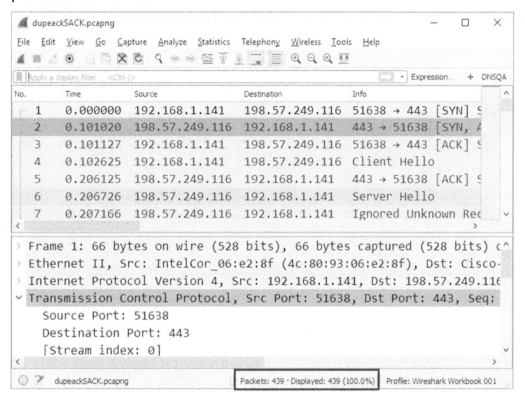

> ### Use dupeackSACK.pcapng (just created by you) to answer Lab 12 – Q6 – Q21.

Lab 12 - A6.   The IP address of the server in this TCP stream is 198.57.249.116.

This is visible in the beginning of the trace file. Not only do we see a SYN/ACK from port 443 (frame 2), but we also see the TLS Server Hello (frame 6).

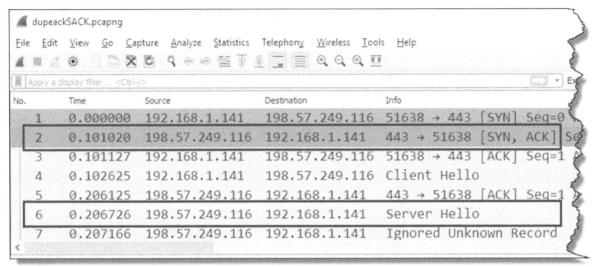

If you had a very large trace file, you'd want to apply a display filter to find the TLS Server Hello packet.

The display filter syntax is `tls.handshake.type==2`.

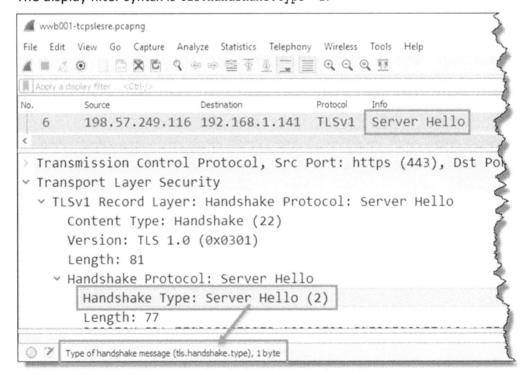

Lab 12 - A7.   The iRTT value for this TCP stream is 0.101127 seconds.

We can't look in the SYN packet for this information. That's the only packet of a TCP conversation that won't contain the iRTT value. After expanding the *[SEQ/ACK analysis]* section of frame 2, we see the iRTT value is 0.101127 seconds.

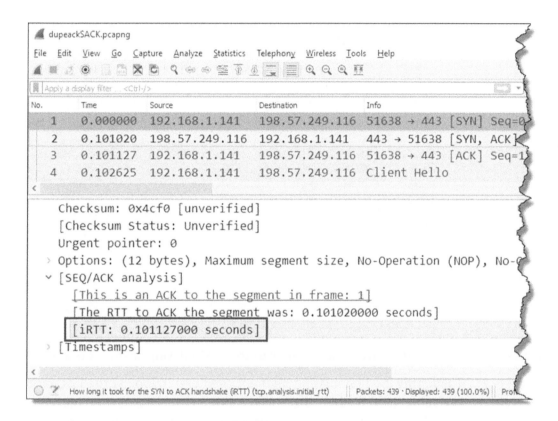

Lab 12 - A8.   The client supports a Maximum Segment Size of 1460, window size multiplier of 4, and Selective ACKs. The Server supports a Maximum Segment Size of 1460, window size multiplier of 128, and Selective ACKs.

Based on this information, both the client and server can send up to 1460 bytes of data to each other in each TCP packet and will use Window Scaling and SACK.

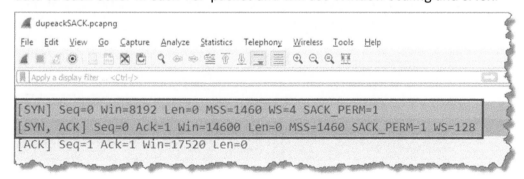

Lab 12 - A9. **Wireshark first indicates that a previous segment was not captured on frame 249.**

This information is visible in the *Expert Information* window. After expanding the *Previous segment(s) not captured* warning, we see frame 249 is the first missing packet indication.

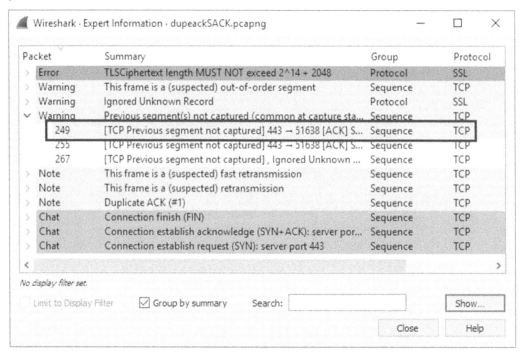

Lab 12 - A10. **The relative sequence number of the first missing segment is 230,549.**

To identify the first missing segment, we need to look at the last packet sent from the server (198.57.249.116) – frame 247. In the following image, we added the *Sequence number* and *Next sequence number* fields as columns.

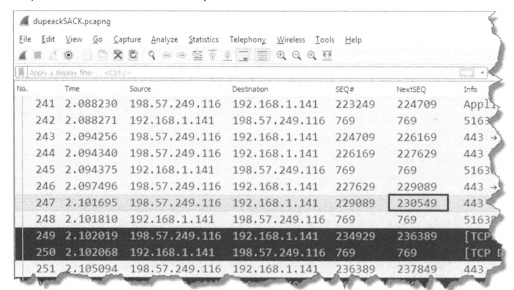

In frame 247, the *Next sequence number* field value is 230,549, and in frame 249, we see sequence number 234,929.

We are using Wireshark's relative sequence numbering which starts the sequence numbers at 0 for TCP SYN and SYN/ACK packets. This is the default setting.

Lab 12 - A11. There are 4,380 bytes missing at this point in the trace file.

Simple math is used in this case. We subtract the *Next sequence number* field value in frame 247 from the *Sequence number* field value in frame 249.

> 234,929 – 230,549 = 4,380 bytes

Looking at the typical data packet size being sent by the server at this point in the trace file (1460 bytes), we can determine that there were probably 3 packets lost.

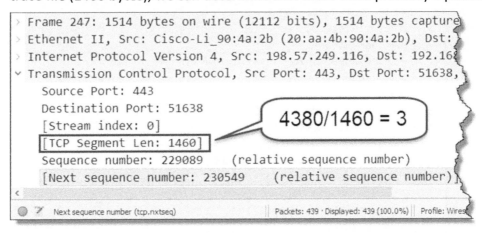

Can we be absolutely certain there were only 3 packets missing at this point in the trace file? No.

We cannot know the exact number of missing packets until they are retransmitted later. We would look for the packets with sequence numbers within the range of the Next expected sequence number and the sequence number that is marked *Previous segment not captured*.

For example, the display filter `tcp.seq >= 230549 && tcp.seq < 234929` displays the three missing packets. Each of the missing packets has a data segment length of 1460 bytes.

Lab 12 - A12. **The SACK Left Edge and Right Edge indicate that the sender of this packet (the client) has received from sequence number 234,929 up to, but not including, byte sequence number 236,389 at this point in the trace file.**

The SACK Left Edge and Right Edge values are labeled as "relative" because Wireshark is using relative sequence numbers.

As additional data packets arrive at the client, the client will increase the SACK Right Edge value to acknowledge receipt of the bytes.

```
> Frame 250: 66 bytes on wire (528 bits), 66 bytes captured (528 bits)
> Ethernet II, Src: IntelCor_06:e2:8f (4c:80:93:06:e2:8f), Dst: Cisco-L
> Internet Protocol Version 4, Src: 192.168.1.141, Dst: 198.57.249.116
∨ Transmission Control Protocol, Src Port: 51638, Dst Port: 443, Seq:
    Source Port: 51638
    Destination Port: 443
    [Stream index: 0]
    [TCP Segment Len: 0]
    Sequence number: 769     (relative sequence number)
    [Next sequence number: 769     (relative sequence number)]
    Acknowledgment number: 230549     (relative ack number)
    1000 .... = Header Length: 32 bytes (8)
  > Flags: 0x010 (ACK)
    Window size value: 37595
    [Calculated window size: 150380]
    [Window size scaling factor: 4]
    Checksum: 0xae34 [unverified]
    [Checksum Status: Unverified]
    Urgent pointer: 0
  ∨ Options: (12 bytes), No-Operation (NOP), No-Operation (NOP), SACK
    > TCP Option - No-Operation (NOP)
    > TCP Option - No-Operation (NOP)
    ∨ TCP Option - SACK 234929-236389
        Kind: SACK (5)
        Length: 10
        left edge = 234929 (relative)
        right edge = 236389 (relative)
        [TCP SACK Count: 1]
  > [SEQ/ACK analysis]
  > [Timestamps]
```

Lab 12 - A13. **The *Acknowledgment number* field remains "stuck" on the first missing segment sequence number value.**

The *Acknowledgment number* field will always indicate the oldest missing sequence number when multiple packets go missing.

In the image below, we applied a `tcp.analysis.duplicate_ack` display filter to the trace file. We also added the *Acknowledgment number* field as a column.

Now it is clear that the *Acknowledgment number* field remains the same until the missing sequence number is received.

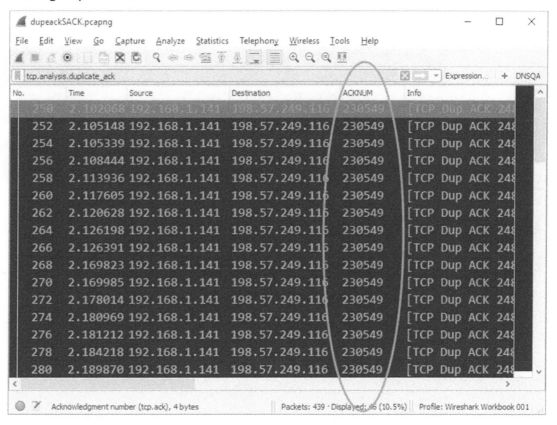

Lab 12 - A14. **The SACK Left Edge value will remain the same as the client receives additional data bytes.**

The SACK Left Edge value remains the same because it is the beginning sequence number of the data that is still being received.

In the image that follows, we added columns for the TCP *SACK Left Edge* and *SACK Right Edge* fields to examine the field values in the Duplicate ACKs.

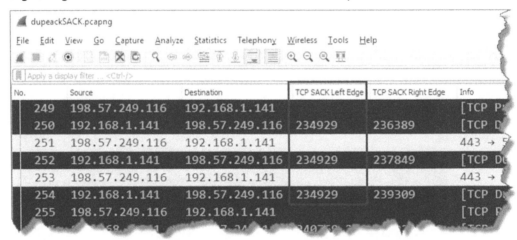

Lab 12 - A15. **The SACK Right Edge will increase as the client receives additional contiguous data bytes.**

As additional data packets arrive at the client, the client increases the SACK Right Edge value to acknowledge these newer segments.

In the image that follows, we see the TCP SACK Right Edge increasing by 1460 bytes for each additional data packet received.

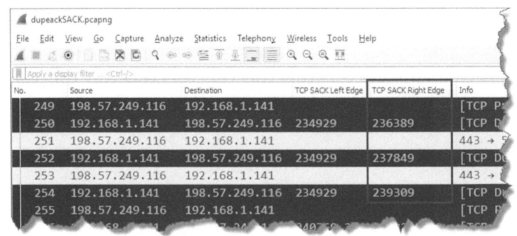

Lab 12 - A16. The second set of missing bytes in this trace file include the relative sequence number 239,309 up to, but not including, 240,769.

By opening the *Expert Information* window, we see the next indication of a missing segment is at frame 255.

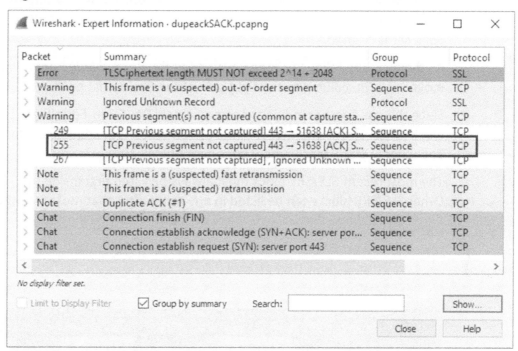

After adding our columns based on the *Sequence number* and *Next sequence number* fields, we see that sequence number 239,309 was expected after frame 253.

Sequence number 240,769 was received instead.

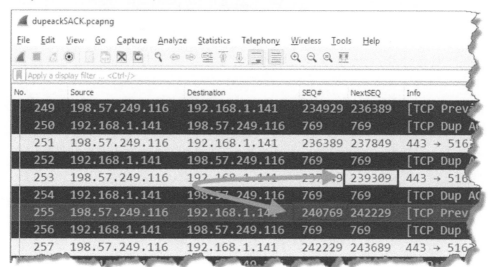

By subtracting the *Next sequence number* field value in frame 253 from the *Sequence Number* field value in frame 255, we see 1460 bytes are missing. We are likely just missing a single packet at this point in the trace file.

Lab 12 - A17. **After the second *[TCP Previous segment not captured]* indication, the *Acknowledgment number* field stays the same and another SACK Left Edge/Right Edge set is created.**

As shown in the following image, we added the *Acknowledgment number* field and moved the *No.* column to the right side of the Packet List pane.

Since there is another missing segment, a new SACK Left Edge/Right Edge (SLE/SRE) block (Block 1) was created. The newest block starts at sequence number 234,929. The older SLE/SRE block is now considered Block 2.

The most recent SLE/SRE block must always be listed first inside the TCP header. Other SLE/SRE blocks can be listed in any order after that most recent block.

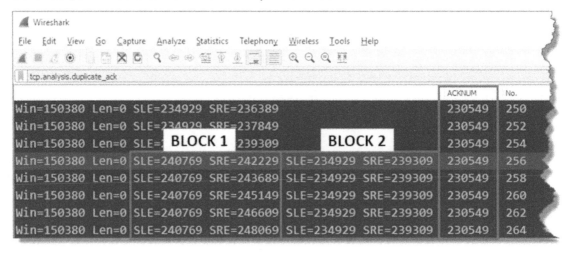

Lab 12 - A18. The client made 43 Duplicate ACK requests for the first missing segment set.

The first missing data bytes began with sequence number 230,549 (as seen in the *Acknowledgment number* field) and ended at 234,928 (one byte before the oldest SACK Left Edge value).

We can create a display filter to answer this question.

The display filter `tcp.analysis.duplicate_ack &&` `tcp.ack==230549` looks for Duplicate ACKs requesting 230,549 in the *Acknowledgment number* field.

Based on this display filter, the client sent 43 requests to find the first missing segment set.

Lab 12 - A19. The first missing segment is received in frame 335.

By filtering on the first missing sequence number, we can see the fast retransmission in frame 335.

The display filter is `tcp.seq==230549`.

Lab 12 - A20. After the first missing data segment is received, the client increases its *Acknowledgment number* field value to request the first byte of the data that is still missing.

Up until this point, the client has been asking for sequence number 230,549 by repeating this value in its *Acknowledgment number* field.

Now that sequence number 230,549 has been received, the client can ask for the next missing sequence number (230,549+1,460=232,009).

In the image below, we filtered on traffic from the client (`ip.src==192.168.1.141`) and added a column for the *Acknowledgment number* field.

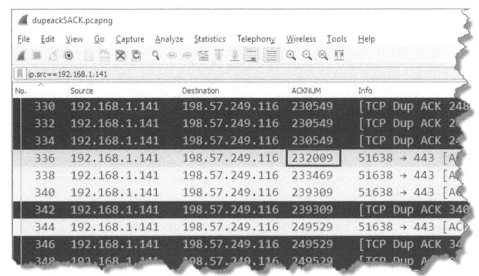

Lab 12 - A21. **Frames 337 and 339 are defined as Out-Of-Order because (1) they were not preceded by two or more Duplicate ACKs requesting their sequence numbers, and (2) they arrived within the iRTT value from the server's previous packets.**

As discussed in *Lab 6: You're Out of Order!* that starts on page 121, Wireshark uses a series of decisions to determine if a packet is a standard retransmission, fast retransmission, or out-of-order.

If the frame is preceded by two or more Duplicate ACKs requesting its sequence number, it will be defined as a fast retransmission.

If not preceded by corresponding Duplicate ACKs, Wireshark looks at the iRTT value. If the frame arrives within the iRTT of the last packet from the host, Wireshark defines it as an out-of-order. If it doesn't arrive that soon, it is defined as a retransmission.

Frames 337 and 339 are actually retransmissions of packets with sequence numbers 232,009 and 233,469. Wireshark only defined them as Out-of-Order packets because the sequence number did not advance from the highest sequence number seen and they arrived within the iRTT of previous packets from the server.

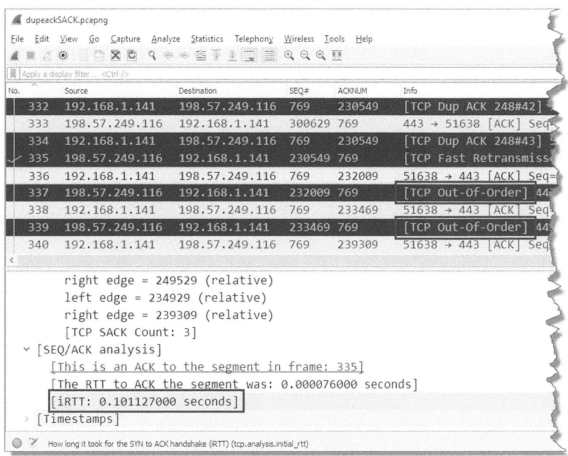

[This page intentionally left blank.]

Lab 13: Just DNS

Objective: Analyze, compare, and contrast various DNS queries and responses to identify errors, cache times, and CNAME (alias) information.

`Trace File: wwb001-justdns.pcapng`

Skills Covered in this Lab

In this lab, you will work with many key functions in Wireshark including, but not limited to:

- Filter based on DNS type
- Filter based on DNS response code
- Locate packets based on keywords
- Use regular expression display filters
- Measure DNS response time
- Count DNS Resource Records (RRs) in responses
- Identify DNS error responses
- Combine display filters for more accurate packet detection
- Analyze DNS cache time
- Follow CNAME details
- Correlate DNS error responses with an application
- Determine why SOA information is included in DNS responses

Before we start this section, I want to call your attention to Statistics | DNS. *Many of the answers to this lab can be obtained using this Statistics window, but I would like you to also obtain the answers by working with display filters. It's great practice and gives you a chance to examine the contents of DNS query and response packets.*

Laura

Lab 13 - Q1. **What is the client's IP address?**

_____

Lab 13 - Q2. **What is the DNS server's IP address?**

_____

Lab 13 - Q3. **Does this client support both IPv4 and IPv6?**

_____

Lab 13 - Q4. **How many DNS queries are in the trace file?**

_____

Lab 13 - Q5. **How many DNS queries relate to _qless.com_ hosts?**

_____

Lab 13 - Q6. **What is the fastest DNS response seen?**

_____

Lab 13 - Q7. **What is the slowest DNS response seen?**

_____

Lab 13 - Q8. **Which DNS response contains the most answer Resource Records (RRs)?**

_____

Lab 13 - Q9. How many DNS error responses are seen?

_____

Lab 13 - Q10. How many DNS queries does the client send for an IPv4 address for _kiosk.us1.qless.com_?

_____

Lab 13 - Q11. How long is the client allowed to cache the IP addresses associated with _scss.adobesc.com_?

_____

Lab 13 - Q12. What content delivery provider does McAfee use?

_____

Lab 13 - Q13. How many DNS responses contain a DNS Time to Live value of less than 5 seconds?

_____

Lab 13 - Q14. How many A record (IPv4) requests are in the trace file?

_____

Lab 13 - Q15. How many AAAA record (IPv6) requests are in the trace file?

_____

Lab 13 - Q16.   **What application is receiving a "No such name" response to some DNS queries it generated?**

_____

Lab 13 - Q17.   **Why did the DNS server reply with SOA information in frame 207?**

_____

Lab 13 Solutions

Trace File: wwb001-justdns.pcapng

Lab 13 - A1. **The client's IP address is 192.168.1.70.**

The first packet in the trace file shows a DNS query made by 192.168.1.70.

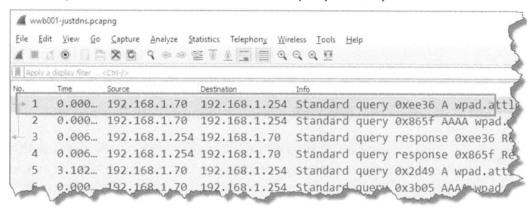

Lab 13 - A2. **The DNS server's IP address is 192.168.1.254.**

Frame 3 is a DNS response from 192.168.1.254. If we wonder if there are other DNS servers in this trace file, we can apply a display filter for dns.flags.response==1.

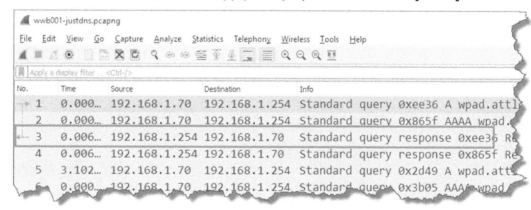

The display filter `dns.flags.response==1` is based on the *Flags* area inside the DNS portion of a packet.

```
> Frame 3: 77 bytes on wire (616 bits), 77 bytes captured (616
> Ethernet II, Src: 2wire_2c:0b:15 (dc:7f:a4:2c:0b:15), Dst: Mi
> Internet Protocol Version 4, Src: 192.168.1.254, Dst: 192.16
> User Datagram Protocol, Src Port: 53, Dst Port: 58757
v Domain Name System (response)
    Transaction ID: 0xee36
    v Flags: 0x8585 Standard query response, Refused
      1... .... .... .... = Response: Message is a response
      .000 0... .... .... = Opcode: Standard query (0)
```
Is the message a response (dns.flags.response) 2 bytes

Lab 13 - A3.   This client is a dual-stack client – it supports both IPv4 and IPv6.

This is evident by looking at the first packets. We see the client send an A record (IPv4 address) request followed by an AAAA, or "quad-A" (IPv6 address) request.

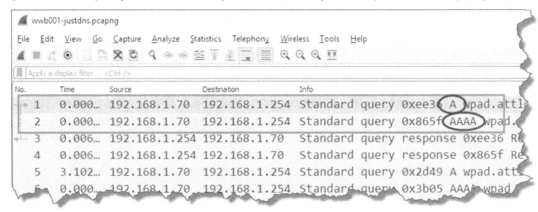

Lab 13 - A4. There are 134 DNS queries in the trace file.

Just as the display filter dns.flags.response==1 can provide a count of DNS responses, dns.flags.response==0 can provide a count of DNS queries.

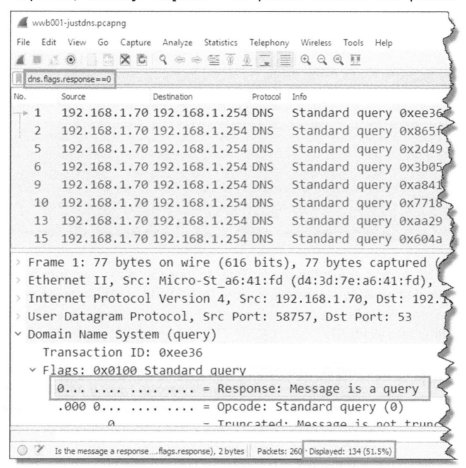

Lab 13 - A5. **There are 57 DNS queries that relate to *qless.com* hosts.**

Now we can expand our DNS queries display filter to include "qless" in it. The new display filter is dns.flags.response==0 && dns contains "qless".

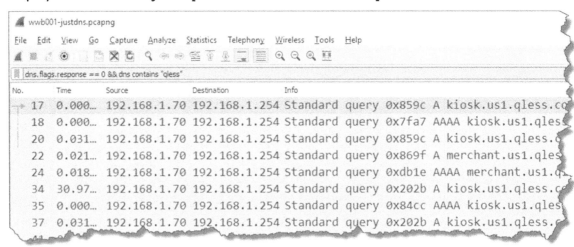

If we want to adjust this display filter to look for "qless" in upper or lower case, we need to move to regular expressions (regex) and use the matches operator. The syntax would be dns.flags.response==0 && dns matches "qless". This display filter also yields 57.

It's always a good idea to look for both uppercase and lowercase characters when you absolutely need to know if an ASCII pattern exists. Consider a network forensics situation when you need to determine if a specific word or phrase exists in the trace file. It may be in any combination of case. Learning to use regex with Wireshark is highly recommended.

In earlier versions of Wireshark (prior to v3), you would need to use dns.flags.response==0 && dns matches "(?i)qless" *adding the* (?i) *modifier to indicate you are interested in upper and lower case characters.*

Current versions of Wireshark do not require the (?i) *modifier—they look for uppercase and lowercase characters by default. If you want to force case sensitivity in newer versions of Wireshark, use the* (?-i) *modifier.*

Lab 13 - A6. **The shortest DNS response time seen is 0.007125 seconds.**

Two steps can be taken to get this information quickly. First, we applied a display filter for DNS responses (dns.flags.response==1). Next, we added the dns.time field as a column for sorting.

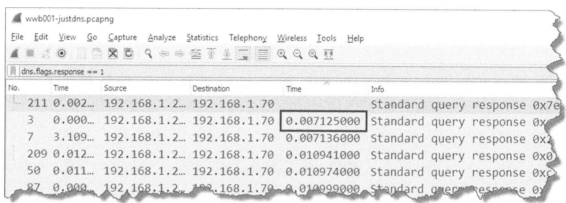

We didn't really need to use the display filter for responses as requests won't even have a dns.time field. Unfortunately, if we don't use that display filter and we sort on the DNS *Time* column, we will have a lot of blank lines above our first numbers.

So why does our filtered result show a blank (DNS) *Time* column on frame 211?

Inside frame 211, there is an indication that the frame is a retransmission and the original response was in frame 207. Wireshark measured the DNS response time based on the first response packet in frame 207, not this frame. That's an excellent call by Wireshark.

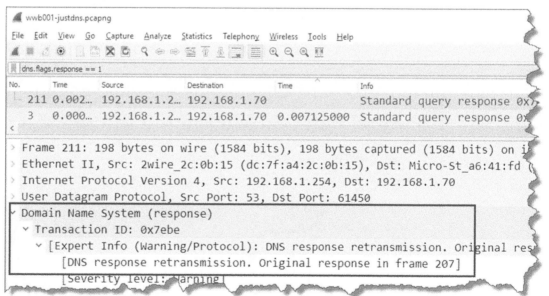

Lab 13 - A7. **The slowest DNS response seen in this trace file is 0.096857 seconds.**

By retaining the display filter for DNS responses and just sorting the (DNS) *Time* column from high to low, we can see the highest response easily.

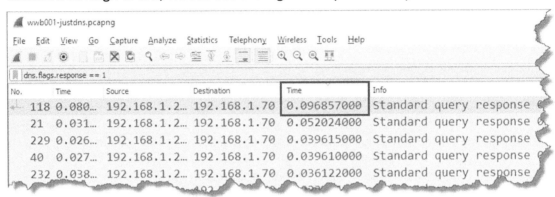

Lab 13 - A8. **Frame 242 contains the most Answer Resource Records (RRs) – 9 Answer RRs.**

You don't need a display filter in place to get this answer. Just add a column based on the *Answer RRs* field and sort that column from high to low. We can quickly determine that the frame that contains the highest number of Answer Resource Records is frame 242.

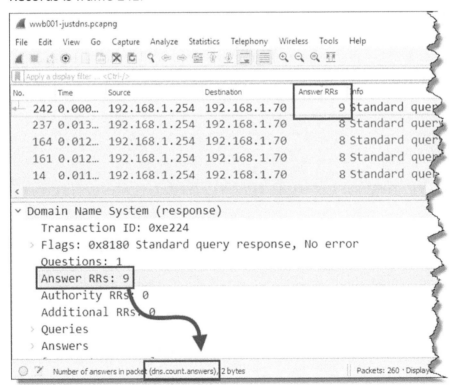

Lab 13 - A9. **There are six DNS error responses in this trace file.**

We are interested in the *Reply code* field which resides inside the DNS *Flags* section. Any value other than 0 in this field indicates an error response. By applying a display filter for `dns.flags.rcode > 0`, we see there are 6 DNS responses that indicate errors.

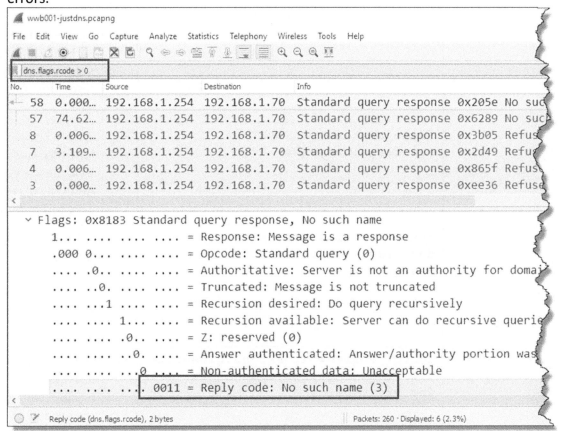

The error responses include:

> No such name
> Refused

The "No such name" responses came in response to DNS queries for *netmon-control.dropbox.com*. This name could not be resolved.

The four Refusals indicate that the DNS server would not try to resolve the name *wpad.attlocal.net*. The "wpad" stands for Web Proxy Auto-Discovery Protocol.

Lab 13 - A10. The client sends 17 DNS queries for an IPv4 address for *kiosk.us1.qless.com*.

Let's go from laziest (casting a "wide net") to most specific in our attempts to get this answer[27].

Display Filter	Hits	Issues
`frame contains "kiosk"`	56	We are looking for any frames with the word "kiosk" in them. Unfortunately, we see AAAA (IPv6) requests and responses. This is too wide of a net.
`frame contains "kiosk" && dns.flags.response==0`	30	We are now also looking only for DNS requests. Unfortunately, we also see AAAA (IPv6) requests. This is a bit better though.
`frame contains "kiosk" && dns.flags.response==0 && dns.qry.type==1`	17	This works perfectly for this trace file. If there were A record queries for *kiosk.something.com*, however, we'd have to be more specific.
`dns.qry.name=="kiosk.us1.qless.com" && dns.flags.response==0 && dns.qry.type==1`	17	This is perfect. We used dns.qry.name specifically because we are looking for the entire DNS name- Wireshark can deal with the dots in the name properly because it is looking at the dissected value in this field. Since we don't want to recreate this every time we are looking for specific A record queries, we'd make this a display filter button and edit the name when desired.

[27] There's nothing wrong with being lazy in analysis – as long as you are only lazy when you can get the answer that way. This is a perfect example of how you can apply a simple filter to see if you can get the answer, but when that doesn't work, you can keep expanding and improving your filter until you get your exact answer.

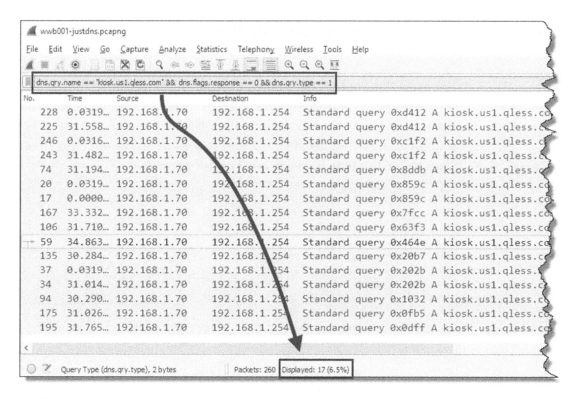

 I cannot stress enough how much display filter buttons speed up your analysis process. You don't have a limit on the number of buttons you can create and you can easily share buttons with other Wireshark systems by simply copying the dfilter_buttons *file from your Wireshark profile directory. To locate this folder, select* Help | About Wireshark | Folders *and jump to your* Personal Configuration *folder. You will see a* profiles *folder that contains all your custom profile directories.*

Lab 13 - A11. **The client is allowed to cache the IP addresses associated with *scss.adobesc.com* for 18 seconds (A records) and 243 seconds (AAAA record).**

To obtain this answer, we applied a display filter for the DNS query name and responses (dns.qry.name=="scss.adobesc.com" && dns.flags.response==1) and then we added a column based on the DNS *Time to Live* (dns.resp.ttl) field. This column is important because a DNS response can have multiple answers and we want to see the time to live in each of the answers.

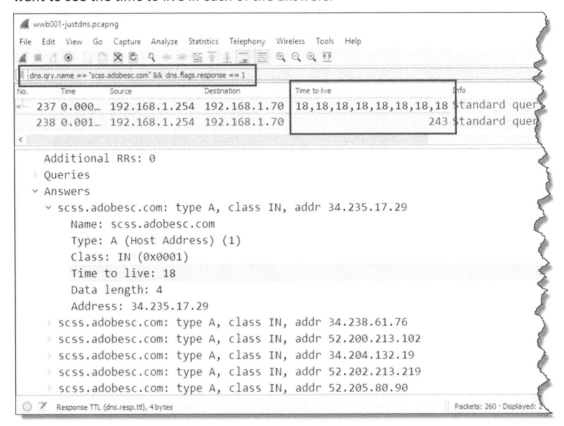

 Columns, columns, columns! Get another monitor or two (or three) so you can see all the important information by adding columns to the Packet List pane. You'll save a lot of time. Although I love looking inside the packets, my main focus is to get the information I need as quickly as possible.

Lab 13 - A12. McAfee uses Akamai as its content delivery provider.

We know this trace file only has DNS packets, so this information must be contained in those DNS packets. We can start with a wide net and look for just packets that contain "mcafee" – `frame contains "mcafee" && dns.flags.response==1`.

This provides us with the answer we need in some of the four packets that match the display filter.

We see several frames with a CNAME (alias) answer. Frame 241, for example, indicates that *ws12.gti.mcafee.com* is actually *ws12.gti.mcafee.akadns.net*.

The domain *akadns.net* refers to Akamai. The *Authority RRs* section defines the responsible authority's mailbox as *hostmaster.akamai.com*.

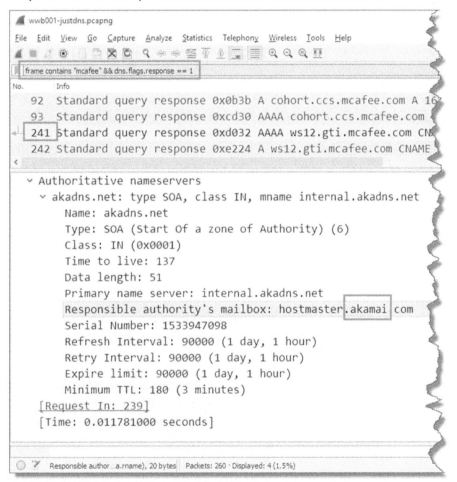

Lab 13 - A13. **There are seven DNS responses that contain a DNS *Time to Live* value of less than 5 seconds.**

We can quickly create and apply a `dns.resp.ttl < 5` display filter to provide this information.

Use the right-click method to build this display filter quickly.[28] Open up any DNS response packet that contains answers (avoid those *wpad.attlocal.net* error packets), expand an *Answer* section and right-click on the *Time to live* field. Choose *Prepare a Filter | Selected*.

Choosing *Prepare a Filter* enables you to edit the display filter before applying it to the trace file. Change the display filter to `dns.resp.ttl < 5` before applying it to the trace file.

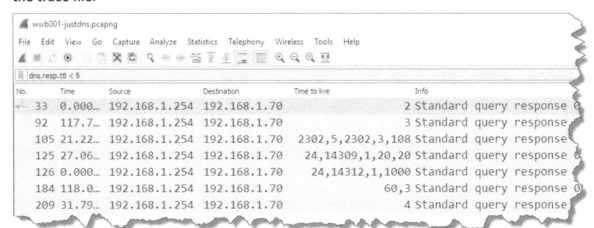

 Your Time to live *column will contains multiple numbers when the DNS response packets contain multiple answers.*

By default, Wireshark displays the values of all occurrences of the field in packets. We can see that frame 105 must have five answers in it. Frame 184 must have two answers in it.

When you right-click on a column header and select Edit column, *one of the column's configuration options is the* Occurrence *option.*

The number 0 in the Occurrence *area indicates that you are interested in all occurrences of the field. If you only want to see the first occurrence of a field, you would enter 1 in this* Occurrence *area.*

---

[28] No "normal" person (grin) memorizes all the fields of frames.

Lab 13 - A14.   There are 67 A record requests in the trace file.

This should be an easy one now. As you've worked on this lab, you've made a lot of display filters looking for A records and looking for requests or responses. You can easily use the right-click method to create this display filter.

In this case, we used (dns.flags.response==0) && (dns.qry.type==1) to get the answer.

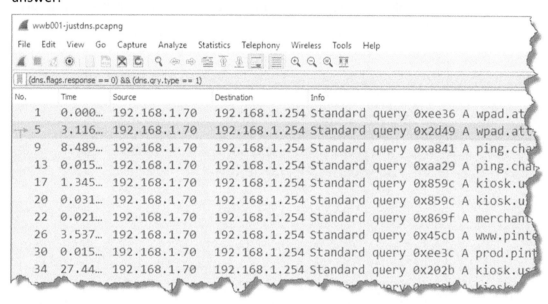

The following table lists some of the most commonly seen DNS *Type* field values.

TYPE	Value	Meaning
A	1	IPv4 host address
NS	2	authoritative name server
CNAME	5	canonical name for an alias
SOA	6	marks the start of authority
PTR	12	domain name pointer (reverse lookup)
HINFO	13	host information
MX	15	mail exchanger
TXT	16	text strings
AAAA	28	IP6 address

Lab 13 - A15. There are 67 AAAA record requests in the trace file.

Just as we did in the previous answer, we used the right-click method to create a simple display filter looking for (1) DNS requests and (2) AAAA types.

The display filter to find this answer is (dns.flags.response==0) && (dns.qry.type==28).

You could also just simply change the dns.qry.type value of your previous display filter to 28.

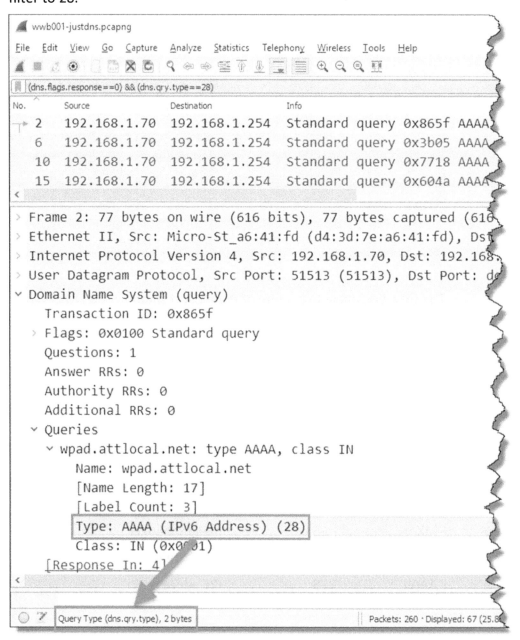

Lab 13 - A16. Dropbox received two "No such name" DNS error responses.

In Lab 13 – A9, we saw a number of error responses when we used the display filter dns.flags.rcode > 0.

We can see a reference to *wpad.attlocal.net* in four of the error responses. As we learned in Lab 13 – A9, these are from the Web Proxy Auto-Discovery Protocol.

There are two error responses that refer to Dropbox as well. You can search for "dropbox netmon control" to learn that "Network control is a security and access feature available to Dropbox Business teams on an Enterprise plan. With this feature, IT admins can manage which Dropbox accounts can be used on their corporate network." If this is a feature that we use on this network, apparently it isn't working too well.

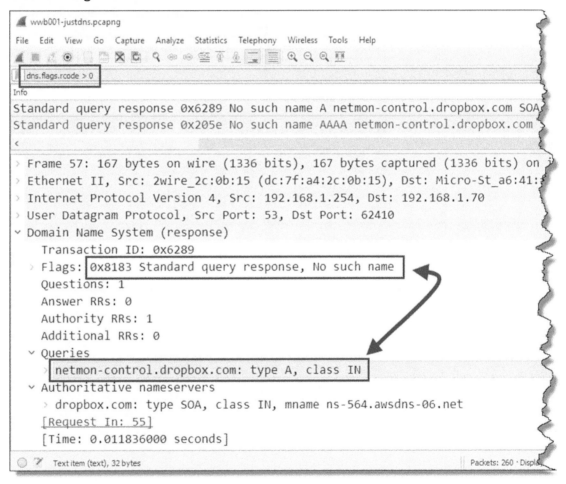

Lab 13 - A17. **In frame 207, the DNS server replied with Start of Authority (SOA) information because there is no IPv6 address associated with the name.**

When there isn't any data for the record type requested, you will typically see DNS servers respond with an SOA record.

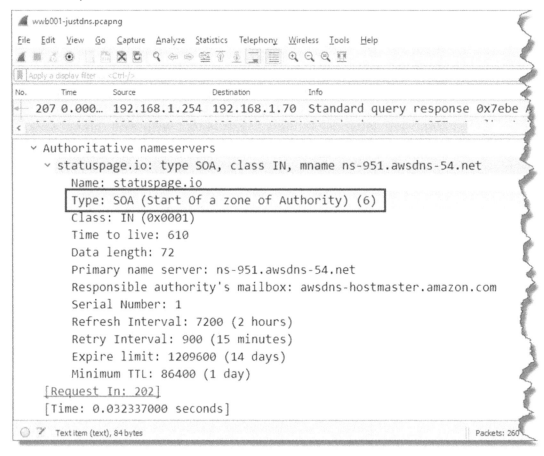

Lab 14: Movie Time

Objective: Use various display filter types, including regular expressions (regex), to analyze HTTP redirections, end-of-field values, object download times, errors, response times and more.

Trace File: wwb001-movietime.pcapng

Skills Covered in this Lab

In this lab, you will work with many key functions in Wireshark including, but not limited to:

- Display filter on TCP SYN packets
- Correlate a host name with an IP address in a sanitized trace file
- Determine if a trace file has been altered with Tracewrangler
- Measure HTTP object download time
- Locate packets based on end-of-field values
- Quickly determine the size of HTTP downloaded objects
- Identify HTTP hosts that are redirecting clients
- Measure, extract, and average HTTP response time
- Reassemble and examine HTTP objects
- Locate "File Not Found" responses based on the HTTP response code
- Identify the fastest responding HTTP servers in a trace file
- Use an inclusion display filter to locate all traffic sent to a set of addresses

Lab 14 - Q1. What are the client's IP addresses?

_____

Lab 14 - Q2. What is the IP address of *www.metacritic.com*?

_____

Lab 14 - Q3. How long did it take to download *CBSI-PLAYER.js*?

_____

Lab 14 - Q4. How many HTTP GET requests were sent to hosts whose names end in *.org*?

_____

Lab 14 - Q5. What is the size of the largest HTTP object downloaded?

_____

Lab 14 - Q6. What host refers the client to *mid.rkdms.com*?

_____

Lab 14 - Q7. What is the average HTTP response time?

_____

Lab 14 - Q8. How long did it take to download *loader.js* from *cdn.taboola.com*?

_____

Lab 14 - Q9. What movie actors are depicted in *dvd_2018_08-180.jpg* and *hulu201808-180.jpg*?

_____

Lab 14 - Q10.   What HTTP request generated a "File Not Found" response?

_____

Lab 14 - Q11.   Which 3 HTTP servers responded fastest to requests?

_____

[This page intentionally left blank.]

Lab 14 Solutions

Trace File: wwb001-movietime.pcapng

Lab 14 - A1. **The client's IPv6 address is 2e3e:cb63:fff2:2e94:6e1c:e314:740:cd8f and its IPv4 address is 10.2.2.2.**

There are lots of ways to get this information. One way to get this information quickly is to apply a display filter for `tcp.flags.syn==1 && tcp.flags.ack==0`. This filter displays all TCP SYN packets in the trace file. Since clients (or client processes) generate these packets, we can see who the sender is with this display filter applied.

By sorting the *Source* column from low to high and then using the quick navigation buttons (⇑ and ⇓) to jump to the top of the list and then to the bottom of the list, we can get both the addresses in the trace file. Alternatively, you can just change the sort order, as shown in the following images.

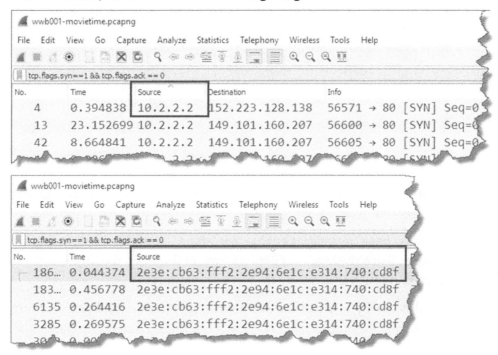

Lab 14 - A2. **The IP address of *www.metacritic.com* is 149.101.160.207.**

You may have started looking for DNS packets with "Metacritic" in a response, but that wouldn't have worked. There are no DNS packets in this trace file.

A simple `frame contains "metacritic"` filter displays 262 frames with a variety of destinations. Many of these frames are HTTP GET requests which contain an HTTP *Host* field in them. By adding this field as a column and sorting the column, we can see HTTP requests made to *www.metacritic.com*.

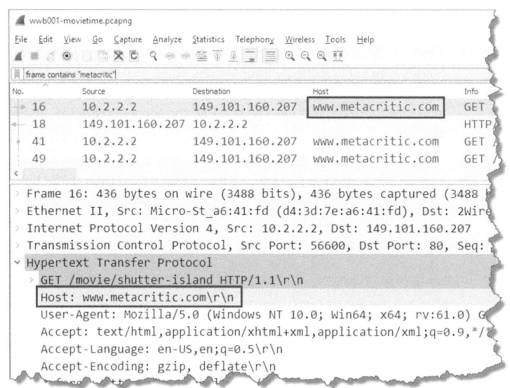

Alternatively, you can apply a `http.host==www.metacritic.com` display filter to view packets sent to this host.

You may have decided to enable Wireshark's name resolution feature to obtain this answer. Since there are no DNS packets in the trace file, however, Wireshark would have to query a DNS server for the information.

Go ahead – if you didn't try this before, try it now. Don't get your hopes up, however.

To enable network name resolution, you can (1) select *View | Name Resolution | Resolve Network Addresses* or (2) select *Edit | Preferences | Name Resolution*. The first option only changes the network name resolution setting temporarily. The change will be lost when you restart Wireshark or move to another profile.

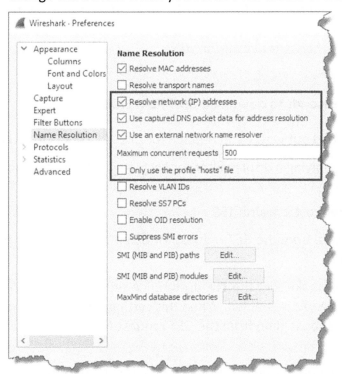

You won't be able to use this technique to resolve the address for *www.metacritic.com* because addresses in this trace file have been sanitized using Tracewrangler.

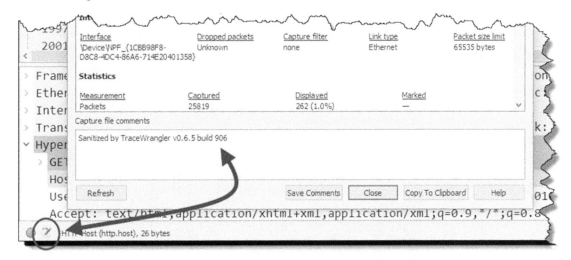

Tracewrangler is a great tool for anonymizing addresses in trace files. Created by Jasper Bongertz and free, the tool is available from *www.tracewrangler.com*.

 Be careful handing out your trace files. Even if you anonymize the IP addresses in the files, there may be an IP address or other sensitive information located inside the payload. Consider using a hex editor to look for other sensitive information.

Lab 14 - A3. **It took 0.057312 seconds to download *CBSI-PLAYER.js*.**

First, we need to find out where the request for *CBSI-PLAYER.js* is in the trace file.

We will begin by applying a display filter for `http.request.uri matches "cbsi-player\.js"`

We see the GET request in frame 155.

We want to measure from the GET request for *CBSI-PLAYER.js* to the final packet of the file download.

In this case, we will make sure the TCP preference setting *Allow subdissector to reassemble TCP streams* is enabled. When this setting is enabled, Wireshark measures HTTP response time from the GET request to the last packet of the file download.

Inside the HTTP section of frame 155, we see the hyperlink to the response frame – frame 330. We cleared our display filter and clicked on this hyperlink to examine the response frame.

```
> Frame 155: 383 bytes on wire (3064 bits), 383 bytes captured (3064
> Ethernet II, Src: DESKTOP-0N5720G (d4:3d:7e:a6:41:fd), Dst: dsldev
> Internet Protocol Version 4, Src: 10.2.2.2, Dst: 190.241.242.229
> Transmission Control Protocol, Src Port: 56611, Dst Port: 80, Seq: 1
v Hypertext Transfer Protocol
  > GET /uvpjs/2.8.3/CBSI-PLAYER.js HTTP/1.1\r\n
    Host: vidtech.cbsinteractive.com\r\n
    User-Agent: Mozilla/5.0 (Windows NT 10.0; Win64; x64; rv:61.0) Ge
    Accept: */*\r\n
    Accept-Language: en-US,en;q=0.5\r\n
    Accept-Encoding: gzip, deflate\r\n
    Referer: http://www.metacritic.com/movie/shutter-island\r\n
    Connection: keep-alive\r\n
    \r\n
    [Full request URI: http://vidtech.cbsinteractive.com/uvpjs/2.8.3/
    [HTTP request 1/4]
    [Response in frame: 330]
    [Next request in frame: 966]
```

Inside the HTTP section of the response frame, we see the *Time since request* value of 0.057312 seconds.

```
> Transmission Control Protocol, Src Port: 80, Dst Port: 56611, Seq: 2073
> [145 Reassembled TCP Segments (207382 bytes): #157(1460), #158(1460), #1
˅ Hypertext Transfer Protocol
   > HTTP/1.1 200 OK\r\n
     Server: Apache\r\n
     ETag: "ffe80da4a589534ffbb17f46d6ef50a3:1522078954"\r\n
     Last-Modified: Mon, 26 Mar 2018 15:42:34 GMT\r\n
     Accept-Ranges: bytes\r\n
     Content-Type: application/x-javascript\r\n
     Vary: Accept-Encoding\r\n
     Content-Encoding: gzip\r\n
   > Content-Length: 206982\r\n
     Cache-Control: max-age=2592000\r\n
     Expires: Mon, 10 Sep 2018 02:01:46 GMT\r\n
     Date: Sat, 11 Aug 2018 02:01:46 GMT\r\n
     Connection: keep-alive\r\n
     \r\n
     [HTTP response 1/4]
     [Time since request: 0.057312000 seconds]
     [Request in frame: 155]
     [Next request in frame: 966]
     [Next response in frame: 987]
     Content-encoded entity body (gzip): 206982 bytes -> 778156 bytes
     File Data: 778156 bytes
```

If the question had asked "What was the response time to the request to download CBSI-PLAYER.js, the answer would be a measurement from the GET request to the 200 OK packet.

With TCP reassembly enabled, in the Info *column, Wireshark shows the "200 OK" in the final packet of the download, which is frame 330 in this case. Wireshark calculates from the request packet to the last packet of the object download (download time).*

However, if you look in the Packet Bytes pane, you can see that the 200 OK is really in frame 157. You must disable TCP reassembly to get the correct HTTP response time. Wireshark calculates from the request packet to the reply packet (response time).

When you disable TCP reassembly, the response is in frame 157 with an http.time *value of 0.012970 seconds.*

Lab 14 - A4. **There are five HTTP GET requests sent to hosts whose names end in _.org_.**

There are several display filters you can use to get this answer.

First, you are looking for HTTP GET requests only. The display filter `http.request.method=="GET"` will provide this information.

We now need to look for _.org_ at the end of the HTTP _Host_ field. We could use `http.host contains ".org"` to find the packets. What if, however, the trace file contained an HTTP GET request sent to _www.organdonor.com_? That packet would be displayed, but it's not what interests us.

This is a perfect time to use regular expressions (regex) in our display filter.

The display filter `http.request.method=="GET" && http.host matches "\.org$"` includes regex that specifically looks for a period (escaped with a leading backslash because the period is a special character). Next, the regex display filter portion looks for the letters "org." A dollar sign "$" is placed last to indicate we are looking at the end of the field. It is that dollar sign that ensures _www.organdonor.com_ doesn't match our display filter.

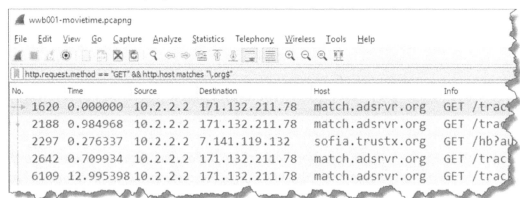

Lab 14 - A5.   **The largest HTTP object download size is 778 kB (*CBSI-PLAYER.js*).**

With the TCP reassembly preferences setting on, select *File | Export Objects | HTTP*.
Sort the table by the *Size* column (high to low) to find the largest object,
CBSI-PLAYER.js.

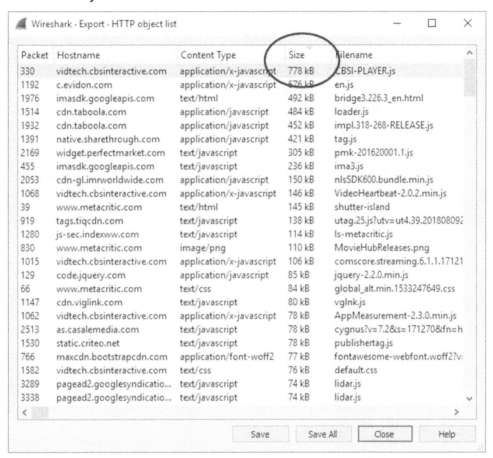

If you left the TCP preference setting Allow subdissector to reassemble
TCP streams *off by mistake, you'd know it immediately. Rather than see a
single entry for a file, you would see separate entries for each packet
containing parts of the file, as shown below.*

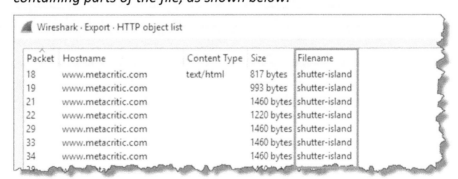

Lab 14 - A6. **The host *www.metacritic.com* refers the client to *mid.rkdms.com*.**

HTTP servers often refer clients to other servers for information. If you look inside the HTTP portion of frame 16, for example, you will see the client sending a request to *www.metacritic.com*. Inside that HTTP request, the client lists the "Referer" as *https://www.google.com/*.

To find out what server referred the client to *mid.rkdms.com*, we need to filter on HTTP traffic sent to *mid.rkdms.com* and then look at the *Referer* field.

The display filter `http.request.method && http.host contains "mid.rkdms.com"` will show us all packets that (1) contain the `http.request.method` field and (2) have *mid.rkdms.com* in the HTTP *Host* field. If we wanted to narrow our display filter, we could add `&& http.referer` to the display filter.

We aren't looking specifically for GET requests – we don't know if the client sent a POST or other HTTP command

Frame 1424 contains the packet of interest.

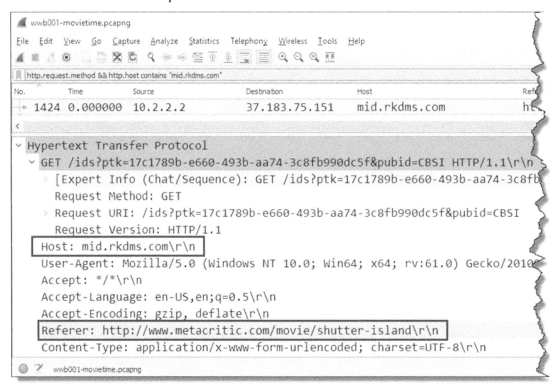

Lab 14 - A7.   The average HTTP response time is 0.086804 seconds.

Now it is important to disable the TCP preference *Allow subdissector to reassemble TCP streams* setting. Right-click on a TCP header in the Packet Details pane and select *Protocol Preferences* to disable this setting.

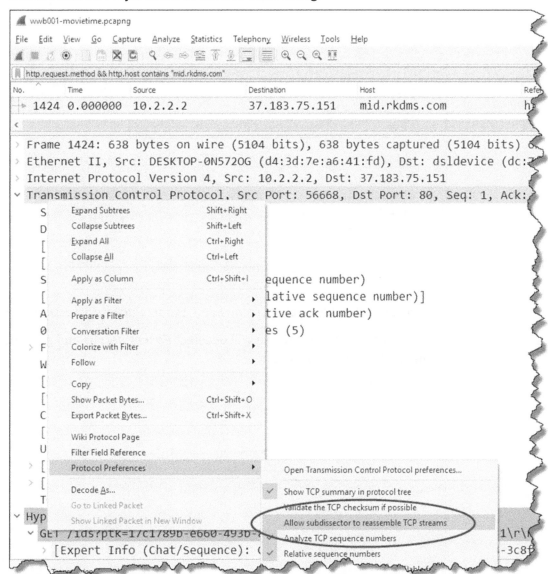

By default, this setting is enabled, and HTTP response time is measured from the request to the last packet of the file download. This is not true response time – this is response time plus download time.

After disabling this setting, we can now add an `http.time` column and apply an `http.time` display filter. We are applying the display filter so we only see packets that contain this field.

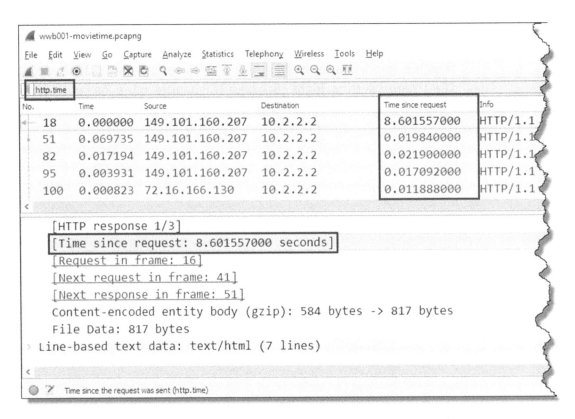

We will extract these packets using *File | Export Packet Dissections | As CSV*.

On the *Export File* window, we will deselect *Packet details* and give the *.csv* file a name, *HTTPResponseTime.csv*.

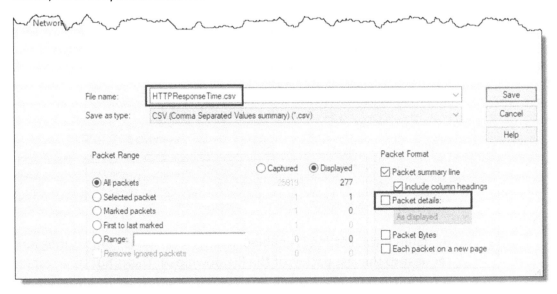

In Excel, we can now average the HTTP *Time Since Request* column. The result is 0.086803866 seconds. Excel offers an answer to the ninth decimal place (nanosecond granularity), but we only provided numbers going to the sixth decimal place. We will round up to the millisecond granularity.

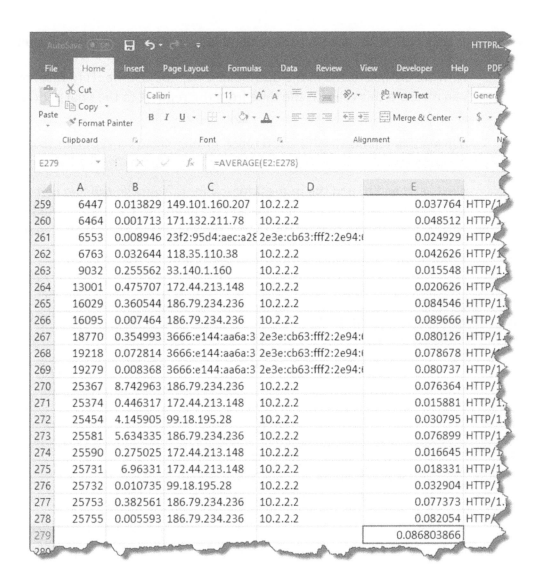

	A	B	C	D		E	
259	6447	0.013829	149.101.160.207	10.2.2.2		0.037764	HTTP/1
260	6464	0.001713	171.132.211.78	10.2.2.2		0.048512	HTTP/1
261	6553	0.008946	23f2:95d4:aec:a28	2e3e:cb63:fff2:2e94:6		0.024929	HTTP/
262	6763	0.032644	118.35.110.38	10.2.2.2		0.042626	HTTP/1
263	9032	0.255562	33.140.1.160	10.2.2.2		0.015548	HTTP/1.
264	13001	0.475707	172.44.213.148	10.2.2.2		0.020626	HTTP/
265	16029	0.360544	186.79.234.236	10.2.2.2		0.084546	HTTP/1.
266	16095	0.007464	186.79.234.236	10.2.2.2		0.089666	HTTP/1
267	18770	0.354993	3666:e144:aa6a:3	2e3e:cb63:fff2:2e94:6		0.080126	HTTP/1.
268	19218	0.072814	3666:e144:aa6a:3	2e3e:cb63:fff2:2e94:6		0.078678	HTTP/
269	19279	0.008368	3666:e144:aa6a:3	2e3e:cb63:fff2:2e94:6		0.080737	HTTP/1
270	25367	8.742963	186.79.234.236	10.2.2.2		0.076364	HTTP/1
271	25374	0.446317	172.44.213.148	10.2.2.2		0.015881	HTTP/1.
272	25454	4.145905	99.18.195.28	10.2.2.2		0.030795	HTTP/1.
273	25581	5.634335	186.79.234.236	10.2.2.2		0.076899	HTTP/1
274	25590	0.275025	172.44.213.148	10.2.2.2		0.016645	HTTP/1
275	25731	6.96331	172.44.213.148	10.2.2.2		0.018331	HTTP/1
276	25732	0.010735	99.18.195.28	10.2.2.2		0.032904	HTTP/1
277	25753	0.382561	186.79.234.236	10.2.2.2		0.077373	HTTP/1.
278	25755	0.005593	186.79.234.236	10.2.2.2		0.082054	HTTP/
279						0.086803866	
280							

Cell E279: =AVERAGE(E2:E278)

Lab 14 - A8.   It took 0.030618 seconds to download *loader.js* from *cdn.taboola.com*.

Now we are interested in the download time, not just the HTTP response time. We can measure this value as the time from the request to the final packet of the download.

We need to enable the TCP preference setting *Allow subdissector to reassemble TCP streams* first.

Next, we need to find the request for *loader.js* from *cdn.taboola.com*. The simple display filter, frame contains "loader.js" identifies two frames. Adding the HTTP *Host* column shows that frame 1465 is the request to *cdn.taboola.com*.

Inside frame 1465, we see the link to the response: frame 1514.

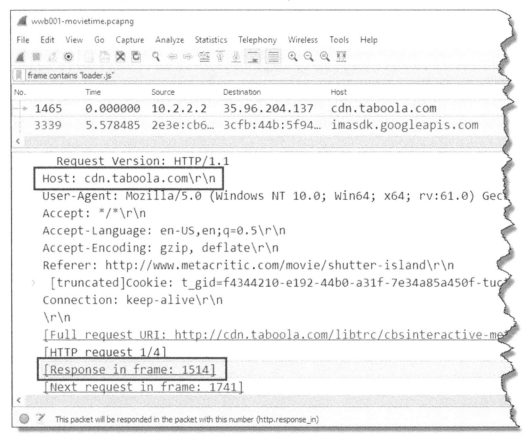

 If you are getting tired of enabling and disabling the TCP preference setting Allow subdissector to reassemble TCP streams, *consider making a copy of your profile, disabling the setting in one profile, and enabling the setting in the other.*

To copy a profile, right-click on the Profile *column in the Status Bar. Select* Manage profiles *and click the* Copy *button* 📋 *. Give your copied profile a name that includes "-noTCPreassembly" at the end of the name.*

After clearing the display filter and jumping to frame 1514, we can obtain the download time of 0.030618 seconds.

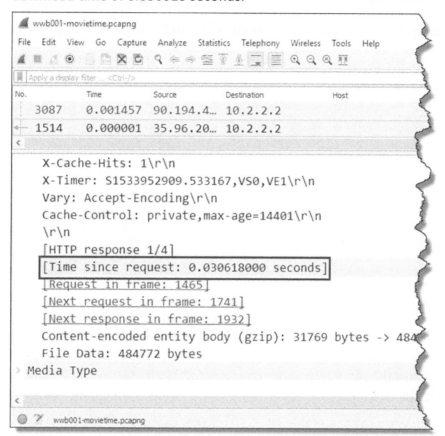

 The Wireshark developers use the syntax [protocol].time *for all the response time fields.*

For example, HTTP response time is displayed in the http.time *field. DNS response time is displayed in the* dns.time *field.*

The SMB dissectors offer two different response time fields: smb.time *and* smb2.time. *The* smb2.time *field covers both SMBv2 and SMBv3.*

Lab 14 - A9.   **Robert Downey, Jr., is depicted in *dvd_2018_08-180.jpg* and Arnold Schwarzenegger is depicted in *hulu201808-180.jpg*.**

This question requires a reassembly of the HTTP objects to find the answer.

Again, you will need the TCP reassembly preference enabled. Selecting *File | Export Objects | HTTP*, we can sort the table by the *Filename* column to find our file quickly.

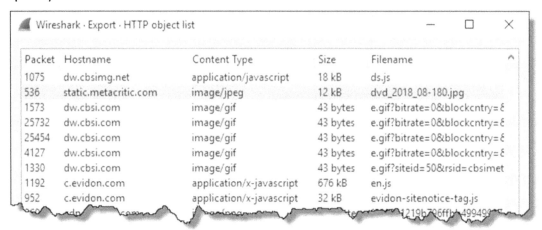

Packet	Hostname	Content Type	Size	Filename
1075	dw.cbsimg.net	application/javascript	18 kB	ds.js
536	static.metacritic.com	image/jpeg	12 kB	dvd_2018_08-180.jpg
1573	dw.cbsi.com	image/gif	43 bytes	e.gif?bitrate=0&blockcntry=&
25732	dw.cbsi.com	image/gif	43 bytes	e.gif?bitrate=0&blockcntry=&
25454	dw.cbsi.com	image/gif	43 bytes	e.gif?bitrate=0&blockcntry=&
4127	dw.cbsi.com	image/gif	43 bytes	e.gif?bitrate=0&blockcntry=&
1330	dw.cbsi.com	image/gif	43 bytes	e.gif?siteid=50&rsid=cbsimet
1192	c.evidon.com	application/x-javascript	676 kB	en.js
952	c.evidon.com	application/x-javascript	32 kB	evidon-sitenotice-tag.js

Select *dvd_2018_08-180.jpg*, click *Save*, and create/select a target directory. Perform the same operation to save *hulu201808-180.jpg*. In this directory, you will find the two files.

If you want to reassemble all HTTP objects captured in the trace file, select *Save All* and create/specify a target directory.

dvd_2018_08-180.jpg   *hulu201808-180.jpg.*

Lab 14 - A10. The HTTP request in frame 8906 generated the "File Not Found" response.

When you apply a display filter for HTTP 404 responses (`http.response.code==404`), you'll find frame 9032. Inside this frame is a link to the request in frame 8906.

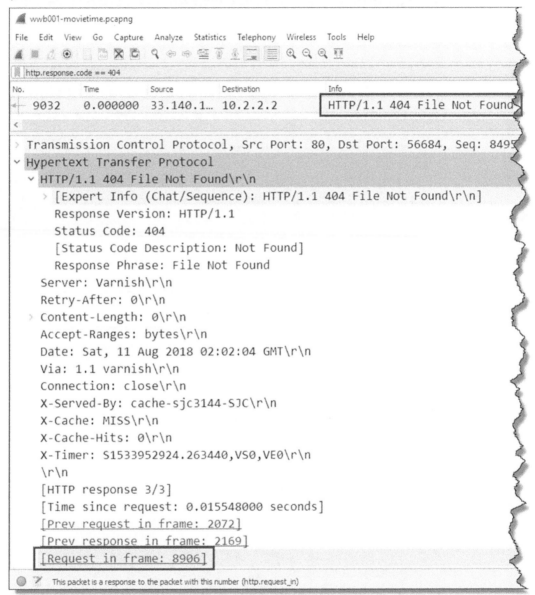

Clearing the display filter and clicking the hyperlink to frame 8906 shows the request was for:

Request URI Path: *∕opt∕tboptevent.html*
Request URI Query: *v=2&a=u&d=%7B%22stp%22%3A%7B%22a%22%3A1%7D%7D*

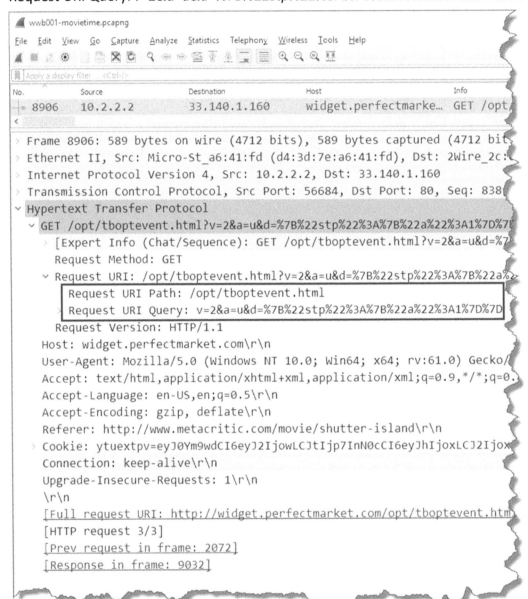

Lab 14 - A11. HTTP servers at 57.21.55.239, 190.241.242.229, and 72.16.166.130 responded fastest to requests.

Since we are interested in response times, we need to disable the TCP preference setting *Allow subdissector to reassemble TCP streams*.

By adding a column based on the HTTP *Time since request* field and adding a display filter for `http.time` (so we only see response packets), we see the fastest HTTP responses come from 57.21.55.239, 190.241.242.229, and 72.16.166.130.

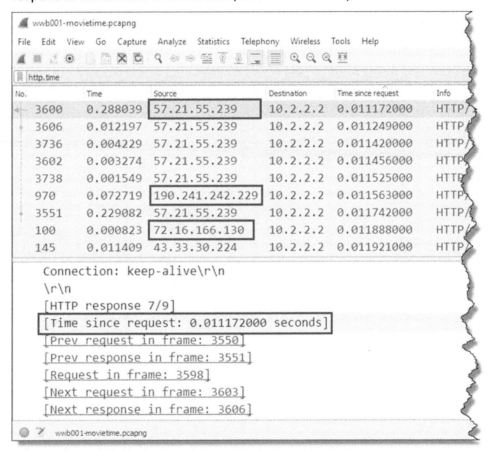

What are the names associated with these servers?

We need to look at HTTP requests to these servers to find the answer in the HTTP *Host* field.

In the image that follows, you may notice a display filter format with which you aren't familiar – a membership display filter.

`ip.dst in {57.21.55.239 190.241.242.229 72.16.166.130}`

This is an interesting display filter. Essentially, adding "in" after a field and a set of values separated by a space and within the curly brackets, you are looking for those values in the specified field. The word in is the membership operator[29].

When we apply this display filter, add and sort an HTTP *Host* column, we can see there are four server names associated with those IP addresses:

- *vidtech.cbsinteractive.com*
- *dw.cbsimg.net*
- *code.jquery.com*
- *c.evidon.com*

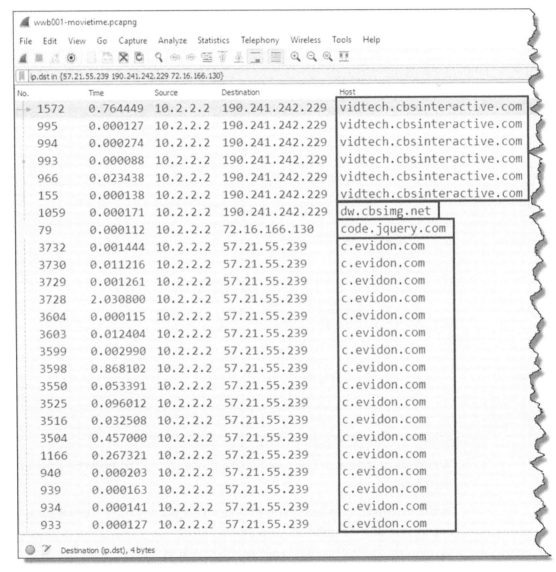

---

[29] We can filter on ranges using the in operator as well. For example, tcp.port in {25..50}

Lab 15: Crafty

Objective: Practice your display filter skills using "contains" operators, ASCII filters, and inclusion/exclusion filters, while analyzing TCP and HTTP performance parameters.

Trace File: wwb001-crafty.pcapng

Skills Covered in this Lab

In this lab, you will work with many key functions in Wireshark including, but not limited to:

- Create and apply display filters using the contains operator
- Perform HTTP response time analysis
- Build and apply ASCII display filters
- Create and apply inclusion display filters
- Create and apply exclusion display filters
- Perform TCP connection analysis to determine which TCP options are supported
- Create display filters based on TCP flag settings
- Differentiate between true out-of-order packets and retransmissions
- Perform TCP Maximum Segment Size (MSS) analysis
- Compare and contrast IPv4 and IPv6 MSS/Maximum Transmission Unit (MTU) values

Lab 15 - Q1. What are the client's IP addresses?

_____

Lab 15 - Q2. What browser is the client using?

_____

Lab 15 - Q3. What Apache versions are seen in this trace file?

_____

Lab 15 - Q4. What HTTP object was not found?

_____

Lab 15 - Q5. To what hosts does the HTTP client try communicating using ports other than 80?

_____

Lab 15 - Q6. What is the name of the slowest-responding HTTP server?

_____

Lab 15 - Q7. What is the average HTTP response time in the trace file?

_____

Lab 15 - Q8. What are the IP addresses of the servers that do not appear to support Selective acknowledgment (SACK)?

_____

Lab 15 - Q9.   **Why did Wireshark mark frame 1735 as an out-of-order frame?**

_____

Lab 15 - Q10.   **How does the server's MSS value affect data transfer in stream 26?**

_____

[This page intentionally left blank.]

Lab 15 Solutions

Trace File: wwb001-crafty.pcapng

Lab 15 - A1.   **The client's IP addresses are 192.168.1.70 and 2600:1700:79e0:1e70:f5dd:e68a:13f2:4adc.**

Just simply looking at the first 30 packets or so can give you this answer.

In frame 19, the client sends a DNS query from 2600:1700:79e0:1e70:f5dd:e68a:13f2:4adc and in frame 24, the client sends a SYN packet from 192.168.1.70.

Lab 15 - A2.   **The client is using Firefox.**

We're looking for the *User-Agent* field in an HTTP request to get this answer. Using a lazy display filter of `http contains "GET"`, frame 88 indicates the client is using Firefox on a Windows 64-bit host.

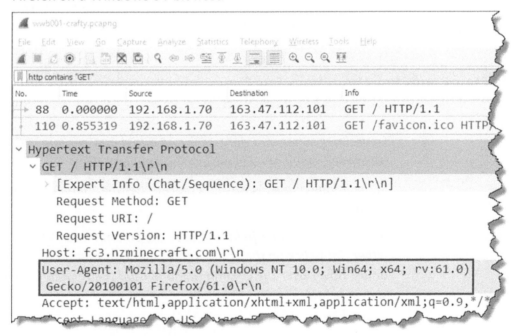

Lab 15 - A3. **Apache versions 2.2.19 (Win32) and 2.4.18 (Ubuntu) are seen in this trace file.**

Now we are interested in HTTP responses as they often contain server information. A simple display filter for `frame contains "Apache"` will work here.

Fifteen packets match this display filter and, by adding and sorting an HTTP *Server* column (`http.server`), we see the two versions listed. Three frames do not mention a version number.

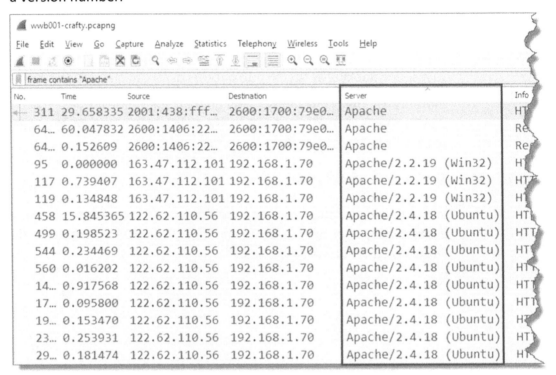

 Sometimes, when you right-click and add a new column, Wireshark will use a very vague or even misleading column title.

In the image above, Wireshark placed the title "Server" on our http.server column.

If you locate another field that uses the column title "Server," you can either right-click on the column titles and edit them to be more specific, or just hover over the column title and read the related field name, as shown below.

Lab 15 - A4. **Favicon.ico is the HTTP object that was not found.**

We'll try a new display filter – `http contains "Not Found"`. (Alternately, we could also look for `http contains "404"`.)

Frames 117 and 119 are HTTP *404 Not Found* responses.

The next step is to locate the related request frames for each of these.

As you see in the following image, frames 110 and 116 are the request frames. We added a column based on the *[Request in frame: x]* field.

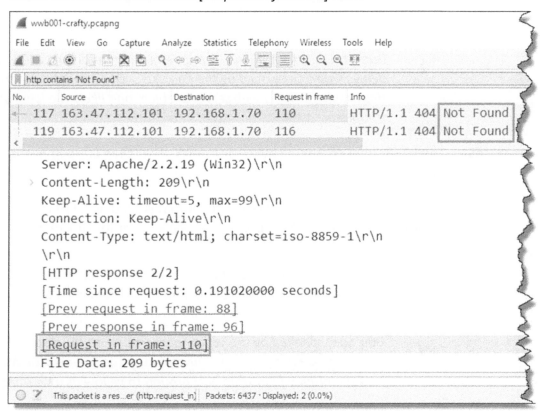

We can use the display filter `frame.number in {110 116}` to just view those two packets. There they are – the *favicon.ico* file could not be found.

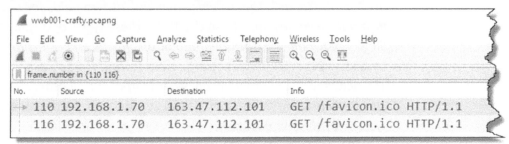

What is a *favicon.ico* file? It's the little icon placed on a browser tab. For example, when you browse to *wireshark.org*, you see the small blue fin on the tab. That icon was obtained when your browser asked for *favicon.ico* from the web server.

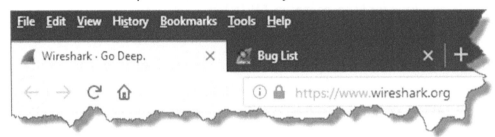

 Don't troubleshoot delays or problems related to favicon.ico. These delays won't be noticed by the end users. Don't spend time trying to fix this problem – it's a web server problem and likely the least of your troubles.

Lab 15 - A5. **The HTTP client communicates using ports other than 80 to *minecraft.geek.nz* and *mc.dirtyores.nz*.**

The question implies that there is a client that is sending HTTP requests to a non-standard port number. We will create a display filter for GET requests to any port other than 80.

A great display filter for this would be `frame contains "GET" and tcp.dstport !=
80`. Essentially, we're looking for those common GET requests, but a destination port number other than 80.

 Don't get spooked by the yellow background on the display filter area when you use this filter. Any time you use the != operator Wireshark will turn the display filter area background to yellow as a warning.

In some instances, the != may not give you what you want. Most often, people use the != to remove traffic to or from a specific IP address, TCP port, or UDP port using the `ip.addr,` `tcp.port,` *or* `udp.port` *fields. These are "combo fields". These fields each look at two fields for source and destination values. Don't use the != for these types of display filters. Simply place the ! before the regular display filter. For example, if you use* `ip.addr==10.2.2.2` *to view traffic to or from this host, use* `!ip.addr==10.2.2.2` *to view all other traffic. For all other, single-occurrence fields (such as the* `tcp.dstport` *field) you can use != as we did for this lab question.*

When we apply this display filter and add the HTTP *Host* field as a column, we can see the destination hosts (and the non-standard port numbers) listed.

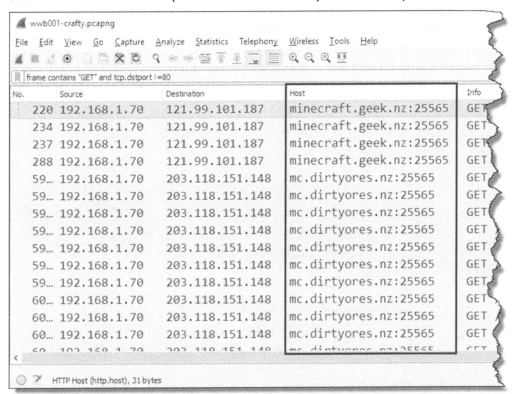

 Did you notice we used the != *in our previous display filter?*

It works great because tcp.dstport *is not a combo field. The field* tcp.dstport *only looks at the TCP destination port field.*

The != *operator should only be avoided when you are working with combo fields, such as:*

> tcp.port: (tcp.srcport || tcp.dstport)
>
> udp.port: (udp.srcport || udp.dstport)
>
> ip.addr: (ip.src || ip.dst)

Lab 15 - A6. **The HTTP server *raidnmc.aternos.me* is the slowest-responding HTTP server in this trace file.**

We are interested in the HTTP response time now. This means we must ensure the TCP preference setting *Allow subdissector to reassemble TCP streams* is disabled. Next, we'll add and sort the `http.time` column.

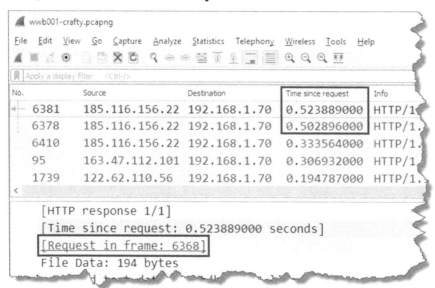

Now that we've identified the slowest response, we need to look at the corresponding request to find out the host name from the HTTP *Host* field. The HTTP request is in frame 6368.

Frame 6368 indicates that the host is *raidnmc.aternos.me*.

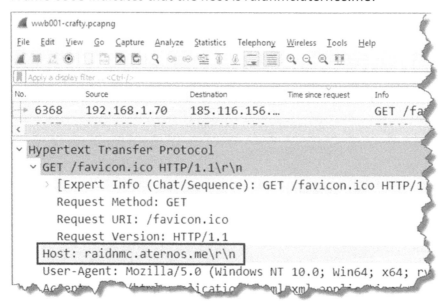

Lab 15 - A7. **The average HTTP response time in the trace file is 0.181502 seconds.**

To get the average HTTP response time, we again must have the TCP preference setting *Allow subdissector to reassemble TCP streams* disabled. We'll add the column for the `http.time` field and then export those response packet dissections to a *.csv* file.

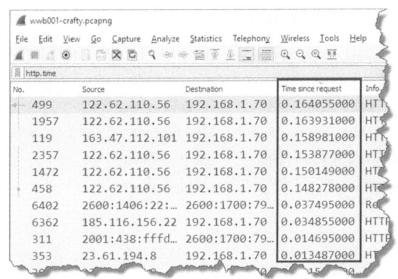

After we select *File | Export Packet Dissections | As .csv* and disable the Packet details export, we can open the file in Excel (or another spreadsheet program). The last step is to obtain the average value for the *Time since request* column.

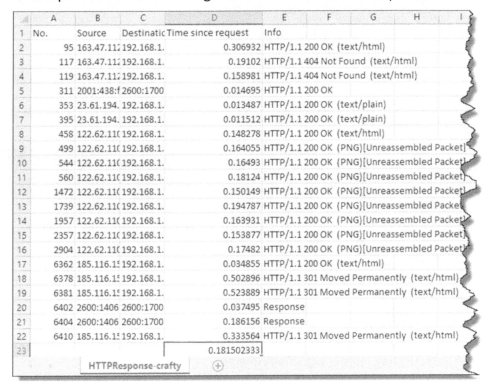

Lab 15 - A8. **The servers at 17.172.224.47 and 185.116.156.22 do not appear to support Selective acknowledgment (SACK).**

To figure this one out, we need to look at the SYN and SYN/ACK packets. We can't just look at the SYN/ACK packets – if a SYN packet doesn't indicate the client supports SACK, the server won't advertise that capability in the SYN/ACK packet.

First let's look at the SYN packets to see what the client supports. Using the display filter `tcp.flags.syn==1 && tcp.flags.ack==0`, we can see the client advertises the following capabilities in its SYN packets:

Starting Window Size:	64,240 bytes (IPv4); 64,800 bytes and 655,535 bytes (IPv6)
Maximum Segment Size:	1460 bytes (IPv4) and 1,440 bytes (IPv6)
Window Size Multiplier:	256 (IPv4/IPv6)
Selective ACK:	Enabled (IPv4/IPv6)

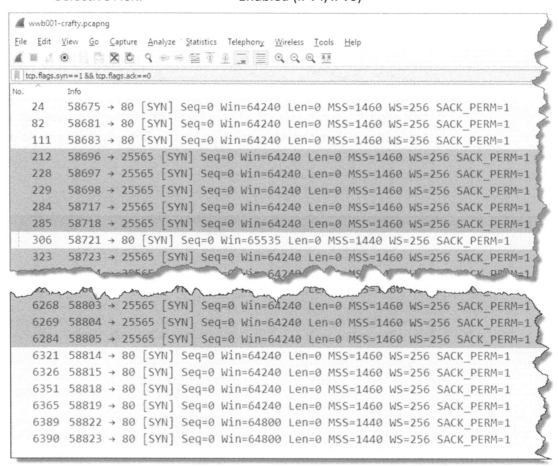

Now that we know what the client can do, let's examine the SYN/ACK packets. Our new display filter is `tcp.flags.syn==1 && tcp.flags.ack==1`.

Sorting the *Info* column can help us here since 64 packets match this new display filter. Looking through these packets, the ones with fewer options appear evident.

Note that we removed the first part of the *Info* column in the image below in order to show the TCP options.

Based on the TCP options shown in the *Info* column, it appears that 17.172.224.47 and 185.116.156.22 are missing some TCP options in their SYN/ACK packets. These hosts only advertise the Maximum Segment Size (MSS) option. They are missing the Window Scaling (WS) and Selective acknowledgment (SACK_PERM) options.

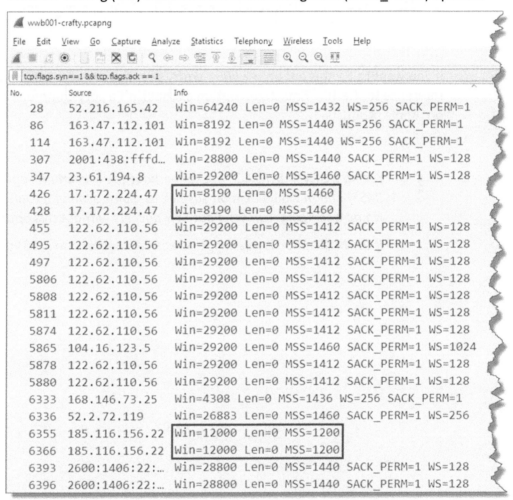

We could also build a single display filter to detect when one of the following options are missing in the TCP handshake packets:

> Maximum Segment Size (TCP Option Kind 2)
> Window Scaling (TCP Option Kind 3)
> Selective acknowledgment (TCP Option Kind 4)
> TCP Timestamps (TCP Option Kind 8)

The display filter would be:

```
tcp.flags.syn==1 && (!tcp.option_kind==2 || !tcp.option_kind==3 ||
!tcp.option_kind==4 || !tcp.option_kind==8)
```

If you want to try this out on *wwb001-crafty.pcapng*, consider removing the reference to the TCP Timestamp option as that isn't a very common option (except on Apple products).

Seeing a SYN or SYN/ACK packet without the Maximum Segment Size (MSS) option would be a bit suspicious. Some scanning tools, such as Nmap and hping, can send out SYN packets without this option.

If the MSS option is missing, the receiver assumes an MSS value of 536.

Lab 15 - A9.   **Wireshark marked frame 1735 as an out-of-order frame because the sequence number decreased, no Duplicate ACK is seen, and the packet arrived within the iRTT of the previous frame from this host.**

The first step is to filter on this one conversation. Right-clicking on this packet and selecting *Conversation Filter | TCP* will show us this one conversation for analysis.

After applying the display filter, consider adding a column for the sequence number.

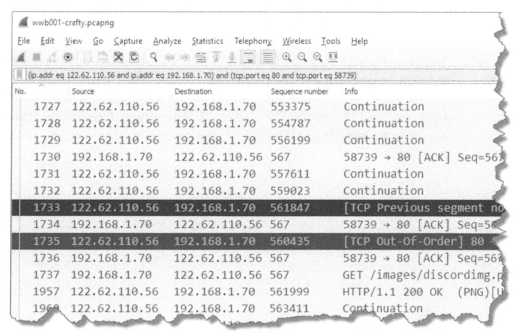

Based on the *Sequence number* column, it appears that the sequence numbers from 122.62.110.56 increment as follows from frame 1731 to frame 1735:

Frame 1731	557,611
Frame 1732	559,023
Frame 1733	561,847
Frame 1735	560,435

Sequence number 560,435 should have appeared before sequence number 561,847.

Sometimes, Wireshark marks fast retransmissions and retransmissions as out-of-order packets. The difference between these designations is (a) whether Duplicate ACKs were seen and (b) how quickly the packet arrived after the previous packet from the same host.

If Duplicate ACKs requesting the sequence number are seen, the packet is marked as a fast retransmission. If not, Wireshark determines that the packet is either a retransmission or an out-of-order packet.

If the packet arrives within the Initial Round-Trip Time (iRTT) value that Wireshark calculates during each TCP handshake process, it is defined as Out-of-Order.

If the packet arrives outside the Initial Round-Trip Time (iRTT) value, it is defined as a retransmission.

If you measure the arrival time from frame 1733 to frame 1735, you will notice that these frames arrived 0.000782 seconds apart. The *Initial Round-trip Time* field (tcp.analysis.initial_rtt) inside the [SEQ/ACK analysis] section TCP header of these packets indicates the iRTT is 0.155716 seconds. This is within the iRTT value, so this packet is defined as Out-of-Order.

Lab 15 - A10. **The server's MSS value of 1,412 will force the client to limit segment sizes to 1,412 bytes in all packets sent to the server.**

First, we need to filter on TCP stream 26. The display filter is tcp.stream==26. Next, we must examine the SYN/ACK from the server (in frame 497) to see the advertised MSS value.

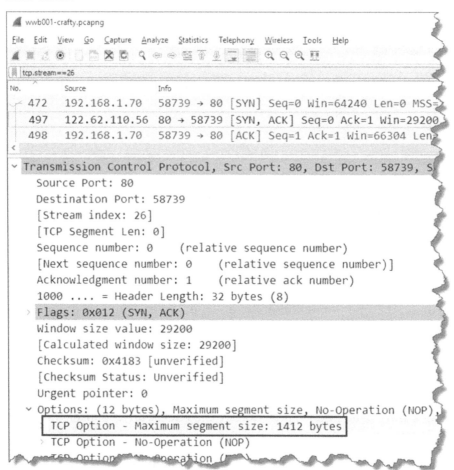

The MSS value advertises the maximum amount of data that a TCP peer can accept in a TCP packet.

In many cases, you'll see an IPv4 host advertise 1460. This is very common for a host on an Ethernet network. It is based on an IP header length of 20 bytes and a TCP header length of 20 bytes.

It's common to see an IPv6 host advertise an MSS of 1,440 bytes. This is based on an IP header length of 40 bytes and a TCP header length of 20 bytes.

IPv4 Structure

Ethernet Header (14)
IPv4 Header (20)
TCP Header (20)
DATA (1460)
Ethernet Trailer (4)

segment packet frame

IPv6 Structure

Ethernet Header (14)
IPv6 Header (40)
TCP Header (20)
DATA (1440)
Ethernet Trailer (4)

segment packet frame

If a standard Ethernet frame will allow for 1460 bytes of data after the TCP header in an IPv4 packet, why is the server is only advertising an MSS of 1,412?

What can reduce the MSS?

Anything that affects the Maximum Transmission Unit (MTU) size, such as a VLAN driver, will affect the MSS size. As the MTU is decreased, so is the MSS.

We must figure that this server, 122.62.110.56, has something running on it that affects the MTU. In turn, this is reducing the MSS size.

We would have to look at the server's configuration to determine what is affecting the MTU and therefore, the MSS.

[This page intentionally left blank.]

Lab 16: Pattern Recognition

Objective: Focus on TCP conversations and endpoints while analyzing TCP sequence numbers, Window Scaling, keep-alive, and Selective Acknowledgment capabilities.

<hr>

Trace File: wwb001-pattern.pcapng

<hr>

Skills Covered in this Lab

In this lab, you will work with many key functions in Wireshark including, but not limited to:

- Identify conversation/host counts using the *Conversations* and *Endpoints* windows
- Identify Selective Acknowledgment capability when TCP handshake information is available
- Work with a trace file that does not contain the Window Scaling setup process
- Interpret *-1* in the TCP *Window Size Scaling Factor* field
- Analyze TCP keep-alive packets
- Analyze the TCP sequence numbers of TCP FIN packets

Lab 16 - Q1. How many IPv4 and IPv6 conversations are seen in this trace file?

_____

Lab 16 - Q2. How many of the hosts support Selective acknowledgment (SACK) and how can you determine that those hosts support SACK?

_____

Lab 16 - Q3. How many TCP conversations are in this trace file?

_____

Lab 16 - Q4. Explain why the TCP _Calculated window size_ field values may be incorrect.

_____

Lab 16 - Q5. In frame 2, Wireshark indicates that the next sequence number from this host should be 2. Why does the host not increment the sequence number to 2 as Wireshark expected?

_____

Lab 16 - Q6. Why did the sequence number change between frame 14 and frame 17?

_____

Lab 16 Solutions

Trace File: wwb001-pattern.pcapng

Lab 16 - A1.   **There is one IPv4 conversation and one IPv6 conversation in this trace file.**

Opening the *Statistics | Conversations* window provides the information on each of the conversations.

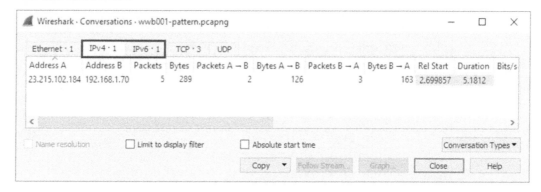

Lab 16 - A2.   **We can determine that all the hosts in this trace file support Selective acknowledgment (SACK) because of the use of SACK Left Edge/Right Edge blocks in their conversations.**

We didn't capture any TCP handshakes in this trace file, so we can't see if SACK_PERM=1 is set in the SYN and SYN/ACK packets (which could have been determined using a tcp.option_kind==4 display filter). Without that, we can only tell if SACK is enabled if the hosts use the feature.

We applied a tcp.options.sack_le display filter to detect the occurrence of a *SACK Left Edge* field. Other filters that would work are tcp.options.sack_re and tcp.options.sack.count.

Since this is a very short trace file, we can easily see SACK Left Edge values sent in three TCP streams (0, 1 and 2).

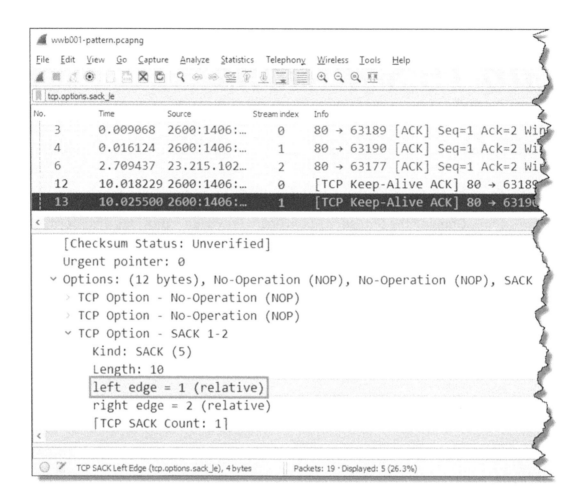

If this was a much larger trace file, we would want to open the *Conversations* window and select *Limit to display filter* to determine which hosts support SACK. In the following image, we can see both the IPv4 and IPv6 conversations support SACK. All hosts in this trace file support SACK.

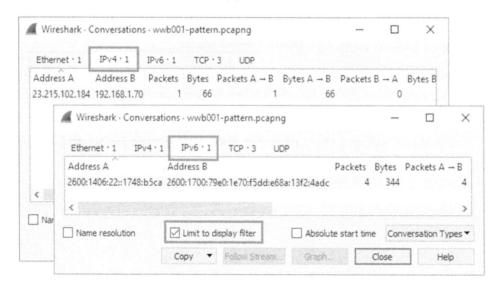

Lab 16 - A3. **There are three TCP conversations are in this trace file.**

Again, opening the *Statistics | Conversations* window provides us with this information.

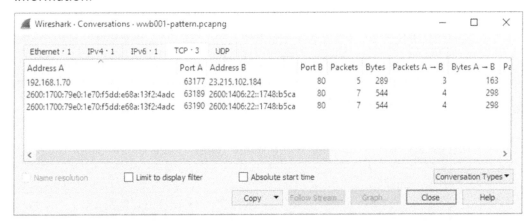

Lab 16 - A4. **The TCP *Calculated window size* field values may incorrect because we did not see the TCP handshake packets, therefore we do not know if Window Scaling is in use, and if it is, what the window size scaling factor is.**

Window scaling is established during the TCP handshake. Since Wireshark did not see the TCP handshake, it notes that the window size scaling factor is "unknown" by placing a -1 in the *Window size scaling factor* field.

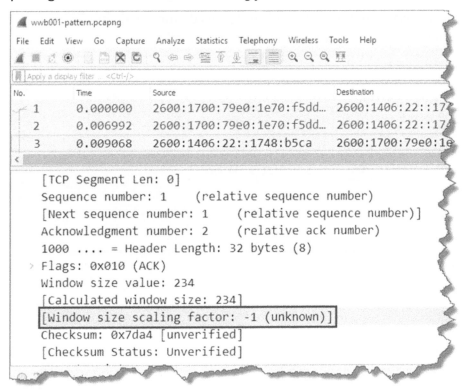

Lab 16 - A5. **The sequence number did not increase in the next frame (frame 11) from this host because it is a keep-alive packet.**

These packets are interesting. In the following image, we've added columns for the *Sequence number* field (SEQ+), the TCP *Segment Length* field (SegLen=), and the *Next sequence number* (NextSEQ) field. We also filtered on tcp.stream==1.

According to the TCP specification, the sequence number value plus the segment length equals the next sequence number to be used. We would expect frame 11 to use sequence number 2, as Wireshark indicates.

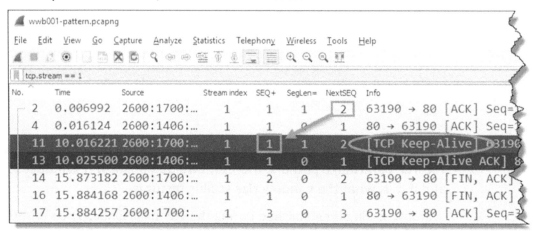

Well, you may see that Wireshark's Expert defined frame 11 as a TCP keep-alive.

Let's examine the developer's notes inside the Wireshark TCP dissector code to see how Wireshark detected these were keep-alives.[30]

```
1952
1953
1954  /* KEEP ALIVE
1955   * a keepalive contains 0 or 1 bytes of data and starts one byte prior
1956   * to what should be the next sequence number.
1957   * SYN/FIN/RST segments are never keepalives
1958   */
1959  if( (seglen==0||seglen==1)
1960  &&   seq==(tcpd->fwd->tcp_analyze_seq_info->nextseq-1)
1961  &&   (flags&(TH_SYN|TH_FIN|TH_RST))==0 ) {
1962      if(!tcpd->ta) {
1963          tcp_analyze_get_acked_struct(pinfo->num, seq, ack, TRUE, tcpd);
1964      }
1965      tcpd->ta->flags|=TCP_A_KEEP_ALIVE;
1966  }
1967
```

---

[30] To access the Wireshark dissector code, visit *wireshark.org* and select *Develop | Browse the Code | epan | dissectors*. Protocol and application dissector file names begin with "*packet-*", followed by the protocol or application name. The files end with ".*c*". For example, the TCP dissector code is contained in *packet-tcp.c*.

In the code, we see that a keep-alive may contain 1 byte of data, but start one byte earlier in the *Sequence number* field. That's why Wireshark defined frame 11 as a keep-alive. Frame 11 started back at sequence number 1 instead of incrementing the sequence number to 2, as expected.

Lab 16 - A6. **The sequence number incremented by 1 between frame 14 and frame 17 because of the phantom byte in the FIN packet (frame 14).**

In the last question, we dealt with unusual sequence number behavior. We are dealing with the same thing in this question.

Notice that frames 14 and 17 are part of the same TCP stream (stream 1).

Again, according to the TCP specification, the sequence number value plus the segment length equals the next sequence number to be used. If that is true, why did the sequence numbers increment by 1 when there was no data inside frame 14?

Just as in the SYN packets, the FIN packets are considered to have a "phantom byte" – a byte of data that really does not exist. Since frame 14 has the FIN bit set, the next frame from this host (frame 17) must increment the sequence number by 1.

The same procedure is in place for TCP stream 0. Frame 15 has the FIN bit set, the next frame from this host (frame 19) must increment the sequence number by 1.

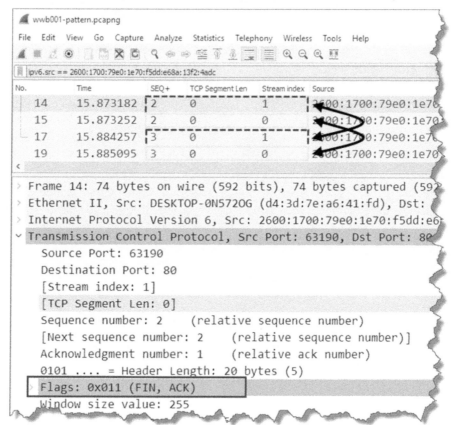

[This page intentionally left blank.]

Index

Lightning Source UK Ltd.
Milton Keynes UK
UKHW032309060320
359927UK00004B/64